4th Workshop on Open-Source Arabic Corpora and Processing Tools with a Shared Task on Offensive Language Detection 2020

Marseille, France
11-16 May 2020

Editors:

Hend Al-Khalifa
Walid Magdy
Kareem Darwish

Tamer Elsayed
Hamdy Mubarak

ISBN: 978-1-7138-1272-2

LREC 2020 Workshop
Language Resources and Evaluation Conference
11–16 May 2020

The 4th Workshop on Open-Source Arabic Corpora and Processing Tools
with a Shared Task on Offensive Language Detection

PROCEEDINGS

Editors:

Hend Al-Khalifa, Walid Magdy, Kareem Darwish, Tamer Elsayed
and Hamdy Mubarak

Proceedings of the LREC 2020
4th Workshop on Open-Source Arabic
Corpora and Processing Tools

with a Shared Task on Offensive Language Detection
(OSACT 2020)

Edited by: Hend Al-Khalifa, Walid Magdy, Kareem Darwish, Tamer Elsayed and Hamdy Mubarak

For more information:
European Language Resources Association (ELRA)
9 rue des Cordelières
75013, Paris
France
http://www.elra.info
Email: lrec@elda.org

Preface

Given the success of the first, second, and third workshops on Open-Source Arabic Corpora and Corpora Processing Tools (OSACT) in LREC 2014, LREC 2016 and LREC 2018, the fourth workshop comes to encourage researchers and practitioners of Arabic language technologies, including computational linguistics (CL), natural language processing (NLP), and information retrieval (IR) to share and discuss their research efforts, corpora, and tools. The workshop gives special attention to Human Language Technologies based on AI/Machine Learning, which is one of LREC 2020 hot topics. In addition to the general topics of CL, NLP and IR, the workshop gives special emphasis to Offensive Language Detection shared task.

OSACT4 had an acceptance rate of 50%, where we received 12 regular papers from which 6 papers were accepted, in addition to 11 shared task papers. We believe that the accepted papers are of high quality and present a mixture of interesting topics.

This year, we introduced the Shared Task on Offensive Language Detection. The shared task attempts to detect such speech in the realm of Arabic social media in two Subtasks. In subtask A, SemEval 2020 Arabic offensive language dataset, which contains 10,000 tweets that were manually annotated for offensiveness was used. Offensive tweets contain explicit or implicit insults or attacks against other people, or inappropriate language. Subtask B targets the identification of Hate Speech. A hate speech tweet contains insults or threats targeting a group based on their nationality, ethnicity, gender, political or sport affiliation, religious belief, or other common characteristics. Subtasks A and B share the same data splits. Subtask B is more challenging than Subtask A as only 5% of the tweets are labeled as hate speech, while 20% of the tweets are labeled as offensive. The shared task attracted many teams from different countries in the Middle East, Europe and US. In all, 40 and 33 teams signed up to participate in Subtasks A and B; among them, 14 and 13 teams submitted their system outputs in the two subtasks respectively.

We would like to thank everyone who in one way or another helped in making this workshop a success. Our special thanks go to the members of the program committee, who did an excellent job in reviewing the submitted papers, and to the LREC organizers. Last but not least, we would like to thank our authors and the workshop participants.

Hend Al-Khalifa, Walid Magdy, Kareem Darwish, Tamer Elsayed, and Hamdy Mubarak

OSACT4 Organizing Committee

Table of Contents

An Arabic Tweets Sentiment Analysis Dataset (ATSAD) using Distant Supervision and Self Training
Kathrein Abu Kwaik, Stergios Chatzikyriakidis, Simon Dobnik, Motaz Saad
and Richard Johansson 1

AraBERT: Transformer-based Model for Arabic Language Understanding
wissam antoun, Fady Baly and Hazem Hajj 9

AraNet: A Deep Learning Toolkit for Arabic Social Media
Muhammad Abdul-Mageed, Chiyu Zhang, Azadeh Hashemi and El Moatez Billah Nagoudi 16

Building a Corpus of Qatari Arabic Expressions
Sara Al-Mulla and Wajdi Zaghouani 24

From Arabic Sentiment Analysis to Sarcasm Detection: The ArSarcasm Dataset
Ibrahim Abu Farha and Walid Magdy 32

Understanding and Detecting Dangerous Speech in Social Media
Ali Alshehri, El Moatez Billah Nagoudi and Muhammad Abdul-Mageed 40

Overview of OSACT4 Arabic Offensive Language Detection Shared Task
Hamdy Mubarak, Kareem Darwish, Walid Magdy, Tamer Elsayed and Hend Al-Khalifa 48

OSACT4 Shared Task on Offensive Language Detection: Intensive Preprocessing-Based Approach
Fatemah Husain 53

ALT Submission for OSACT Shared Task on Offensive Language Detection
Sabit Hassan, Younes Samih, Hamdy Mubarak, Ahmed Abdelali, Ammar Rashed and Shammur
Absar Chowdhury 61

ASU_OPTO at OSACT4 - Offensive Language Detection for Arabic text
Amr Keleg, Samhaa R. El-Beltagy and Mahmoud Khalil 66

OSACT4 Shared Tasks: Ensembled Stacked Classification for Offensive and Hate Speech in Arabic Tweets
Hafiz Hassaan Saeed, Toon Calders and Faisal Kamiran 71

Arabic Offensive Language Detection with Attention-based Deep Neural Networks
Bushr Haddad, Zoher Orabe, Anas Al-Abood and Nada Ghneim 76

Offensive language detection in Arabic using ULMFiT
Mohamed Abdellatif and Ahmed Elgammal 82

Multitask Learning for Arabic Offensive Language and Hate-Speech Detection
Ibrahim Abu Farha and Walid Magdy 86

Combining Character and Word Embeddings for the Detection of Offensive Language in Arabic
Abdullah I. Alharbi and Mark Lee 91

Multi-Task Learning using AraBert for Offensive Language Detection
Marc Djandji, Fady Baly, wissam antoun and Hazem Hajj 97

Leveraging Affective Bidirectional Transformers for Offensive Language Detection
AbdelRahim Elmadany, Chiyu Zhang, Muhammad Abdul-Mageed and Azadeh Hashemi 102

Quick and Simple Approach for Detecting Hate Speech in Arabic Tweets
Abeer Abuzayed and Tamer Elsayed. 109

Workshop Program

An Arabic Tweets Sentiment Analysis Dataset (ATSAD) using Distant Supervision and Self Training
Kathrein Abu Kwaik, Stergios Chatzikyriakidis, Simon Dobnik, Motaz Saad and Richard Johansson

AraBERT: Transformer-based Model for Arabic Language Understanding
wissam antoun, Fady Baly and Hazem Hajj

AraNet: A Deep Learning Toolkit for Arabic Social Media
Muhammad Abdul-Mageed, Chiyu Zhang, Azadeh Hashemi and El Moatez Billah Nagoudi

Building a Corpus of Qatari Arabic Expressions
Sara Al-Mulla and Wajdi Zaghouani

From Arabic Sentiment Analysis to Sarcasm Detection: The ArSarcasm Dataset
Ibrahim Abu Farha and Walid Magdy

Understanding and Detecting Dangerous Speech in Social Media
Ali Alshehri, El Moatez Billah Nagoudi and Muhammad Abdul-Mageed

Overview of OSACT4 Arabic Offensive Language Detection Shared Task
Hamdy Mubarak, Kareem Darwish, Walid Magdy, Tamer Elsayed and Hend Al-Khalifa

OSACT4 Shared Task on Offensive Language Detection: Intensive Preprocessing-Based Approach
Fatemah Husain

ALT Submission for OSACT Shared Task on Offensive Language Detection
Sabit Hassan, Younes Samih, Hamdy Mubarak, Ahmed Abdelali, Ammar Rashed and Shammur Absar Chowdhury

ASU_OPTO at OSACT4 - Offensive Language Detection for Arabic text
Amr Keleg, Samhaa R. El-Beltagy and Mahmoud Khalil

OSACT4 Shared Tasks: Ensembled Stacked Classification for Offensive and Hate Speech in Arabic Tweets
Hafiz Hassaan Saeed, Toon Calders and Faisal Kamiran

Arabic Offensive Language Detection with Attention-based Deep Neural Networks
Bushr Haddad, Zoher Orabe, Anas Al-Abood and Nada Ghneim

Offensive language detection in Arabic using ULMFiT
Mohamed Abdellatif and Ahmed Elgammal

Multitask Learning for Arabic Offensive Language and Hate-Speech Detection
Ibrahim Abu Farha and Walid Magdy

Combining Character and Word Embeddings for the Detection of Offensive Language in Arabic
Abdullah I. Alharbi and Mark Lee

Multi-Task Learning using AraBert for Offensive Language Detection
Marc Djandji, Fady Baly, wissam antoun and Hazem Hajj

Leveraging Affective Bidirectional Transformers for Offensive Language Detection
AbdelRahim Elmadany, Chiyu Zhang, Muhammad Abdul-Mageed and Azadeh Hashemi

Quick and Simple Approach for Detecting Hate Speech in Arabic Tweets
Abeer Abuzayed and Tamer Elsayed

Proceedings of the 4th Workshop on Open-Source Arabic Corpora and Processing Tools, pages 1–8
with a Shared Task on Offensive Language Detection.
Language Resources and Evaluation Conference (LREC 2020), Marseille, 11–16 May 2020
© European Language Resources Association (ELRA), licensed under CC-BY-NC

An Arabic Tweets Sentiment Analysis Dataset (ATSAD) using Distant Supervision and Self Training

Kathrein Abu Kwaik[*], **Motaz Saad**[†], **Stergios Chatzikyriakidis**[*],
Simon Dobnik[*], **Richard Johansson**[¶]

[*]CLASP, Department of Philosophy, Linguistics and Theory of Science, University of Gothenburg, Sweden
[¶]Department of Computer Science and Engineering, University of Gothenburg, Sweden
[†]The Islamic University of Gaza, Palestine

{kathrein.abu.kwaik,richard.johansson,stergios.chatzikyriakidis,simon.dobnik}@gu.se , motaz.saad@gmail.com

Abstract

As the number of social media users increases, they express their thoughts, needs, socialise and publish their opinions. For good social media sentiment analysis, good quality resources are needed, and the lack of these resources is particularly evident for languages other than English, in particular Arabic. The available Arabic resources lack of from either the size of the corpus or the quality of the annotation. In this paper, we present an Arabic Sentiment Analysis Corpus collected from Twitter, which contains 36K tweets labelled into positive and negative. We employed distant supervision and self-training approaches into the corpus to annotate it. Besides, we release an 8K tweets manually annotated as a gold standard. We evaluated the corpus intrinsically by comparing it to human classification and pre-trained sentiment analysis models. Moreover, we apply extrinsic evaluation methods exploiting sentiment analysis task and achieve an accuracy of 86%.

Keywords: Sentiment Analysis, Distant Supervision, Self Training

1. Introduction

Companies and businesses stakeholders reach out to their customers through Social Media not only for advertising and marketing purposes, but also to get customer feedback concerning products or services. This is one of the main reasons that sentiment analysis applications have become increasingly sought out by the industry field. Even though sentiment analysis programs are widely used in the commercial sector, they have many other important uses, including political orientation analysis, electoral programs and decision-making. Sentiment Analysis is the process of automatically mining attitudes, opinions, views and emotions from the text, speech, tweets using Natural Language Processing (NLP) and machine learning (Liu, 2012). Sentiment analysis involves classifying opinions into different classes like positive, negative, mixed or neutral. It can also refer to Subjectivity Analysis, i.e. the task of distinguishing between objective and subjective text.

There are so many Arabic speakers in the world and they speak different varieties of Arabic depending on the region but with only one variety that is standardised namely, Modern Standard Arabic MSA. Social media is prevalent and it is particularly this domain where the local varieties are used and for which the resources are most limited. The total number of monthly active Twitter users in the Arab region is estimated at 11.1 million in March 2017, generating 27.4 million tweets per day according to weedoo.[1] Arabic, especially dialects, still looking for more efficient resources that can be used for the needs of NLP tasks.

One of the biggest challenges in the construction of Arabic NLP resources is the big variation found in Arabic language where there are Modern Standard Arabic (MSA), Classical Arabic (CA) and the dialects. This has the result, that, in some tasks, it might be necessary to build stand-alone resources for each individual variation where the available

tools have been built for MSA can not be adapted for dialects and vice-verse (Qwaider et al., 2019). In addition, building resources requires sufficient time and funding to produce highly efficient resources. Moreover, deep learning NLP methods require a huge amount of data. As a result of the unique Twitter features that are widely used to express opinions, views, thoughts and feelings, we therefore present Arabic Tweets Sentiment Analysis Dataset (ATSAD) contains 36k tweets classified as positive or negative.

The contributions of this paper can be highlighted under two headings: a) resource creation and b) resource evaluation. Regarding resource creation, we introduce a sentiment analysis dataset collected from Twitter, and as for resource evaluation, we introduce a method that combines the distant supervision approach with self-training to build a dataset that satisfies the size and quality requirements. In order to annotate a large number of tweets, we employ the distant supervision approach where the emojis are used as a weak noisy label. We manually annotate a subset of 8k tweets of the dataset and offer it as gold standard dataset. In order to improve the quality of the corpus, we apply the self-training techniques on the dataset and combine it with the distant supervision approach as a *double check approach*. Using our proposed double check approach, we achieve an accuracy of 86% on the sentiment analysis task. The dataset is available online for research usage.[2]

The rest paper is organised as follows: Section 2 reviews some related works in term of sentiment analysis and social media resources. In Section 3, the challenges of processing Twitter text are presented and in Section 4, the details of collecting and creating the tweets dataset are presented. We evaluate the dataset in Section 5. Sections 6 and 7 are the conclusion and future work sections respectively.

---

[1]https://weedoo.tech/twitter-arab-world-statistics-feb-2017/

[2]https://github.com/motazsaad/arabic-sentiment-analysis

2. Related Work

Arabic Sentiment analysis (ASA) has received considerable attention in terms of resource creation (Rushdi-Saleh et al., 2011; Aly and Atiya, 2013; Abdul-Mageed et al., 2014; El-nagar et al., 2018). These resources are collected from different sources such as (blogs, reviews, tweets, comments, etc.) and involve a mix of Arabic vernacular and classical Arabic. Furthermore, they have been used extensively in research on SA for Arabic such as (Al Shboul et al., 2015; Obaidat et al., 2015; Al-Twairesh et al., 2016). Most NLP work on SA uses machine learning classifiers with feature engineering. For example (Azmi and Alzanin, 2014; El-Beltagy et al., 2016) used machine learning classifiers on polarity and subjectivity classifications. However, recent papers (Al Sallab et al., 2015; Dahou et al., 2016; Alayba et al., 2018) investigated the use of Deep Neural Networks for Arabic sentiment analysis. Most of the datasets are collected from web blogs and customer reviews. Some are manually annotated following a specific annotation guidelines, while other corpora like LABR (Aly and Atiya, 2013) depend on the stars ratings done by users where the stars are used as polarity labels, the 5 stars denote a high positive, 1 star denotes a high negative and the 3 stars indicate the neutral and mixed label.

In the AraSenTi-tweets corpus (Al-Twairesh et al., 2017), many approaches to collect the tweets were adopted, e.g the utilisation of emoticons, sentiment hashtags as well as the sentiment keywords. Then, the authors only keep the tweets that have their location set to a Saudi location. The dataset is manually annotated and sets some annotation guidelines. It contains 17 573 tweets each of which is classified to one of four classes (positive, negative, mixed or neutral). A sentiment baseline is built depending on TFIDF and using SVM with a linear kernel which achieved an F-score of 60.05%.

In (Nabil et al., 2015), the authors presented the Arabic Sentiment Tweets Dataset (ASTD). It is a dataset of 10,000 Egyptian tweets. It is composed of 799 positive, 1,684 negative, 832 mixed and 6,691 neutral tweets. The authors also conducted a set of benchmark experiments for four way sentiment classification as (positive, negative, mixed, neutral) and two-way sentiment classification as (positive, negative). When focusing on two-way classification, the corpus is unbalanced and small to be useful for the two-way sentiment analysis task.

A corpus for Jordanian tweets is also presented in (Atoum and Nouman, 2019). The authors collected tweets according to location, and then they filtered them to collect different types of terminologies to identify Jordanian Arabic dialect keywords efficiently. The corpus contains 3,550 Jordanian dialect tweets manually annotated as follows: 616 positive tweets, 1,313 negative tweets, and 1,621 neutral tweets. They conducted several experiments both with and without stemming/rooting applying them to several models with uni-grams/bi-grams and trying NB and SVM classifiers. The result shows that the SVM classifier performs better than the NB classifier. The ROC performance reached an average of 0.71, 0.77 on NB and SVM respectively on all experiments. A similar corpus for Levantine dialects is presented in Shami-Senti (Qwaider et al., 2019).

It has approximately 2.5k posts from social media sites in general topics classified manually as positive, negative and neutral. The corpus is still under development.

Recently, a 40K tweets dataset is presented in (Mohammed and Kora, 2019). The authors extracted tweets written in Arabic. After that, they reprocessed the tweets and cleaned them very carefully by two experts, they corrected every misspelling words and removed all the repeating characters, in addition to the normal cleaning steps like normalisation. The total size of the dataset is 40,000 tweets classified into positive and negative equally. The corpus is considered a reliable resource but by manually cleaning all the data, it turns to a very hard crafted corpus where the resulted clean corpus differ than the real tweets, where the goal of cleaning is to normalise text and remove spelling mistakes but keep the style of the author. This has been normalised too much in this corpus and hence important information was lost.

Even though in most of the Arabic tweet corpus creation procedures, the authors used the emoticons to extract as many sentiment tweets as possible such as (Al-Twairesh et al., 2017; Refaee and Rieser, 2014), however none of them using the emojis and the emoticons as a sentiment label. An emoticon is built from keyboard characters that when put together in a certain way represent a facial expression like :) ;) :(and so on, while an emoji is an actual image[3]. The Stanford Twitter Sentiment (STS), is one of the most well-known dataset for English Twitter sentiment analysis (Go et al., 2009). The dataset provides training and testing sets. The tweets were collected on the condition to contain at least one emoticon. Then they automatically classified the tweets in regard to the emoticons to positive and negative. The process resulted in a training set of 1.6 million annotated tweets and a test set of 359 manually annotated tweets that are used as a gold standard. The data set has been extensively used for different tasks related to sentiment analysis and subjectivity classification (Bravo-Marquez et al., 2013; Saif et al., 2012; Bakliwal et al., 2012; Speriosu et al., 2011). Refaee and Rieser (2014) presented Arabic subsets of tweets using emoticons, hashtags and keywords. They apply distant supervision on the emoticons subset. After the evaluation process, they get an accuracy 95% and 51% for subjectivity analysis and sentiment classification respectively. They comment that emoticons can be used efficiently with subjectivity detection but not for the polarity classification task.

As obvious from the previous discussion, these corpora or dataset have lacked some aspect. They have some limitation in term of the size of the corpus as ASTD, the number of presented dialects as AraSenti and the annotation procedure like LABR. We are looking for Arabic sentiment analysis corpus that concerns the Arabic social media text and that handles multiple dialects in a reasonable number of instances size to conduct experiments and find a way to do the annotation as accurate as possible. In this paper, and similarly to STS (Go et al., 2009), we constructed a dataset based on emojis for extracting and classifying tweets. Additionally, we manually annotated 20% of this data, which

---

[3]https://grammarist.com/new-words/emoji-vs-emoticon/

can then be used as a gold standard for any tweets sentiment analysis task and as the test set for our corpus.

3. Challenges of processing text from social media

Natural language processing must be adapted to the type of text to be processed (formal, scientific, colloquial), but furthermore, humans differ in the way they write in that specific type of text. This variety in writing style has increased with the advent of social media, where people are using their style of writing and daily conversational language to post, reply, or tweet more often. In addition to specific idiosyncrasies of Arabic in terms of processing, Twitter has unique features that make tweets have different characteristics from other social media (Alwakid et al., 2017; Giachanou and Crestani, 2016). Detecting sentiment in social media text in general and Twitter in particular is a non-trivial task. There are many challenges as follows:

- The short text length is the unique characteristics of tweets, which can be up to 280 characters.

- Due to the constraint on the length of the tweet (280 characters), users tend to employ abbreviations in the tweets to make room for other words.

- Tweets, as well as other social media text, are an example of *User Generated Content*, and contain unstructured language, orthographic mistakes, use of slang words, a lot of ironic and sarcastic sentences, abbreviations and many idiomatic expressions.

- Analysing Arabic tweets in specific is a challenging task due to the use of Arabic dialects in tweets which (due to the lack of standard orthography) results to a lot of spelling inconsistencies. Moreover, the lack of capitalisation and diacritics, as well as the usage of connected words like إنشاالله increase the complexity of processing Arabic tweets.

- The extensive of use of misspellings Arabic result in a Data Sparsity, that has an impact on the overall performance of SA systems. Saif et al. (2012) propose a semantic smoothing model by extracting semantically hidden concepts from tweets and then incorporate them into supervised classifier training through interpolation to reduce the sparseness in English tweets.

- Many Arabic tweets are verses from the Holy Quran. There prayers to refer to different situations with different meanings are used, for example, ماما بشتاقلك كتير. الله يرحمك ويجمعنا معك في الجنة, which in English means *Mam I miss you a lot. I ask God to have mercy on you and to bring us together in heaven*, even though it ostensibly carries a positive meaning of empathy and paradise, it carries negative feelings of longing and loss due to death.

4. Arabic Tweets Sentiment Analysis Dataset (ATSAD)

To create and build the sentiment analysis corpus or datasets, we first build a sentiment emoji lexicon. The lexicon contains both positive and negative emojis expressing the feelings corresponding to different sentiment categories. We collect the emojis as well as their indicated sentiment from "Emojis Sentiment Ranking Lexicon" (Kralj Novak et al., 2015) which is available at `http://kt.ijs.si/data/Emoji_sentiment_ranking/` and Emojipedia[4]. Then, this lexicon is employed as the seed for the Twitter retrieval procedure. The Lexicon is composed of 91 negative emojis and 306 positive emojis.

Instead of collecting tweets by hashtags or query terms we exploit the emojis and their assigned sentiment and condition the tweet language set to Arabic. We extracted 59k of the tweets using the Twitter API in April 2019. The corpus contains multiple dialects from all over the Arab world as it is not geographically constrained. To automatically annotate the tweets either as positive or negative, we use the emojis as a noisy (weak) label. If the tweet is fetched by the positive emojis from the lexicon like ☺ then it is labelled as positive and the tweets fetched by the negative lexicon are labelled as negative.

More specifically, we perform the following cleaning actions:

1. Remove all metadata generated by Twitter API like tweet_id, username, time, location, RT

2. Remove all special characters but not emojis

3. Remove non-Arabic characters

4. Remove links

5. Remove diacritics from the text

6. Remove duplicated tweets

Table 1 shows the statistics of the corpus before and after the pre-processing phase which gives us 36K tweets.

	Positive	Negative	Total	Vocabs	Words
Before	30,607	29,232	59,839	95,538	76,2673
After	18,173	18,695	36,868	95,057	41,8857

Table 1: Statistics of the Twitter sentiment analysis corpus (ATSAD) before and after the pre-processing

5. Corpus Evaluation

The process of building a resource is not limited to data collection, but it must be checked and verified in order to be trustworthy and used as a resource. In this section, we evaluate the Tweets corpus by introducing two well-known methodologies: Intrinsic and extrinsic evaluations.

In intrinsic evaluation, the corpus is directly evaluated in terms of its accuracy and quality. We check whether the rule-based annotation (simply an emojis annotation) can be used to build a reliable corpus and use it effectively in the desired functionality. On the other hand, in extrinsic evaluation, the dataset is going to be assessed with respect to its

---

[4]https://emojipedia.org/people/emojis

impact on an external task which in our case is the sentiment analysis model (Resnik and Lin, 2010).

To check the quality of the corpus, we have asked two annotators, one an NLP expert, the second an educated native Arabic speaker, to annotate subsets of the corpus. We start with a random sample containing 180 instances (1% of the data) for both positive and negative classes. When the annotation was completed, the two annotators agreed on the 90% of the sample.

In case of disagreement, we choose the expert annotator's choice as the class label. The annotation process is cumulative, in the sense that we pick random samples every time from the corpus and ask the annotators to annotate. For each sample we calculate the number of mismatched labels between the emoji-based annotation and the human annotation, and we also compute the accuracy of the emoji-based annotation by taking the number of right classified instances divided by the total number of the sample. Table 2 shows the number of errors (mismatches) and accuracy for annotation samples in the range from 1% to 10% of the corpus. Figure 1 plots the accuracy results. It is clear that after manually annotating 10% of the whole corpus, the percentage of matches tweets between the human and the emoji-based annotation is 77.2%.

Obtaining 77.2% is not good enough to use it for a task to predict the real sentiment of the tweets even though it is less time-consuming compared to manual annotation. Therefore, later we are going to present a combination method of self training and distant supervision to improve the quality of the dataset.

Sample %	Samples	#errors	Accuracy
1%	360	106	70.5%
2%	720	200	72.2%
3%	1,080	293	72.9%
4%	1,400	370	74.3%
5%	1,800	450	75%
10%	3,608	823	77.2%

Table 2: Human annotation accuracy compared to the emojis based annotation. The first two columns show the percentage and number of the sampled tweets, #_error shows the number of mismatched samples and the Accuracy column calculates the percentage of the matches between both annotations.

Moreover, we check the quality of the corpus with pretrained sentiment analysis models that have been built and trained on existing datasets. The following datasets are used in our experiments and shown in Table 3:

- 40k dataset (Mohammed and Kora, 2019): as mentioned in the related work section, this is a tweets dataset containing 40,000 instances. It is manually annotated into positive and negative and the tweets are subsequently manually cleaned.

- LABR (Aly and Atiya, 2013): a large SA dataset for Arabic sentiment analysis. The data are extracted from a book review website and contain over 63k book reviews written in MSA with some dialectal phrases.

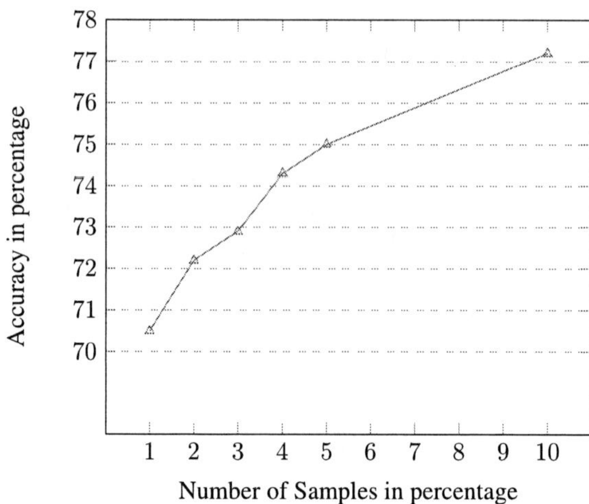

Figure 1: Accuracy of dataset comparing to human annotation

Given that our corpus concerns two-way classification, we only use the binary balanced subsets of LABR. LABR can be considered to be a human annotated corpus, where the users rate books using the stars system (1 to 5).

Ratings of 4 and 5 stars are considered positive, ratings of 1 and 2 stars negative and 3-star ratings are taken as neutral. In the binary classification case, 3-star ratings are ignored, keeping only the positive and negative labels.

- ASTD (Nabil et al., 2015): an Arabic SA corpus collected from Twitter and focusing on Egyptian Arabic. It consists of approximately 10k tweets which are classified as objective, subjective positive, subjective negative, and subjective mixed. We use only the positive and negative subset.

- Shami-Senti (Qwaider et al., 2019): a Levantine SA corpus. It contains approximately 2.5k posts from social media sites in general topics classified manually as positive, negative and neutral from the four main countries where Levantine is spoken: Palestine, Syria, Lebanon and Jordan.

Corpus	NEG	POS
40k tweets	20,002	19,998
LABR 2 Balanced	6,578	6,580
ASTD	1,496	665
Shami-Senti	935	1,064

Table 3: The number of instances per category in the corpora used in our experiments

We build a model on each corpus and apply the resulting model to our Twitter corpus. The model uses a combination of (1-3) word grams and a LinearSVC classifier. Table 4 shows the accuracy of the models built (trained and tested) on the original datasets, while the ASTAD column shows the accuracy of the trained model when we use it to predict the class on our Twitter dataset. It is clear that none of the models works for this dataset and the accuracy does not exceed 60%. This is an expected result, given that the data are from a very different domain, i.e. book reviews. Even though both ASTD and the ATSAD share the same domain, the ASTD only contains Egyptian dialects. In the case of the Shami corpus, it only contains Levantine dialects with a limited number of examples (2k). The 40k tweets model and ATSAD also share the same domain (tweets) but the manual hard prepossessing and cleaning of the data make it hard to predict real tweets as people post it, also the 40k corpus only has Egyptian dialect.

	Same corpus	ATSAD
40k tweets	79%	60%
LABR	82%	54%
ASTD	81%	59%
SHAMI-SENTI	84%	59%

Table 4: Accuracy of models trained on different SA corpora; the same corpus column indicates the accuracy of the model when the train dataset and the test dataset are both from the same corpus, the last column for the accuracy when we test the models on the ATSAD

Summing up, it is clear from the previous discussion that the ATSAD is a challenge for the models trained on the available datasets that are standardised and regularised. Therefore we have to create an ML model that would be successful on this ATSAD. To achieve a good accuracy on the model, then the dataset should be improved in term of the data quality and annotation quality.

6. Self training on Distant supervision Corpus

Creating a good resource requires the collection of a big amount of data that are preprocessed and annotated. The annotation is usually done by hiring annotators and specifying annotation rules they have to follow to produce a reasonable annotation agreement. This process is time and money consuming. There is another approach to build a large enough dataset more quickly. The process is called Distant supervision or weak supervision (Yao et al., 2010). Distant supervision involves heuristically matching the contents of a database to the corresponding text (Hoffmann et al., 2011). In our case, we use the emojis in the tweets to work as weak labels with which we can annotate the 36K tweets automatically. Although this is sometimes not producing high-quality dataset, it works in some tasks.

We annotate the 36k tweets by distant supervision and then extract 4k tweets (10% of the total dataset). We ask the two annotators to label them manually. We compute the number of agreed annotation between the human annotation and the emojis annotation we have an agreement of 77.2%.

To use the human annotation dataset as a gold standard we extract other 4K tweets and also manually annotate them, upgrading the final manually annotated dataset to 8k tweets of which 3705 are classified as positive, 3911 negative and 384 instances are mixed. We exclude the mixed class from our experiments.

We build a baseline with TF-IDF unigram word model and a Linear-SVC classifier. Moreover, we build another complex model -from some previous work - by combining word n-grams (1-5), character n-grams (2-5) with and without word boundary consideration (Qwaider et al., 2019). The models are built for sentiment analysis and the problem is recognised as two-way classification, so every tweet is classified either as positive or negative. Table 5 shows the number of tweets per class for the human annotation dataset and the remaining tweets in the emojis dataset which were weakly annotated by the distant supervision.

	Human annotated	Emojis annotated
	Label Distribution	
#Positive	3,705	14,468
#Negative	3,911	14,784
	Train/Test Distribution	
#Train_set	6,092	23,401
#Test_set	1,524	5,851
#Total_set	7,616	29,252

Table 5: Statistics of the human annotation subset and the emojis distant supervision subset after subtract the human dataset

We apply both the baseline and the complex model on the manually annotated dataset and we get an accuracy of %71 and %79 respectively. We refer to this experiment as (Manual experiment). To check again the quality of the emojis based dataset we applied the previous model trained on the human labels on the emojis dataset of 29k tweets to predict the label. After testing the two models, the resulted accuracy is %63 and %76 for both the baseline and the complex model respectively (Mixed experiment). The mixed experiment is to some extent similar to the agreement between the manual annotation and the emojis annotation experiment we have done first and got an accuracy of 76% using 4k subset.

To improve the quality of the automatic annotation and therefore the proposed tweets corpus, we will exploit the manual annotation dataset to enhance the entire dataset. Therefore, a self-training approach is to be employed on the data to improve the classification and increase the accuracy of the annotation. Self-training is a commonly used method for semi-supervised learning (Yarowsky, 1995; Abney, 2002). The idea of Self-training is to train a classifier with a small amount of labelled data and incrementally retrain the classifier by adding the most confidently labelled instances that were previously unlabelled as a new data. This process continues until most of the unlabelled data becomes labelled (Gao et al., 2014). We can implement a self-training technique with little modification of the existing configuration: our dataset is not completely unlabelled but has weak emoji-based annotations. From the mixed model experiments, rather than extracting the instances predicted with the highest confidence, we extract instances where the

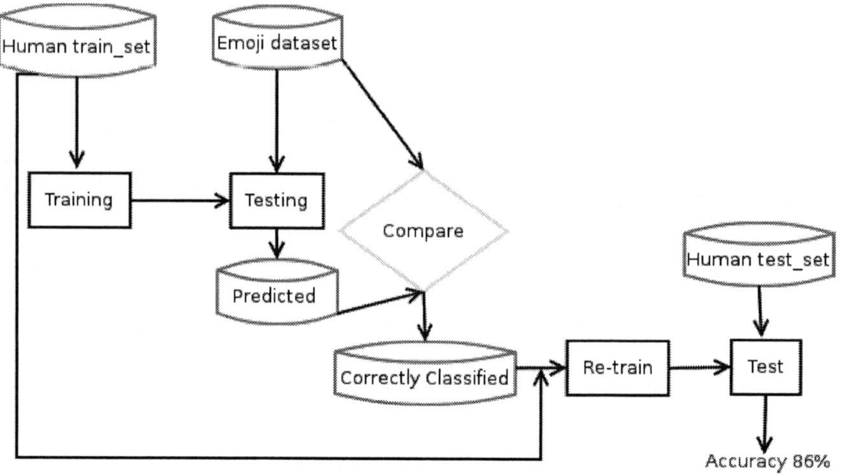

Figure 2: Self training (double-check) approach applied on the TSAD

model prediction label matches the emojis label. This is the case for 22,542 out of 29,252 tweets in the dataset. We add these tweets to the training set which consists of the human annotated dataset (6,092). Thus, to re-train the classifier we have a total of 22,542 + 6,092 = 28,634 tweets. We call this experiment (double check) where we combine the self training with distant supervision. The 28K tweets are now a dataset with strong supervised labelling where the small amount of human annotation dataset and distant supervising from emojis helps to annotate more data. We re-build both the baseline and the complex models and retrain them on the dataset we produced from the double check experiment (28k tweets), then apply the model to the test set from the human annotation dataset (1,524 tweets).We use the same dataset across all the experiments in order to allow for the comparison. The baseline and the complex model accuracy increases to 77% and 86% respectively. Figure 2 shows the diagram for the self-training approach.

To evaluate our self-training experiment and our method to extract only those instances where the model prediction matches the emojis annotation, we conduct a small experiment of self-training called (Non-check) where we:

1. Use the model from the (mixed experiment) to predict the label for the automatically labelled dataset (29k tweets).

2. Retrain the model with the human annotated training dataset in addition to the predicted labelled dataset (from the previous model). Thus, this re-train dataset consists of 6,092 + 29,252 = 35,341 tweets.

3. Use the manually annotated test set (1524 tweets) and use the model to predict the sentiment.

4. The accuracy of the baseline is 70% and 81% for the complex model.

Consequently, it is clear that (i) using the emojis as a noisy label, (ii) matching with the human annotation and (iii) apply the self training technique to annotate the dataset leads to an improvement of the data. Table 6 shows the performance of the models on different datasets. These are represented as plots in Figure 3.

Experiment	#Train	#test	Baseline	Complex
Manual	6,092	1,524	71%	79%
Mixed	6,092	29,252	63%	76%
double-check	28,634	1,524	**77%**	**86%**
Non-check	35,341	1,524	70%	81%

Table 6: The performance of the baseline and complex models on different datasets.

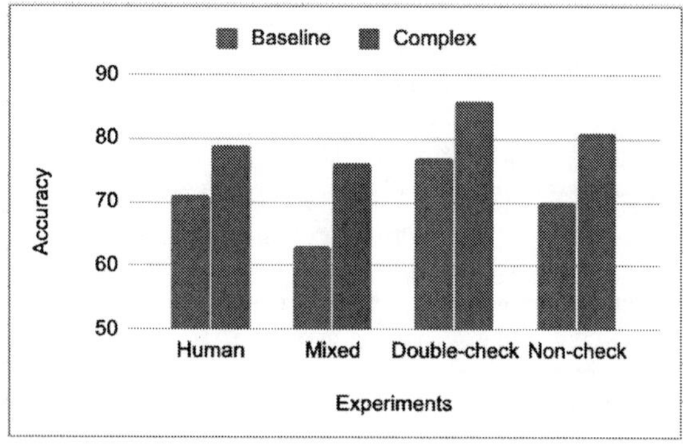

Figure 3: plotting the accuracy for all the experiments for both the baseline and complicated models

When we were done with the experiments, we extracted all the emojis and examined the emoji frequencies per category. We found some emojis are shared between the positive and the negative class, such as the smiley face with tears. We also discover that people used the black smiley face to indicate the negative feeling more often than the positive. These emojis are considered tricky emojis and they decrease the quality of the annotation. We modified our conditions by removing all the misleading emojis to collect more accurate data. Up to now we have collected over 200k tweets. Table 7 views the number of occurrence for the most 10 frequent emojis per sentiment category.

	Positive Class		Negative Class	
	Emoji	#	Emoji	#
1		2938		4249
2		1442		2178
3		1303		1126
4		931		1070
5		834		905
6		716		845
7		662		619
8		503		608
9		424		501
10		385		468
Total		22757		23969

Table 7: Number of occurrence for the most 10 frequent emojis per category, the last row show the total number of the whole emojis in the dataset per category

7. Future work

Based on our emojis analysis and the subsequent modification of the data collection and annotation conditions, we are planning to further increase the size of the dataset and use it for different tasks like building custom sentiment word embeddings and to fine-tune deep learning networks.

8. Conclusion

To extend the limited Dialectal Arabic resources, we collected an Arabic Tweets Sentiment Analysis Dataset (AT-SAD). The corpus has been collected from Twitter during April 2019 and employs emojis as seeds for extraction of candidate instances. After the pre-processing, we apply distant supervision using emojis as weak labels to annotate the entire dataset. In addition, we commissioned two annotators to manually annotate a subset of 8k tweets. We evaluate the corpus by comparing the emoji-based annotation with the human annotation and we get an observed agreement of 77.2%. We built a sentiment analysis machine learning model with the unigram features as a baseline and another complex model that utilises word grams and character grams. We exploit the human annotation dataset to help us improve the annotation of the automatically labelled dataset by self-training approaches. Over several experiments we achieve an accuracy of 86%.

Using the distant supervision approaches for automatically data annotation process can saves us a lot of effort, time and money. Distant supervision is a very valuable method to annotate large number of instances automatically, in our case based on emojis to denote the category. The self training approach can be used together with a small number of manually annotated instances to improve the quality of the automatically labelled dataset.

Acknowledgements

Kathrein Abu Kwaik, Stergios Chatzikyriakidis and Simon Dobnik are supported by grant 2014-39 from the Swedish Research Council, which funds the Centre for Linguistic Theory and Studies in Probability (CLASP) in the Department of Philosophy, Linguistics, and Theory of Science at the University of Gothenburg. Richard Johansson was funded by the Swedish Research Council under grant 2013–4944.

9. Bibliographical References

Abdul-Mageed, M., Diab, M., and Kübler, S. (2014). Samar: Subjectivity and sentiment analysis for Arabic social media. *Computer Speech & Language*, 28(1):20–37.

Abney, S. (2002). Bootstrapping. In *Proceedings of the 40th annual meeting of the Association for Computational Linguistics*, pages 360–367.

Al Sallab, A., Hajj, H., Badaro, G., Baly, R., El Hajj, W., and Shaban, K. B. (2015). Deep learning models for sentiment analysis in Arabic. In *Proceedings of the second workshop on Arabic natural language processing*, pages 9–17.

Al Shboul, B., Al-Ayyoub, M., and Jararweh, Y. (2015). Multi-way sentiment classification of Arabic reviews. In *2015 6th International Conference on Information and Communication Systems (ICICS)*, pages 206–211. IEEE.

Al-Twairesh, N., Al-Khalifa, H., and Al-Salman, A. (2016). AraSenTi: Large-Scale Twitter-Specific Arabic Sentiment Lexicons. In *Proceedings of the 54th Annual Meeting of the Association for Computational Linguistics (Volume 1: Long Papers)*, pages 697–705, Berlin, Germany, August. Association for Computational Linguistics.

Al-Twairesh, N., Al-Khalifa, H., Al-Salman, A., and Al-Ohali, Y. (2017). Arasenti-tweet: A corpus for Arabic sentiment analysis of saudi tweets. *Procedia Computer Science*, 117:63–72.

Alayba, A. M., Palade, V., England, M., and Iqbal, R. (2018). A combined CNN and LSTM model for Arabic sentiment analysis. In *International Cross-Domain Conference for Machine Learning and Knowledge Extraction*, pages 179–191. Springer.

Alwakid, G., Osman, T., and Hughes-Roberts, T. (2017). Challenges in sentiment analysis for Arabic social networks. *Procedia Computer Science*, 117:89–100.

Aly, M. and Atiya, A. (2013). Labr: A large scale Arabic book reviews dataset. In *Proceedings of the 51st Annual Meeting of the Association for Computational Linguistics (Volume 2: Short Papers)*, volume 2, pages 494–498.

Atoum, J. O. and Nouman, M. (2019). Sentiment Analysis of Arabic Jordanian Dialect Tweets. *(IJACSA) International Journal of Advanced Computer Science and Applications*, 10:256–262.

Azmi, A. M. and Alzanin, S. M. (2014). Aara'–a system for mining the polarity of Saudi public opinion through e-newspaper comments. *Journal of Information Science*, 40(3):398–410.

Bakliwal, A., Arora, P., Madhappan, S., Kapre, N., Singh, M., and Varma, V. (2012). Mining sentiments from tweets. In *Proceedings of the 3rd Workshop in Computational Approaches to Subjectivity and Sentiment Analysis*, pages 11–18.

Bravo-Marquez, F., Mendoza, M., and Poblete, B. (2013). Combining strengths, emotions and polarities for boosting twitter sentiment analysis. In *Proceedings of the Second International Workshop on Issues of Sentiment Discovery and Opinion Mining*, page 2. ACM.

Dahou, A., Xiong, S., Zhou, J., Haddoud, M. H., and Duan, P. (2016). Word embeddings and convolutional neural network for Arabic sentiment classification. In *Proceedings of coling 2016, the 26th international conference on computational linguistics: Technical papers*, pages 2418–2427.

El-Beltagy, S. R., Khalil, T., Halaby, A., and Hammad, M. (2016). Combining lexical features and a supervised learning approach for Arabic sentiment analysis. In *International Conference on Intelligent Text Processing and Computational Linguistics*, pages 307–319. Springer.

Elnagar, A., Khalifa, Y. S., and Einea, A. (2018). Hotel Arabic-reviews dataset construction for sentiment analysis applications. In *Intelligent Natural Language Processing: Trends and Applications*, pages 35–52. Springer.

Gao, W., Li, S., Xue, Y., Wang, M., and Zhou, G. (2014). Semi-supervised sentiment classification with self-training on feature subspaces. In *Workshop on Chinese Lexical Semantics*, pages 231–239. Springer.

Giachanou, A. and Crestani, F. (2016). Like It or Not: A Survey of Twitter Sentiment Analysis Methods. *ACM Comput. Surv.*, 49(2):28:1–28:41, June.

Go, A., Bhayani, R., and Huang, L. (2009). Twitter sentiment classification using distant supervision. *CS224N Project Report, Stanford*, 1(12):2009.

Hoffmann, R., Zhang, C., Ling, X., Zettlemoyer, L., and Weld, D. S. (2011). Knowledge-based weak supervision for information extraction of overlapping relations. In *Proceedings of the 49th Annual Meeting of the Association for Computational Linguistics: Human Language Technologies-Volume 1*, pages 541–550. Association for Computational Linguistics.

Kralj Novak, P., Smailović, J., Sluban, B., and Mozetič, I. (2015). Sentiment of emojis. *PLoS ONE*, 10(12):e0144296.

Liu, B. (2012). Sentiment analysis and opinion mining. *Synthesis lectures on human language technologies*, 5(1):1–167.

Mohammed, A. and Kora, R. (2019). Deep learning approaches for Arabic sentiment analysis. *Social Network Analysis and Mining*, 9(1):52.

Nabil, M., Aly, M., and Atiya, A. (2015). ASTD: Arabic Sentiment Tweets Dataset. In *Proceedings of the 2015 Conference on Empirical Methods in Natural Language Processing*, pages 2515–2519.

Obaidat, I., Mohawesh, R., Al-Ayyoub, M., Mohammad, A.-S., and Jararweh, Y. (2015). Enhancing the determi-nation of aspect categories and their polarities in Arabic reviews using lexicon-based approaches. In *2015 IEEE Jordan Conference on Applied Electrical Engineering and Computing Technologies (AEECT)*, pages 1–6. IEEE.

Qwaider, C., Chatzikyriakidis, S., and Dobnik, S. (2019). Can Modern Standard Arabic Approaches be used for Arabic Dialects? Sentiment Analysis as a Case Study. In *Proceedings of the 3rd Workshop on Arabic Corpus Linguistics*, pages 40–50.

Refaee, E. and Rieser, V. (2014). Evaluating distant supervision for subjectivity and sentiment analysis on Arabic twitter feeds. In *Proceedings of the EMNLP 2014 workshop on Arabic natural language processing (ANLP)*, pages 174–179.

Resnik, P. and Lin, J. (2010). 11. evaluation of NLP systems. *The handbook of computational linguistics and natural language processing*, 57.

Rushdi-Saleh, M., Martín-Valdivia, M. T., Ureña-López, L. A., and Perea-Ortega, J. M. (2011). OCA: Opinion Corpus for Arabic. *Journal of the American Society for Information Science and Technology*, 62(10):2045–2054.

Saif, H., He, Y., and Alani, H. (2012). Alleviating data sparsity for twitter sentiment analysis. CEUR Workshop Proceedings (CEUR-WS. org).

Speriosu, M., Sudan, N., Upadhyay, S., and Baldridge, J. (2011). Twitter polarity classification with label propagation over lexical links and the follower graph. In *Proceedings of the First workshop on Unsupervised Learning in NLP*, pages 53–63. Association for Computational Linguistics.

Yao, L., Riedel, S., and McCallum, A. (2010). Collective cross-document relation extraction without labelled data. In *Proceedings of the 2010 Conference on Empirical Methods in Natural Language Processing*, pages 1013–1023. Association for Computational Linguistics.

Yarowsky, D. (1995). Unsupervised word sense disambiguation rivaling supervised methods. In *33rd annual meeting of the association for computational linguistics*, pages 189–196.

Proceedings of the 4th Workshop on Open-Source Arabic Corpora and Processing Tools, pages 9–15
with a Shared Task on Offensive Language Detection.
Language Resources and Evaluation Conference (LREC 2020), Marseille, 11–16 May 2020
© European Language Resources Association (ELRA), licensed under CC-BY-NC

AraBERT: Transformer-based Model for
Arabic Language Understanding

Wissam Antoun*, Fady Baly*, Hazem Hajj
American University of Beirut
{wfa07, fgb06, hh63}@aub.edu.lb

Abstract

The Arabic language is a morphologically rich language with relatively few resources and a less explored syntax compared to English. Given these limitations, Arabic Natural Language Processing (NLP) tasks like Sentiment Analysis (SA), Named Entity Recognition (NER), and Question Answering (QA), have proven to be very challenging to tackle. Recently, with the surge of transformers based models, language-specific BERT based models have proven to be very efficient at language understanding, provided they are pre-trained on a very large corpus. Such models were able to set new standards and achieve state-of-the-art results for most NLP tasks. In this paper, we pre-trained BERT specifically for the Arabic language in the pursuit of achieving the same success that BERT did for the English language. The performance of AraBERT is compared to multilingual BERT from Google and other state-of-the-art approaches. The results showed that the newly developed AraBERT achieved state-of-the-art performance on most tested Arabic NLP tasks. The pretrained araBERT models are publicly available on github.com/aub-mind/araBERT hoping to encourage research and applications for Arabic NLP.

Keywords: Arabic, transformers, BERT, AraBERT, Language Models

1. Introduction

Pretrained contextualized text representation models have enabled massive advances in Natural Language Understanding (NLU) tasks, and achieved state-of-the-art performances in multiple NLP tasks (Howard and Ruder, 2018; Devlin et al., 2018). Early pretrained text representation models aimed at representing words by capturing their distributed syntactic and semantic properties using techniques like Word2vec (Mikolov et al., 2013) and GloVe (Pennington et al., 2014). However, these models did not incorporate the context in which a word appears into its embedding. This issue was addressed by generating contextualized representations using models like ELMO (Peters et al., 2018)). Recently, there has been a focus on applying transfer learning by fine-tuning large pretrained language models for downstream NLP/NLU tasks with a relatively small number of examples, resulting in notable performance improvement for these tasks. This approach takes advantage of the language models that had been pre-trained in an unsupervised manner (or sometimes called self-supervised). However, this advantage comes with drawbacks, particularly the huge corpora needed for pre-training, in addition to the high computational cost of days needed for training (latest models required 500+ TPUs or GPUs running for weeks (Conneau et al., 2019; Raffel et al., 2019; Adiwardana et al., 2020)). These drawbacks restricted the availability of such models to English mainly and a handful of other languages. To remedy this gap, multilingual models have been trained to learn representations for +100 languages simultaneously, but still fall behind single-language models due to little data representation and small language-specific vocabulary. While languages with similar structure and vocabulary can benefit from the shared representations (Conneau et al., 2019), this is not the case for other languages, like Arabic, which differ in morphological and syntactic structure and share very little with other abundant Latin-based languages.

In this paper, we describe the process of pretraining the BERT transformer model (Devlin et al., 2018) for the Arabic language, and which we name ARABERT. We evaluate ARABERT on three Arabic NLU downstream tasks that are different in nature: (*i*) Sentiment Analysis (SA), (*ii*) Named Entity Recognition (NER), and (*iii*) Question Answering (QA). The experiments results show that ARABERT achieves state-of-the-art performances on most datasets, compared to several baselines including previous multilingual and single-language approaches. The datasets that we considered for the downstream tasks contained both Modern Standard Arabic (MSA) and Dialectal Arabic (DA).

Our contributions can be summarized as follows:

- A methodology to pretrain the BERT model on a large-scale Arabic corpus.

- Application of ARABERT to three NLU downstream tasks: Sentiment Analysis, Named Entity Recognition and Question Answering.

- Publicly releasing ARABERT on popular NLP libraries.

The rest of the paper is structured as follows. Section 2. provides a concise literature review of previous work on language representation for English and Arabic. Section 3. describes the methodology that was used to develop ARABERT. Section 4. describes the downstream tasks and benchmark datasets that are used for evaluation. Section 5. presents the experimental setup and discusses the results. Finally, section 6. concludes and points to possible directions for future work.

2. Related Works
2.1. Evolution of Word Embeddings

The first meaningful representations for words started with the word2vec model developed by (Mikolov et al., 2013).

---

*Equal Contribution

Since then, research started moving towards variations of word2vec like of GloVe (Pennington et al., 2014) and fastText (Mikolov et al., 2017). While major advances were achieved with these early models, they still lacked contextualized information, which was tackled by ELMO (Peters et al., 2018). The performance over different tasks improved noticeably, leading to larger structures that had superior word and sentence representations. Ever since, more language understanding models have been developed such as ULMFit (Howard and Ruder, 2018), BERT (Devlin et al., 2018), RoBERTa (Liu et al., 2019), XLNet (Yang et al., 2019), ALBERT (Lan et al., 2019), and T5 (Raffel et al., 2019), which offered improved performance by exploring different pretraining methods, modified model architectures and larger training corpora.

2.2. Non-contextual Representations for Arabic

Following the success of the English word2vec (Mikolov et al., 2013), the same feat was sought by NLP researchers to create language specific embeddings. Arabic word2vec was first attempted by (Soliman et al., 2017), and then followed by a Fasttext model (Bojanowski et al., 2017) trained on Wikipedia data and showing better performance than word2vec. To tackle dialectal variations in Arabic (Erdmann et al., 2018) presented techniques for training multidialectal word embeddings on relatively small and noisy corpora, while (Abu Farha and Magdy, 2019; Abdul-Mageed et al., 2018) provided Arabic word embeddings trained on ∼250M tweets.

2.3. Contextualized Representations for Arabic

For non-English languages, Google released a multilingual BERT (Devlin et al., 2018) supporting 100+ languages with solid performance for most languages. However, pre-training monolingual BERT for non-English languages proved to provide better performance than the multilingual BERT such as Italian BERT Alberto (Polignano et al., 2019) and other publicly available BERTs (Martin et al., 2019; de Vries et al., 2019). Arabic specific contextualized representations models, such as hULMonA (ElJundi et al., 2019), used the ULMfit structure, which had a lower performance that BERT on English NLP Tasks.

3. ARABERT: Methodology

In this paper, we develop an Arabic language representation model to improve the state-of-the-art in several Arabic NLU tasks. We create ARABERT based on the BERT model, a stacked Bidirectional Transformer Encoder (Devlin et al., 2018). This model is widely considered as the basis for most state-of-the-art results in different NLP tasks in several languages. We use the BERT-base configuration that has 12 encoder blocks, 768 hidden dimensions, 12 attention heads, 512 maximum sequence length, and a total of ∼110M parameters[1]. We also introduced additional preprocessing prior to the model's pre-training, in order to better fit the Arabic language. Below, we describe the pre-training setup, the pre-training dataset for ARABERT,

the proposed Arabic-specific preprocessing, and the fine-tuning process.

3.1. Pre-training Setup

Following the original BERT pre-training objective, we employ the *Masked Language Modeling* (MLM) task by adding whole-word masking where; 15% of the N input tokens are selected for replacement. Those tokens are replaced 80% of the times with the [MASK] token, 10% with a random token, and 10% with the original token. Whole-word masking improves the pre-training task by forcing the model to predict the whole word instead of getting hints from parts of the word. We also employ the *Next Sentence Prediction* (NSP) task that helps the model understand the relationship between two sentences, which can be useful for many language understanding tasks such as Question Answering.

3.2. Pre-training Dataset

The original BERT was trained on 3.3B words extracted from English Wikipedia and the Book Corpus (Zhu et al., 2015). Since the Arabic Wikipedia Dumps are small compared to the English ones, we manually scraped Arabic news websites for articles. In addition, we used two publicly available large Arabic corpora: (1) the 1.5 billion words Arabic Corpus (El-Khair, 2016), which is a contemporary corpus that includes more than 5 million articles extracted from ten major news sources covering 8 countries, and (2) OSIAN: the Open Source International Arabic News Corpus (Zeroual et al., 2019) that consists of 3.5 million articles (∼1B tokens) from 31 news sources in 24 Arab countries.

The final size of the pre-training dataset, after removing duplicate sentences, is 70 million sentences, corresponding to ∼24GB of text. This dataset covers news from different media in different Arab regions, and therefore can be representative of a wide range of topics discussed in the Arab world. It is worth mentioning that we preserved words that include Latin characters, since it is common to mention named entities, scientific or technical terms in their original language, to avoid information loss.

3.3. Sub-Word Units Segmentation

Arabic language is known for its lexical sparsity which is due to the complex concatenative system of Arabic (Al-Sallab et al., 2017). Words can have different forms and share the same meaning. For instance, while the definite article "ال - *Al*", which is equivalent to "the" in English, is always prefixed to other words, it is not an intrinsic part of that word. Hence, when using a BERT-compatible tokenization, tokens will appear twice, once with "*Al-*" and

---

[1] Further details about the transformer architecture can be found in (Vaswani et al., 2017)

once without it. For instance, both "كتاب‎- *kitAb*" and "الكتاب‎-*AlkitAb*" need to be included in the vocabulary, leading to a significant amount of unnecessary redundancy.

To avoid this issue, we first segment the words using Farasa (Abdelali et al., 2016) into stems, prefixes and suffixes. For instance, "اللّغة‎ - *Alloga*" becomes ال‎ +لغ‎ +ة‎ - *Al+ log +a*". Then, we trained a SentencePiece (an unsupervised text tokenizer and detokenizer (Kudo, 2018)), in unigram mode, on the segmented pre-training dataset to produce a subword vocabulary of ∼60K tokens. To evaluate the impact of the proposed tokenization, we also trained SentencePiece on non-segmented text to create a second version of ARABERT (AraBERTv0.1) that does not require any segmentation. The final size of vocabulary was 64k tokens, which included nearly 4K unused tokens to allow further pre-training, if needed.

3.4. Fine-tuning

Sequence Classification To fine-tune AraBERT for sequence classification, we take the final hidden state of the first token, which corresponds to the word embedding of the special "[CLS]" token prepended to the start of each sentence. We then add a simple feed-forward layer with standard Softmax to get the probability distribution over the predicted output classes. During fine-tuning, the classifier and the pre-trained model weights are trained jointly to maximize the log-probability of the correct class.

Named Entity Recognition For the NER task, each token in the sentence is labeled with the IOB2 format (Ratnaparkhi, 1998), where the "B" tag corresponds to the first word of the entity, the "I" tag corresponds to the rest of the words of the same entity, and the "O" tag indicates that the tagged word is not a desired named entity. Hence, we treat the system as a multi-class classification process, which allows us to use some text classification methods to label the tokens. Furthermore, after using the AraBERT tokenizer, we only input the first sub-token of each word to the model.

Question Answering In the QA, given a question and a passage containing the answer, the model needs to select a span of text that contains the answers. This is done by predicting a "start" token and an "end" token on condition that the "end" token should appear after the "start" token. During training, the final embedding of every token in the passage is fed into two classifiers, each with a single set of weights, which are applied to every token. The dot product of the output embeddings and the classifier is then fed into a softmax layer to produce a probability distribution over all the tokens. The token with the highest probability of being a "start" toke is then selected, and the same process is repeated for the "end" token.

4. Evaluation

We evaluated ARABERT on three Arabic language understanding downstream tasks: Sentiment Analysis, Named Entity Recognition, and Question Answering. As a baseline, we compared ARABERT to the multilingual version of BERT, and to other state-of-art results on each task.

4.1. Sentiment Analysis

We evaluated ARABERT on the following Arabic sentiment datasets that cover different genres, domains and dialects.

- **HARD:** The Hotel Arabic Reviews Dataset (Elnagar et al., 2018) contains 93,700 hotel reviews written in both Modern Standard Arabic (MSA) and in dialectal Arabic. Reviews are split into positive and negative reviews, where a negative review has a rating of 1 or 2, a positive review has a rating of 4 or 5, and neutral reviews with rating of 3 were ignored.

- **ASTD:** The Arabic Sentiment Twitter Dataset (Nabil et al., 2015) contains 10,000 tweets written in both MSA and Egyptian dialect. We tested on the balanced version of the dataset, referred to as ASTD-B.

- **ArSenTD-Lev:** The Arabic Sentiment Twitter Dataset for LEVantine (Baly et al., 2018) contains 4,000 tweets written in Levantine dialect with annotations for sentiment, topic and sentiment target. This is a challenging dataset as the collected tweets are from multiple domains and discuss different topics.

- **LABR:** The Large-scale Arabic Book Reviews dataset (Aly and Atiya, 2013) contains 63,000 book reviews written in Arabic. The reviews are rated between 1 and 5. We benchmarked our model on the unbalanced two-class dataset, where reviews with ratings of 1 or 2 are considered negative, while those with ratings of 4 or 5 are considered positive.

- **AJGT:** The Arabic Jordanian General Tweets dataset (Alomari et al., 2017) contains 1,800 tweets written in Jordanian dialect. The tweets were manually annotated as either positive or negative.

Baselines: Sentiment Analysis is a popular Arabic NLP task. Previous approaches relied on sentiment lexicons such as ArSenL (Badaro et al., 2014), which is a large-scale lexicon of MSA words that is developed using the Arabic WordNet in combination with the English SentiWordNet. Recurrent and recursive neural networks were explored with different choices of Arabic-specific processing (Al Sallab et al., 2015; Al-Sallab et al., 2017; Baly et al., 2017). Convolutional Neural Networks (CNN) were trained with pre-trained word embeddings (Dahou et al., 2019a). A hybrid model was proposed by (Abu Farha and Magdy, 2019), where CNNs were used for feature extraction, and LSTMs were used for sequence and context understanding. Current state-of-the-art results are achieved by the hULMonA model (ElJundi et al., 2019), which is an Arabic language model that is based on the ULMfit architecture (Howard and Ruder, 2018). We compare the results of ARABERT to those of hULMonA.

4.2. Named Entity Recognition

This task aims to extract and detect named entities in the text. It is framed as a word-level classification (or tagging) task, where the classes correspond to pre-defined categories such as names, locations, organizations, events and time expressions. For evaluation, we use the Arabic NER corpus (ANERcorp) (Benajiba and Rosso, 2007). This dataset contains 16.5K entity mentions distributed among 4 entities categories, *person* (39%), *organization*: (30.4%), *location*: (20.6%), and *miscellaneous*: (10%).

Baselines: Advances in the NER task have been focusing on English, namely on the CoNLL 2003 (Sang and De Meulder, 2003) dataset. Initially, NER was tackled with Conditional Random Fields (CRF) (Lafferty et al., 2001). Later on, CRFs were used on top of Bi-LSTM models (Huang et al., 2015; Lample et al., 2016) presenting significant improvements over standalone CRFs. Bi-LSTM-CRF structures were then used with contextualized embeddings that displayed further improvements (Peters et al., 2018). Lastly, large pre-trained transformers showed slight improvement, setting the current state-of-the-art performance (Devlin et al., 2018). As for Arabic, We compare ARABERT performance with Bi-LSTM-CRF baseline that set the previous state-of-the-art performance (El Bazi and Laachfoubi, 2019), and with BERT multilingual.

4.3. Question Answering

Open-domain Question Answering (QA) is one of the goals of artificial intelligence, this goal can be achieved by leveraging natural language understanding and knowledge gathering (Kwiatkowski et al., 2019). English QA research has been fueled by the release of large datasets such as Stanford Question Answering Dataset (SQuAD) (Rajpurkar et al., 2016). On the other hand, research in Arabic QA has been hindered by the lack of such massive datasets, and by the fact that Arabic presents its own challenges such as:

- Inconsistent name spelling (ex: Syria in Arabic can be written as "سوريا - *sOriyA*" and "سورية - *sOriyT*")

- Name de-spacing (ex: The name is written as " عبدالعزيز - *AbdulAzIz*" in the question, and " عبد العزيز - *Abdul AzIz*" in the answer)

- Dual form " المثنى", which can have multiple forms (ex: "قلمان - *qalamAn*" or "قلمين - *qalamyn*" meaning *"two pencils"*)

- Grammatical gender variation: all nouns, animate and inanimate objects are classified under two genders either masculine or feminine (ex: "كبير - *kabIr*" and " كبيرة - *kabIrT*"

We evaluate ARABERT on the Arabic Reading Comprehension Dataset (ARCD) (Mozannar et al., 2019) , where the task is to find the span of the answer in a document for a given question. ARCD contains 1395 questions on Wikipedia articles along with 2966 machine translated questions and answers from the SQuAD dubbed (Arabic-SQuAD). We train on the whole Arabic-SQuAD and on 50% of ARCD and test on the remaining 50% of ARCD.

Baselines Multilingual BERT had previously achieved state of the art results on ARCD.

5. Experiments

5.1. Experimental Setup

Pretraining In our experiments, the original implementation of BERT on TensorFlow was used. The data for pre-training was sharded, transformed into TFRecords, and then stored on Google Cloud Storage. Duplication factor was set to 10, a random seed of 34, and a masking probability of 15%. The model was pre-trained on a TPUv2-8 pod for 1,250,000 steps. To speed up the training time, the first 900K steps were trained on sequences of 128 tokens, and the remaining steps were trained on sequences of 512 tokens. The decision of stopping the pre-training was based on the performance of downstream tasks. We follow the same approach taken by the open-sourced German BERT (DeepsetAI,). Adam optimizer was used, with a learning rate of 1e-4, batch size of 512 and 128 for sequence length of 128 and 512 respectively. Training took 4 days, for 27 epochs over all the tokens.

Fine-tuning Fine-tuning was done independently using the same configuration for all tasks. We do not run extensive grid search for the best hyper-parameters due to computational and time constraints. We use the splits provided by the dataset's authors when available. and the standard 80% and 20% when not[2].

5.2. Results

Table 1 illustrates the experimental results of applying AraBERT to multiple Arabic NLU downstream tasks, compared to state-of-the-art results and the multilingual BERT model (mBERT).

Sentiment Analysis For Arabic sentiment analysis, the results in Table 1 show that both versions of AraBERT outperform mBERT and other state-of-the-art approaches on most tested datasets. Even though AraBERT was trained on MSA, the model was able to preform well on dialects that were never seen before.

Named Entity Recognition Results in Table 1 show that AraBERTv0.1 improved results by 2.53 points in F1 score scoring 84.2 compared with the Bi-LSTM-CRF model, making AraBERT the new state-of-the-art for NER on ANERcorp. Testing AraBERT with tokenized suffixes and prefixes showed results similar to that of the Bi-LSTM-CRF model. We believe that the reason this happened is that the start token (B-label) is referenced to the suffixes most of the

---

[2]The scripts used to create the datasets are available on our Github repo https://github.com/aub-mind/arabert

Table 1: Performance of AraBERT on Arabic downstream tasks compared to mBERT and previous state of the art systems

Task	metric	prev. SOTA	mBERT	AraBERTv0.1/ v1
SA (HARD)	Acc.	95.7*	95.7	**96.2** / 96.1
SA (ASTD)	Acc.	86.5*	80.1	92.2 / **92.6**
SA (ArsenTD-Lev)	Acc.	52.4*	51.0	58.9 / **59.4**
SA (AJGT)	Acc.	92.6**	83.6	93.1 / **93.8**
SA (LABR)	Acc.	**87.5**[†]	83.0	85.9 / 86.7
NER (ANERcorp)	macro-F1	81.7[††]	78.4	**84.2** / 81.9
QA (ARCD)	Exact Match	mBERT	**34.2**	30.1 / 30.6
	macro-F1		61.3	61.2 / **62.7**
	Sent. Match		90.0	**93.0** / 92.0

* (ElJundi et al., 2019)
** (Dahou et al., 2019b)
[†] (Dahou et al., 2019b)
[††] Previous state of the art performance by BiLSTM-CRF model

time. An example of this, "الجامعة" with a label B-ORG becomes "الـ", "جامعة" with labels B-ORG, I-ORG respectively, providing misleading starting cues to the model. Testing multilingual BERT, it proved inefficient as we got results lower than the baseline model.

Question Answering While the results in Table 1 show an improvement in F1-score, the exact match scores were significantly lower. Upon further examination of the results, the majority of the erroneous answers differed from the true answer by one or two words with no significant impact on the semantics of the answer. Examples are shown in Tables 2 and 3. We also report a 2% absolute increase in the sentence match score over mBERT, which is the previous state-of-the-art. Sentence Match (SM) measures the percentage of predictions that are within the same sentence as the ground truth answer.

Table 2: Example of an erroneous results from the ARCD test set: the only difference is the preposition "في - *In*".

Question	أين تأسست منظمة الأم المتحدة؟
	where was the united nations established?
Ground Truth	*In San Francisco* – في سان فرنسيسكو
Predicted Answer	*San Francisco* – سان فرنسيسكو

Table 3: Another example of an erroneous results from the ARCD test set: the predicted answer does not include "introductory" words.

Question	ما هو النظام الخاص بدولة النمسا؟
	What is the type of government in Austria?
Ground Truth	*Austria is a federal republic* – النمسا هي جمهورية فيدرالية
Predicted Answer	*A federal republic* – جمهورية فيدرالية

5.3. Discussion

AraBERT achieved state-of-the-art performance on sentiment analysis, named entity recognition, and the question answering tasks. This adds truth to the assumption that pretrained language models on a single language only surpass the performance of a multilingual model. This jump in performance has many explanations. First, data size is a clear factor for the boost in performance. AraBERT used around 24GB of data in comparison with the 4.3G Wikipedia used for the multilingual BERT. Second, the vocab size used in the multilingual BERT is 2k tokens in comparison with 64k vocab size used for developing AraBERT. Third, with the large data size, the pre-training distribution has more diversity. As for the fourth point, the pre-segmentation applied before BERT tokenization improved performance on SA and QA tasks but reduced it on the NER task. It is also noted that the pre-processing applied to the pre-training data took into consideration the complexities of the Arabic language. Hence, increased the effective vocabulary by excluding unnecessary redundant tokens that come with certain common prefixes, and help the model learn better by reducing the language complexity. We believe these factors helped to reach state-of-the-art results on 3 different tasks and 8 different datasets. Obtained results indicate that the advantage we got in the datasets considered are better understood in a monolingual model than of a general language model trained on Wikipedia crawls such as multilingual BERT.

6. Conclusion

AraBERT sets a new state-of-the-art for several downstream tasks for Arabic language. It is also 300MB smaller than multilingual BERT. By publicly releasing our AraBERT models, we hope that it will be used to serve as the new baseline for the various Arabic NLP tasks, and hope that this work will act as a footing stone to building and improving future Arabic language understanding models. We are currently working on publishing an AraBERT version that won't depend on external tokenizers. We are also in the process of training models with a better understanding of the various dialects that the Arabic language has across different Arabic countries.

7. Acknowledgments

We would like to express special thanks to Dr. Ramy Baly (Massachusetts Institute of Technology) for the useful discussions and suggestions, to Dr. Dirk Goldhahn (Universität Leipzig) for access to the OSIAN dataset, to TFRC for the free access to cloud TPUs, and to As-Safir newspaper, and Yakshof for providing us with their news articles.

8. References

Abdelali, A., Darwish, K., Durrani, N., and Mubarak, H. (2016). Farasa: A fast and furious segmenter for arabic. In *Proceedings of the 2016 Conference of the North American Chapter of the Association for Computational Linguistics: Demonstrations*, pages 11–16.

Abdul-Mageed, M., Alhuzali, H., and Elaraby, M. (2018). You tweet what you speak: A city-level dataset of arabic dialects. In *Proceedings of the Eleventh International Conference on Language Resources and Evaluation (LREC 2018)*.

Abu Farha, I. and Magdy, W. (2019). Mazajak: An online Arabic sentiment analyser. In *Proceedings of the Fourth*

Arabic Natural Language Processing Workshop, pages 192–198, Florence, Italy, August. Association for Computational Linguistics.

Adiwardana, D., Luong, M.-T., So, D. R., Hall, J., Fiedel, N., Thoppilan, R., Yang, Z., Kulshreshtha, A., Nemade, G., Lu, Y., and Le, Q. V. (2020). Towards a human-like open-domain chatbot.

Al Sallab, A., Hajj, H., Badaro, G., Baly, R., El-Hajj, W., and Shaban, K. (2015). Deep learning models for sentiment analysis in arabic. In *Proceedings of the second workshop on Arabic natural language processing*, pages 9–17.

Al-Sallab, A., Baly, R., Hajj, H., Shaban, K. B., El-Hajj, W., and Badaro, G. (2017). Aroma: A recursive deep learning model for opinion mining in arabic as a low resource language. *ACM Transactions on Asian and Low-Resource Language Information Processing (TALLIP)*, 16(4):1–20.

Alomari, K. M., ElSherif, H. M., and Shaalan, K. (2017). Arabic tweets sentimental analysis using machine learning. In *International Conference on Industrial, Engineering and Other Applications of Applied Intelligent Systems*, pages 602–610. Springer.

Aly, M. and Atiya, A. (2013). LABR: A large scale Arabic book reviews dataset. In *Proceedings of the 51st Annual Meeting of the Association for Computational Linguistics (Volume 2: Short Papers)*, pages 494–498, Sofia, Bulgaria, August. Association for Computational Linguistics.

Badaro, G., Baly, R., Hajj, H., Habash, N., and El-Hajj, W. (2014). A large scale arabic sentiment lexicon for arabic opinion mining. In *Proceedings of the EMNLP 2014 workshop on arabic natural language processing (ANLP)*, pages 165–173.

Baly, R., Hajj, H., Habash, N., Shaban, K. B., and El-Hajj, W. (2017). A sentiment treebank and morphologically enriched recursive deep models for effective sentiment analysis in arabic. *ACM Transactions on Asian and Low-Resource Language Information Processing (TALLIP)*, 16(4):1–21.

Baly, R., Khaddaj, A., Hajj, H., El-Hajj, W., and Shaban, K. B. (2018). Arsentd-lev: A multi-topic corpus for target-based sentiment analysis in arabic levantine tweets. In *OSACT 3: The 3rd Workshop on Open-Source Arabic Corpora and Processing Tools*, page 37.

Benajiba, Y. and Rosso, P. (2007). Anersys 2.0: Conquering the ner task for the arabic language by combining the maximum entropy with pos-tag information. In *IICAI*, pages 1814–1823.

Bojanowski, P., Grave, E., Joulin, A., and Mikolov, T. (2017). Enriching word vectors with subword information. *Transactions of the Association for Computational Linguistics*, 5:135–146.

Conneau, A., Khandelwal, K., Goyal, N., Chaudhary, V., Wenzek, G., Guzmán, F., Grave, E., Ott, M., Zettlemoyer, L., and Stoyanov, V. (2019). Unsupervised cross-lingual representation learning at scale.

Dahou, A., Elaziz, M. A., Zhou, J., and Xiong, S. (2019a). Arabic sentiment classification using convolutional neural network and differential evolution algorithm. *Computational intelligence and neuroscience*, 2019.

Dahou, A., Xiong, S., Zhou, J., and Elaziz, M. A. (2019b). Multi-channel embedding convolutional neural network model for arabic sentiment classification. *ACM Transactions on Asian and Low-Resource Language Information Processing (TALLIP)*, 18(4):1–23.

de Vries, W., van Cranenburgh, A., Bisazza, A., Caselli, T., van Noord, G., and Nissim, M. (2019). Bertje: A dutch bert model. *arXiv preprint arXiv:1912.09582*.

DeepsetAI.). Open sourcing german bert.

Devlin, J., Chang, M.-W., Lee, K., and Toutanova, K. (2018). Bert: Pre-training of deep bidirectional transformers for language understanding. *arXiv preprint arXiv:1810.04805*.

El Bazi, I. and Laachfoubi, N. (2019). Arabic named entity recognition using deep learning approach. *International Journal of Electrical & Computer Engineering (2088-8708)*, 9(3).

El-Khair, I. A. (2016). 1.5 billion words arabic corpus. *arXiv preprint arXiv:1611.04033*.

ElJundi, O., Antoun, W., El Droubi, N., Hajj, H., El-Hajj, W., and Shaban, K. (2019). hulmona: The universal language model in arabic. In *Proceedings of the Fourth Arabic Natural Language Processing Workshop*, pages 68–77.

Elnagar, A., Khalifa, Y. S., and Einea, A. (2018). Hotel arabic-reviews dataset construction for sentiment analysis applications. In *Intelligent Natural Language Processing: Trends and Applications*, pages 35–52. Springer.

Erdmann, A., Zalmout, N., and Habash, N. (2018). Addressing noise in multidialectal word embeddings. In *Proceedings of the 56th Annual Meeting of the Association for Computational Linguistics (Volume 2: Short Papers)*, pages 558–565.

Howard, J. and Ruder, S. (2018). Universal language model fine-tuning for text classification. *arXiv preprint arXiv:1801.06146*.

Huang, Z., Xu, W., and Yu, K. (2015). Bidirectional lstm-crf models for sequence tagging. *arXiv preprint arXiv:1508.01991*.

Kudo, T. (2018). Subword regularization: Improving neural network translation models with multiple subword candidates.

Kwiatkowski, T., Palomaki, J., Redfield, O., Collins, M., Parikh, A., Alberti, C., Epstein, D., Polosukhin, I., Kelcey, M., Devlin, J., Lee, K., Toutanova, K. N., Jones, L., Chang, M.-W., Dai, A., Uszkoreit, J., Le, Q., and Petrov, S. (2019). Natural questions: a benchmark for question answering research. *Transactions of the Association of Computational Linguistics*.

Lafferty, J. D., McCallum, A., and Pereira, F. C. (2001). Conditional random fields: Probabilistic models for segmenting and labeling sequence data. In *ICML*.

Lample, G., Ballesteros, M., Subramanian, S., Kawakami, K., and Dyer, C. (2016). Neural architectures for named entity recognition. *arXiv preprint arXiv:1603.01360*.

Lan, Z., Chen, M., Goodman, S., Gimpel, K., Sharma,

P., and Soricut, R. (2019). Albert: A lite bert for self-supervised learning of language representations.

Liu, Y., Ott, M., Goyal, N., Du, J., Joshi, M., Chen, D., Levy, O., Lewis, M., Zettlemoyer, L., and Stoyanov, V. (2019). Roberta: A robustly optimized bert pretraining approach.

Martin, L., Muller, B., Suárez, P. J. O., Dupont, Y., Romary, L., Éric Villemonte de la Clergerie, Seddah, D., and Sagot, B. (2019). Camembert: a tasty french language model.

Mikolov, T., Sutskever, I., Chen, K., Corrado, G. S., and Dean, J. (2013). Distributed representations of words and phrases and their compositionality. In *Advances in neural information processing systems*, pages 3111–3119.

Mikolov, T., Grave, E., Bojanowski, P., Puhrsch, C., and Joulin, A. (2017). Advances in pre-training distributed word representations. *arXiv preprint arXiv:1712.09405*.

Mozannar, H., Maamary, E., El Hajal, K., and Hajj, H. (2019). Neural arabic question answering. In *Proceedings of the Fourth Arabic Natural Language Processing Workshop*, pages 108–118.

Nabil, M., Aly, M., and Atiya, A. (2015). ASTD: Arabic sentiment tweets dataset. In *Proceedings of the 2015 Conference on Empirical Methods in Natural Language Processing*, pages 2515–2519, Lisbon, Portugal, September. Association for Computational Linguistics.

Pennington, J., Socher, R., and Manning, C. (2014). Glove: Global vectors for word representation. In *Proceedings of the 2014 conference on empirical methods in natural language processing (EMNLP)*, pages 1532–1543.

Peters, M. E., Neumann, M., Iyyer, M., Gardner, M., Clark, C., Lee, K., and Zettlemoyer, L. (2018). Deep contextualized word representations. In *Proceedings of NAACL-HLT*, pages 2227–2237.

Polignano, M., Basile, P., de Gemmis, M., Semeraro, G., and Basile, V. (2019). AlBERTo: Italian BERT Language Understanding Model for NLP Challenging Tasks Based on Tweets. In *Proceedings of the Sixth Italian Conference on Computational Linguistics (CLiC-it 2019)*, volume 2481. CEUR.

Raffel, C., Shazeer, N., Roberts, A., Lee, K., Narang, S., Matena, M., Zhou, Y., Li, W., and Liu, P. J. (2019). Exploring the limits of transfer learning with a unified text-to-text transformer.

Rajpurkar, P., Zhang, J., Lopyrev, K., and Liang, P. (2016). Squad: 100,000+ questions for machine comprehension of text. *arXiv preprint arXiv:1606.05250*.

Ratnaparkhi, A. (1998). Maximum entropy models for natural language ambiguity resolution.

Sang, E. F. and De Meulder, F. (2003). Introduction to the conll-2003 shared task: Language-independent named entity recognition. *arXiv preprint cs/0306050*.

Soliman, A. B., Eissa, K., and El-Beltagy, S. R. (2017). Aravec: A set of arabic word embedding models for use in arabic nlp. *Procedia Computer Science*, 117:256–265.

Vaswani, A., Shazeer, N., Parmar, N., Uszkoreit, J., Jones, L., Gomez, A. N., Kaiser, L., and Polosukhin, I. (2017). Attention is all you need.

Yang, Z., Dai, Z., Yang, Y., Carbonell, J., Salakhutdinov, R., and Le, Q. V. (2019). Xlnet: Generalized autoregressive pretraining for language understanding.

Zeroual, I., Goldhahn, D., Eckart, T., and Lakhouaja, A. (2019). OSIAN: Open source international Arabic news corpus - preparation and integration into the CLARIN-infrastructure. In *Proceedings of the Fourth Arabic Natural Language Processing Workshop*, pages 175–182, Florence, Italy, August. Association for Computational Linguistics.

Zhu, Y., Kiros, R., Zemel, R., Salakhutdinov, R., Urtasun, R., Torralba, A., and Fidler, S. (2015). Aligning books and movies: Towards story-like visual explanations by watching movies and reading books.

Proceedings of the 4th Workshop on Open-Source Arabic Corpora and Processing Tools, pages 16–23
with a Shared Task on Offensive Language Detection.
Language Resources and Evaluation Conference (LREC 2020), Marseille, 11–16 May 2020
© European Language Resources Association (ELRA), licensed under CC-BY-NC

AraNet: A Deep Learning Toolkit for Arabic Social Media

Muhammad Abdul-Mageed, Chiyu Zhang, Azadeh Hashemi, El Moatez Billah Nagoudi
Natural Language Processing Lab, University of British Columbia
{muhammad.mageeed, azadeh.hashemi, moatez.nagoudi}@ubc.ca
chiyuzh@mail.ubc.ca

Abstract

We describe AraNet, a collection of deep learning Arabic social media processing tools. Namely, we exploit an extensive host of both publicly available and novel social media datasets to train bidirectional encoders from transformers (BERT) focused at social meaning extraction. AraNet models predict age, dialect, gender, emotion, irony, and sentiment. AraNet either delivers state-of-the-art performance on a number of these tasks and performs competitively on others. AraNet is exclusively based on a deep learning framework, giving it the advantage of being feature-engineering free. To the best of our knowledge, AraNet is the first to performs predictions across such a wide range of tasks for Arabic NLP. As such, AraNet has the potential to meet critical needs. We publicly release AraNet to accelerate research, and to facilitate model-based comparisons across the different tasks.

1. Introduction

The proliferation of social media has made it possible to study large online communities at scale. This offers opportunities to make important discoveries, facilitate decision making, guide policies, improve health and well-being, aid disaster response, attend to population needs in pandemics such as the current COVID-19, etc. The wide host of languages, languages varieties, and dialects used on social media and the nuanced differences between users of various backgrounds (e.g., different age groups, gender identities) make it especially difficult to derive sufficiently valuable insights based on single prediction tasks. For these reasons, it is highly desirable to develop natural language processing (NLP) tools that can help piece together more complete pictures of events impacting individuals of different identities across different geographic regions. In this work, we propose AraNet , a suit of tools that has the promise to play such a role of Arabic social media processing.

For Arabic, a collection of languages and varieties spoken by a wide population of $\sim$ 400 million native speakers covering a vast geographical region (shown in Figure 1), no such suite of tools currently exists. Many works have focused on sentiment analysis, e.g., (Abdul-Mageed et al., 2014a; Nabil et al., 2015; ElSahar and El-Beltagy, 2015; Al Sallab et al., 2015; Al-Moslmi et al., 2018; Al-Smadi et al., 2019; Al-Ayyoub et al., 2019; Farha and Magdy, 2019) and dialect identification (Elfardy and Diab, 2013; Zaidan and Callison-Burch, 2011; Zaidan and Callison-Burch, 2014; Cotterell and Callison-Burch, 2014; Zhang and Abdul-Mageed, 2019b; Bouamor et al., 2019a). However, there is rarity of tools for other tasks such as gender and age detection. This motivates our toolkit, which we hope can meet the current critical need for studying Arabic communities online. This is especially valuable given the waves of protests, uprisings, and revolutions that have swept the region during the last decade.

Although we create new models for tasks such as sentiment analysis and gender detection as part of AraNet, our primary focus is to provide strong baselines across the various tasks. We believe this will facilitate comparisons across models. This is particularly useful due to absence of standardization across datasets for many of the tasks, and given

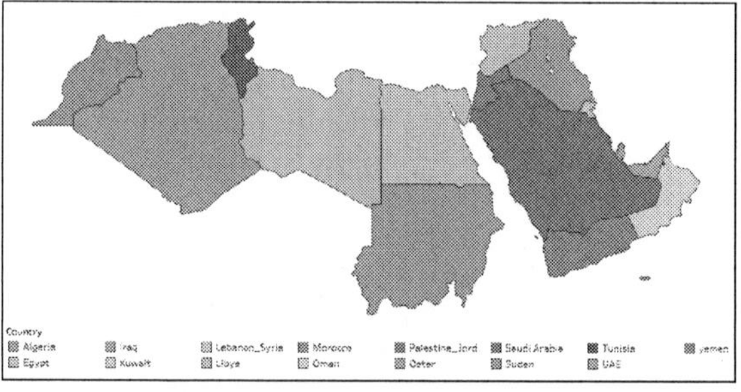

Figure 1: A map of Arab countries. Our different datasets cover varying regions of the Arab world as we describe in each section.

```
import aranet
identifier = aranet.DialectId()
# predict a text dialect
prediction = identifier.predict(text=text_string, with_dist=False)
print("Predict a text dialect:")
print(prediction)

# predict a file line by line
predictions = identifier.predict(path=path_to_tsv_file)
print("Predict a file line by line:")
print(predictions)

                    Output

Predict a text dialect:
[('Qatar', 0.74)]

Predict a file line by line:
[('Qatar', 0.74), ('UAE', 0.14), ('KSA', 0.11), ('Egypt', 0.05)]
```

Figure 2: AraNet usage and output as a Python library.

the somewhat ephemeral nature of parts of some types of these data. In particular, many tasks are developed based on social media posts such as tweets that are distributed under restrictive conditions. For example, Twitter terms require release of data only in the form of tweet ids, making it challenging to acquire 100% of these tweets especially once the data are several months old. These reasons make *model-based comparisons* appealing, as a way to measure research progress in absence of easy benchmarking. Our general approach is to adopt sensible baselines across the various AraNet tasks, but we do not necessarily explicitly compare to all previous research. This is the case since most existing works either exploit *smaller data* (and so it will not be a fair comparison), use *methods pre-dating BERT* (and so will likely be outperformed by our models). In addition, we note that although it would have been possible to acquire better results by feature engineering (especially on smaller datasets), our main goal is to keep our models free of laborious feature engineering. In some tasks, we even acquire better results that what is reported here by adopting more involved methods. But, again, we do our best here to keep all models relatively comparable (and as simple as possible) in terms of the methods employed to acquire them. Our hope is that, by adopting model-based comparisons, we can help accelerate progress on Arabic social media processing. For these reasons, we also package models from our recent works on dialect (Zhang and Abdul-Mageed, 2019b) and irony (Zhang and Abdul-Mageed, 2019a) as part of AraNet.

The rest of the paper is organized as follows: In Section 2. we describe our methods. In Section 3., we describe or refer to published literature for the data we exploit for each task. Also in Section 3., we provide results from our models. Section 4. is about AraNet design and use, and Section 5. is about ethical considerations. We overview related works in Section 6., and conclude in Section 7..

2. Methods

2.1. Supervised BERT

Transformer. Across all our tasks, we use Bidirectional Encoder Representations from Transformers (BERT). BERT is based on the Transformer architecture of (Vaswani et al., 2017), which we briefly introduce here. The Transformer depends solely on self-attention, thus allowing for parallelizing the network (unlike RNNs). It is an encoder-decoder architecture where the *encoder* takes a sequence of symbol representations $x^{(i)} \ldots x^{(n)}$, maps them into a sequence of continuous representations $z^{(i)} \ldots x^{(n)}$ that are then used by the *decoder* to generate an output sequence $y^{(i)} \ldots y^{(n)}$, one symbol at a time. This is performed using *self-attention*, where different positions of a single sequence are related to one another. The Transformer employs an attention mechanism based on a function that operates on *queries*, *keys*, and *values*. The attention function maps a query and a set of key-value pairs to an output, where the output is a weighted sum of the values. For each value, a weight is computed as a compatibility function of the query with the corresponding key. This particular version of attention is a scaled dot product of queries and keys (each of d_k) that is scaled by a factor of $\frac{1}{\sqrt{d_k}}$ on which a softmax is applied to acquire the weights on the values. The scaled dot product attention is computed as as a set of queries, keys, and values in three matrices Q, K, and V, respectively, follows:

$$Attention\,(\textbf{Q, K, V}) = softmax\left(\frac{QK^T}{\sqrt{d_k}}\right)V \quad (1)$$

Encoder of the Transformer in (Vaswani et al., 2017) has 6 attention layers, each of which has h attention heads (*multihead attention*) to allow the model to jointly attend to information from different representation subspaces across different positions. Each of the 6 layers also has a simple,

fully-connected feed-forward network (FFN) that is applied to each position separately and identically that different parameters across the different layers. Decoder of the Transformer is similar to the encoder but has a third sub-layer that performs multi-head attention over the encoder stack. Since the Transformer discards with both recurrence and convolution, it resorts to the so-called *positional encoding* (based on sin and cosine functions) at the bottoms of the encoder and decoder stacks as a way to capture order of the sequence. We now introduce BERT.

BERT. BERT involves two self-supervised learning tasks, (1) *masked language models (Masked LM)* and (2) *next sentence prediction*. Since BERT uses bidirectional conditioning, a given percentage of random input tokens are masked and the model attempts to predict these masked tokens. This is the Masked LM task, where masked tokens are simply replaced by a string [MASK] . (Devlin et al., 2018) mask 15% of the tokens (the authors use WordPieces) and feed the final hidden vectors of these masked tokens to an output softmax over the vocabulary. The next sentence prediction task is just binary classification. For a given sentence S, two sentences A and B are generated where A (positive class) is an actual sentence from the corpus and B is a randomly chosen sentence (negative class). Once trained on an unlabeled dataset, BERT can then be fine-tuned with supervised data for a downstream task (e.g., text classification, question answering).

All our models are trained in a fully supervised fashion, with dialect id being the only task where we leverage semi-supervised learning. We briefly outline our semi-supervised methods next.

2.2. Self-Training

Only for the dialect id task, we investigate augmenting our human-labeled training data with automatically-predicted data from self-training. Self-training is a wrapper method for semi-supervised learning (Triguero et al., 2015; Pavlinek and Podgorelec, 2017) where a classifier is initially trained on a (usually small) set of labeled samples D^l, then is used to classify an unlabeled sample set D^u. Most confident predictions acquired by the original supervised model are added to the labeled set, and the model is iteratively re-trained. We perform self-training using different confidence thresholds and choose different percentages from predicted data to add to our dialect training set. We only report best settings here, and the reader is referred to our winning system on the MADAR shared task for more details on these different settings (Zhang and Abdul-Mageed, 2019b).

2.3. Implementation & Models Parameters

For all our tasks, we use the BERT-Base Multilingual Cased model released by the authors [1]. The model is trained on 104 languages (including Arabic) with 12 layer, 768 hidden units each, 12 attention heads, and has 110M parameters in entire model. The model has 119,547 shared WordPieces vocabulary, and was pre-trained on the entire

---

[1] https://github.com/google-research/bert/blob/master/multilingual.md

Wikipedia for each language. For fine-tuning, we use a maximum sequence size of 50 tokens and a batch size of 32. We set the learning rate to $2e - 5$ and train for 15 epochs [2] and choose the best model based on performance on a development set. We use the same hyper-parameters in all of our BERT models. We fine-tune BERT on each respective labeled dataset for each task. For BERT input, we apply WordPiece tokenization, setting the maximal sequence length to 50 words/WordPieces. For all tasks, we use a TensorFlow implementation. An exception is the sentiment analysis task, where we used a PyTorch implementation with the same hyper-parameters but with a learning rate $2e - 6$. [3]

Pre-processing. Most of our training data in all tasks come from Twitter. Exceptions are in some of the datasets we use for sentiment analysis, which we point out in Section 3.5.. Our pre-processing thus incorporates methods to clean tweets, other datasets (e.g., from the news domain) being much less noisy. For pre-processing, we remove all usernames, URLs, and diacritics in the data.

3. Data and Models

3.1. Age and Gender

Arab-Tweet. For modeling age and gender, we use Arap-Tweet (Zaghouani and Charfi, 2018) [4], which we will refer to as *Arab-Tweet*. Arab-tweet comprises 11 Arabic regions from 17 different countries. [5] For each region, data from 100 Twitter users were crawled. Users needed to have posted at least 2,000 tweets and were selected based on an initial list of seed words characteristic of each region. The seed list included words such as برشة /barsha/ 'many' for Tunisian Arabic and وايد /wayed/ 'many' for Gulf Arabic. (Zaghouani and Charfi, 2018) employed human annotators to verify that users do belong to each respective region. Annotators also assigned gender labels from the set *male, female* and age group labels from the set *under-25, 25-to34, above-35* at the user-level, which in turn is the tag for tweet level. Tweets with less than 3 words and re-tweets were removed. Refer to (Zaghouani and Charfi, 2018) for details about how annotation was carried out. We provide a description of the data in Table 1. Table 1 also provides class breakdown across our splits.We note that (Zaghouani and Charfi, 2018) do not report classification models exploiting the data. Although age and gender are user-level tasks, note that we train *tweet-level* age and gender models. However, tweet-level models can easily be ported to user-level by simply taking the majority class based on softmax-thresholding as we show in (Zhang and Abdul-Mageed, 2019b). [6]

We shuffle the Arab-tweet dataset and split it into 80% training (TRAIN), 10% development (DEV), and 10% test (TEST). The distribution of classes in our splits is in Table 1. For pre-processing, we reduce 2 or more consecutive repetitions of the same character into only 2 and remove diacritics. With this dataset, we train a small unidirectional GRU (*small-GRU*) with a single 500-units hidden layer and dropout$= 0.5$ as a baseline. Small-GRU is trained with the TRAIN set, batch size = 8, and up to 30 words of each sequence. Each word in the input sequence is represented as a trainable 300-dimension vector. We use the top 100K words from TRAIN which are weighted by mutual information as our vocabulary in the embedding layer. We evaluate the model on the blind TEST set. Table 2 shows that small-GRU obtains 36.29% acc. on age classification, and 53.37% acc. on gender detection. Table 2 also shows performance of the fine-tuned BERT model. BERT significantly outperforms our baseline on the two tasks. It improves 15.13% acc. (for age) and 11.93% acc. (for gender) over the small-GRU.

UBC Twitter Gender Dataset. We also develop an in-house Twitter dataset for gender. We manually labeled 1,989 users from each of the 21 Arab countries. The data had 1,246 "male", 528 "female", and 215 unknown users. We remove the "unknown" category and balance the dataset to have 528 from each of the two "male" and "female" categories. We ended with 69,509 tweets for "male" and 67,511 tweets for "female". We split the users into 80% TRAIN (110,750 tweets for 845 users), 10% DEV (14,158 tweets for 106 users), and 10% TEST (12,112 tweets for 105 users). We then model this dataset with BERT and evaluate on DEV and TEST. Table 3 shows that fine-tuned model obtains 62.42% acc. on DEV and 60.54% acc. on TEST. These results are 2.89% and 4.76% less than performance on Arab-Tweet, perhaps reflecting more diversity in UBC-Gender data which also makes it more challenging. Another potential reason for this accuracy drop could be that, for this tweet-level task, some tweets from the same user occur across our TRAIN/DEV/TEST splits. This was unavoidable since Arab-Tweet is distributed without user ids, thus not making it possible for us to prevent user-level data leakage into the two tweet-level classification tasks of age and gender we report here. We alleviate this issue for gender by annotating and developing on UBC-Gender where we control for user-level data distribution across the splits as explained earlier.

We also combine the Arab-tweet gender dataset with our UBC-Gender dataset for gender on training, development, and test, respectively, to obtain new TRAIN, DEV, and TEST. We fine-tune BERT on the combined TRAIN and evaluate on combined DEV and TEST. As Table 3 shows, the model obtains 65.32% acc. on combined DEV, and 65.32% acc. on combined TEST. This is the model we package in AraNet.

3.2. Dialect

The dialect identification model in AraNet is based on our winning system in the MADAR shared task 2 (Bouamor et al., 2019b) as described in (Zhang and Abdul-Mageed, 2019b). The corpus is divided into training, development,

---

[2]For dialect id, we trained only for 10 epochs. This was based on monitoring loss on a development set.

[3]We find this learning rate to work better when we use PyTorch.

[4]The resource is an Arabic **p**rofiling dataset, and hence the sequence "Arap" with an "p".

[5]Counts are based on the distribution we received from the authors.

[6]Arab-Tweet is also distribute only with tweet-level labels (i.e., without user ids), thus making it not possible to model age and gender at the user level exploiting the data.

Data split	Under 25		25 until 34		35 and up		# of tweets
	Female	Male	Female	Male	Female	Male	
TRAIN	215,950	213,249	207,184	248,769	174,511	226,132	1,285,795
DEV	27,076	26,551	25,750	31,111	21,942	28,294	160,724
TEST	26,878	26,422	25,905	31,211	21,991	28,318	160,725
ALL	269,904	266,222	258,839	311,091	218,444	282,744	1,607,244

Table 1: Distribution of age and gender classes in our Arab-Tweet data splits

	Age		Gender	
	DEV	TEST	DEV	TEST
small-GRU	36.13	36.29	53.39	53.37
BERT	50.95	51.42	65.31	65.30

Table 2: Model performance in accuracy of Arab-Tweet age and gender classification tasks.

	DEV	TEST
UBC_TW_Gender	62.42	60.54
Gender_comb	65.32	65.32

Table 3: Model performance in accuracy. UBC_TW_Gender refers to the model trained on UBC Twitter Gender dataset. Gender_Comb denotes the model trained on the Arab-Tweet and UBC-Gender combined TRAIN data split. Each model is evaluated on the corresponding DEV and TEST sets.

and test; and the organizers masked test set labels. We lost some tweets from TRAIN when we crawled using tweet ids, ultimately acquiring 2,036 (TRAIN-A), 281 (DEV) and 466 (TEST). We also make use of the task 1 corpus (95,000 sentences (Bouamor et al., 2018)). More specifically, we concatenate the task 1 data to the training data of task 2, to create TRAIN-B. Again, note that TEST labels were only released to participants after the official task evaluation. Table 4 shows statistics of the data. More information about the data is in (Bouamor et al., 2018). We use TRAIN-A to perform supervised modeling with BERT and TRAIN-B for self training, under various conditions. We refer the reader to (Zhang and Abdul-Mageed, 2019b) for more information about our different experimental settings on dialect id. We acquire our best results with self-training, with a classification accuracy of 49.39% and F_1 score at 35.44. This is the winning system model in the MADAR shared task and we showed in (Zhang and Abdul-Mageed, 2019b) that our tweet-level predictions can be ported to user-level prediction. On user-level detection, our models perform superbly, with 77.40% acc. and 71.70% F_1 score on unseen MADAR TEST.

	# of tweets		
	TRAIN	DEV	TEST
TRAIN-A	193,086	26,588	43,909
TRAIN-B	288,086	–	–

Table 4: Distribution of classes within the MADAR twitter corpus.

3.3. Emotion

We make use of two datasets, LAMA-DINA and LAMA-DIST (Alhuzali et al., 2018). The LAMA-DINA dataset is a Twitter dataset with a combination of gold labels from (Abdul-Mageed et al., 2016) and distant supervision labels. The tweets are labeled with the Plutchik 8 primary emotions from the set: {*anger, anticipation, disgust, fear, joy, sadness, surprise, trust*}. The distant supervision approach depends on use of seed phrases with the Arabic first person pronoun انا (Eng. "I") + a seed word expressing an emotion, e.g., فرحان (Eng. "happy"). The manually labeled part of the data comprises tweets carrying the seed phrases verified by human annotators $9,064$ tweets for inclusion of the respective emotion. LAMA-DIST ($182,605$ tweets) [7] is only labeled using distant supervision. For more information about the dataset, readers are referred to (Alhuzali et al., 2018). The data distribution over the emotion classes is in Table 5. We combine LAMA+DINA and LAMA-DIST training set and refer to this new training set as LAMA-D2 ($189,903$ tweets). We fine-tune BERT on the LAMA-D2 and evaluate the model with same DEV and TEST sets from LAMA+DINA. On DEV set, the fine-tuned BERT model obtains 61.43% acc. and 58.83 F_1. On TEST set, we acquire 62.38% acc. and 60.32% F_1.

	LAMA+DINA		LAMA-DIST	
	#	%	#	%
anger	1,038	11.45	3,650	2.00
anticipation	933	10.29	24,672	13.51
disgust	1,069	11.79	2,478	1.36
fear	1,434	15.82	28,315	15.51
happy	1,364	15.05	55,253	30.26
sad	1,195	13.18	27,584	15.11
surprise	1,167	12.88	15,106	8.27
trust	864	9.53	25,547	13.99
total	9,064	100.00	182,605	100.00

Table 5: Emotion class distribution in LAMA+DINA and LAMA-DIST datasets.

3.4. Irony

We use the dataset for irony identification on Arabic tweets released by IDAT@FIRE2019 shared task (Ghanem et al., 2019). The shared task dataset contains $5,030$ tweets related to different political issues and events in the Middle East taking place between 2011 and 2018. Tweets are

---

[7] These statistics are based on minor cleaning of the data to remove short tweets < 3 words and residuals of the seeds used for collecting the data.

collected using pre-defined keywords (i.e., targeted political figures or events) and the positive class involves ironic
hashtags such as #sokhria, #tahakoum, and #maskhara
(Arabic variants for "irony"). Duplicates, retweets, and
non-intelligible tweets are removed by organizers. Tweets
involve both MSA as well as dialects at various degrees of
granularity such as *Egyptian*, *Gulf*, and *Levantine*.
IDAT@FIRE2019 (Ghanem et al., 2019) is set up as a binary classification task where tweets are assigned labels
from the set {*ironic, non-ironic*}. A total of $4,024$ tweets
were released by organizers as training data. In addition,
a total of $1,006$ tweets were used by organizers as TEST
data. TEST labels were not release; and teams were expected to submit the predictions produced by their systems
on the TEST split. For our models, we split the $4,024$ released training data into 90% TRAIN ($n = 3,621$ tweets;
'ironic'$= 1,882$ and 'non-ironic'$= 1,739$) and 10% DEV
($n = 403$ tweets; 'ironic'$= 209$ and 'non-ironic'$= 194$).
We use the same small-GRU architecture of Section 3.1
as our baselines. We fine-tune BERT on our TRAIN, and
evaluate on DEV. The small-GRU obtain 73.70% acc. and
73.47% F_1 score. BERT model significantly outperforms
the small-GRU, acquiring 81.64% acc. and 81.62% F_1
score.

	Acc	F_1
small-GRU	73.70	73.47
BERT	**81.64**	**81.62**

Table 6: Model performance on irony detection.

3.5. Sentiment

We collect 15 datasets related to sentiment analysis of Arabic, including MSA and dialects (Abdul-Mageed and Diab,
2012; Abdulla et al., 2013; Abdul-Mageed et al., 2014b;
Nabil et al., 2015; Kiritchenko et al., 2016; Aly and Atiya,
2013; Salameh et al., 2015; Rosenthal et al., 2017; Alomari
et al., 2017; Mohammad et al., 2018; Baly et al., 2019).
Table 8 shows all the corpora we use. The datasets involve
different types of sentiment analysis tasks such as binary
classification (i.e., negative or positive), 3-way classification (i.e., negative, neutral, or positive), and subjective language detection. To combine these datasets for binary sentiment classification, we normalize different types of labels
to binary tags in the set {*'positive'*, *'negative'*} using the
following rules:

- Map {Positive, Pos, or High-Pos} to 'positive'

- Map {Negative, Neg, or High-Neg} to 'negative'

- Exclude samples whose label is not 'positive' or 'negative' such as 'obj', 'mixed', 'neut', or 'neutral'.

After label normalization, we obtain $126,766$ samples. We
split this resulting dataset into 80% training (TRAIN), 10%
development (DEV), and 10% test (TEST). The distribution
of classes in our splits is presented in Table 7. We fine-
tune pre-trained BERT on the TRAIN set using PyTorch
implementation with $2e - 6$ learning rate and 15 epochs,
as explained in Section 2.. Our best model on the DEV set

obtains 80.24% acc. and 80.24% F_1. We evaluate this best
model on TEST set and obtain 77.31% acc. and 76.67%
F_1.

	TRAIN	DEV	TEST
# pos	61,555	7,030	7,312
# neg	39,044	7,314	4,511
Total	100,599	14,344	11,823

Table 7: Distribution of sentiment classes in our data splits.

4. AraNet Design and Use

AraNet consists of identifier tools including age, gender, dialect,
emotion, irony and sentiment. Each tool comes with an embedded
model. The tool comes with modules for performing normalization and tokenization. AraNet can be used either as (1) a Python
library or (2) a command-line and interactive tool, as follows:

AraNet as a Python Library: Importing AraNet module as a
Python library provides identifier functions. Prediction is based
on a text input or a path to a file, and returns the identified class
label. The library also returns the probability distribution over all
available class labels if needed. This probability is the outcome of
the softmax function applied to the last layer (with logits) in each
model. Figure 2 shows two examples of using the tool as Python
library.

AraNet as a Command-Line and Interactive Tool: AraNet
provides scripts supporting both command-line and interactive
mode. Command-line mode accepts a text or file path. Interaction mode is good for quick interactive line-by-line experiments
and also pipeline re-directions.

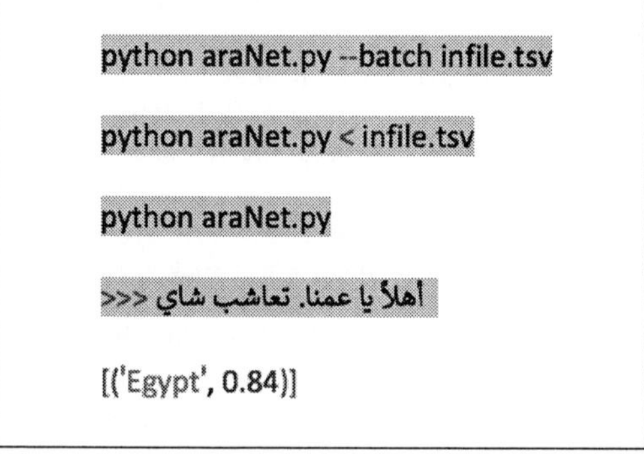

Figure 3: AraNet usage examples as command-line mode,
pipeline, and interactive mode.

AraNet is available through pip or from source on GitHub [12] with
detailed documentation.

5. Ethical Considerations

AraNet is trained on data collected from publicly available
sources. The distribution of classes across the different tasks are
reasonably balanced as listed in the respective sections in the current paper. Meanwhile, we note that we have not used AraNet in
real-world situations, nor tested any bias its decisions could involve. As a result, we advise against using AraNet in decision

---

[12]https://github.com/UBC-NLP/aranet

Authors	Task	Sources	# Data	#Class	Classes	MSA/DIA
Abdul-Mageed and Diab (2012)	SSA	Wiki.[8], PAT[9], Forums	5,382	4	Obj, Subj, Pos, Neg and Neut	MSA
Abdulla et al. (2013)	SA	Twitter,	2000	2	Pos, Neg	MSA
Abdul-Mageed et al. (2014b)	SSA	Maktoob[10], Twitter	11918	3	Obj, Subj Pos, Subj Neg and Subj Mixed	MSA+DIA
Nabil et al. (2015)	SSA	Twitter	10000	4	Obj, Subj Pos, Subj Neg and Subj Mixed	MSA
Kiritchenko et al. (2016)	SI	Twitter	1,366	–	Regression [0,1]	MSA
Aly and Atiya (2013)	SA	Book reviews	63,000	3	Pos, Neg, or Neut	MSA
Salameh et al. (2015)	SA	BBN Parallel Text[11]	1200	3	Pos, Neg, or Neut	DIA
Salameh et al. (2015)	SA	Twitter	2000	3	Pos, Neg, or Neut	DIA
Rosenthal et al. (2017)	SA	Twitter	9,500	2	Pos, or Neg	MSA
Rosenthal et al. (2017)	SA	Twitter	3,400	3	Pos, Neut, or Neg	MSA
Rosenthal et al. (2017)	SA	Twitter	9,450	5	High-Pos, Pos, Neut, Neg, Hihg-Neg	MSA
Alomari et al. (2017)	SA	Twitter	1800	3	Pos or Neg	DIA
Mohammad et al. (2018)	SA	Twitter	1,800	7	Various levels of Pos, Neg or Neut [-3,3]	MSA
Saad (2019)[*]	SA	Twitter	58,751	2	Pos, or Neg	DIA
Baly et al. (2019)	SA	Twitter	4,000	5	High-Pos, Pos, Neut, Neg, Hihg-Neg	DIA

Table 8: Sentiment analysis datasets. **SA**: Sentiment analysis. **SSA**: Subjectivity and sentiment analysis. [*]Dataaet from Saad (2019) is available at `https://www.kaggle.com/mksaad/arabic-sentiment-twitter-corpus`.

making without prior research as to what its deployment could involve and how best it can be tested. *We also do not approve any use of the AraNet or its decisions in any form for manipulative, unfair, malicious, dangerous, or otherwise unlawful (including by international standards) causes by individuals or organizations.* Our conviction is that machine-learning-based software can be very powerful and useful, if not at times necessary, but must be tested and deployed *only* carefully and ethically. AraNet is no exception.

6. Related Works

As we pointed out earlier, there are several works on some of the tasks but less on others. By far, Arabic sentiment analysis has been the most popular task. Works focused on both MSA (Abdul-Mageed et al., 2011; Abdul-Mageed et al., 2014a) and dialects (Nabil et al., 2015; ElSahar and El-Beltagy, 2015; Al Sallab et al., 2015; Al-Moslmi et al., 2018; Al-Smadi et al., 2019; Al-Ayyoub et al., 2019; Farha and Magdy, 2019). A number of studies have been published on dialect detection, including (Zaidan and Callison-Burch, 2011; Zaidan and Callison-Burch, 2014; Elfardy and Diab, 2013; Cotterell and Callison-Burch, 2014). Some works took as their target the tasks of age detection (Zaghouani and Charfi, 2018; Rangel et al., 2019), gender detection (Zaghouani and Charfi, 2018; Rangel et al., 2019), irony identification (Karoui et al., 2017; Ghanem et al., 2019), and emotion analysis (Abdul-Mageed et al., 2016; Alhuzali et al., 2018).

A number of resources and tools exist for Arabic natural language processing, including Penn Arabic treebank (Maamouri et al., 2004), Buckwalter Morphological Analyzer (Buckwalter, 2002), segmenters (Abdelali et al., 2016), POS taggers (Abumalloh et al., 2016; Diab et al., 2004), morpho-syntactic analyzers (Abdul-Mageed et al., 2013; Pasha et al., 2014), subjectivity and sentiment analysis (Abdul-Mageed, 2019; Farha and Magdy, 2019), offensive and hateful language (Elmadany et al., 2020), and

dangerous speech (Alshehri et al., 2020).

7. Conclusion

We presented AraNet, a deep learning toolkit for a host of Arabic social media processing. AraNet predicts age, dialect, gender, emotion, irony, and sentiment from social media posts. It delivers either state-of-the-art or competitive performance on these tasks. It also has the advantage of using a unified, simple framework based on the recently-developed BERT model. AraNet has the potential to alleviate issues related to comparing across different Arabic social media NLP tasks, by providing one way to test new models against AraNet predictions (i.e., model-based comparisons). Our toolkit can be used to make important discoveries about the Arab world, a vast geographical region of strategic importance. It can enhance also enhance our understating of Arabic online communities, and the Arabic digital culture in general.

8. Bibliographic References

Abdelali, A., Darwish, K., Durrani, N., and Mubarak, H. (2016). Farasa: A fast and furious segmenter for arabic. In *Proceedings of the 2016 Conference of the North American Chapter of the Association for Computational Linguistics: Demonstrations*, pages 11–16.

Abdul-Mageed, M. and Diab, M. T. (2012). Awatif: A multi-genre corpus for modern standard arabic subjectivity and sentiment analysis. In *LREC*, volume 515, pages 3907–3914. Citeseer.

Abdul-Mageed, M., Korayem, M., and YoussefAgha, A. (2011). "yes we can?": Subjectivity annotation and tagging for the health domain. In *Proceedings of RANLP2011*.

Abdul-Mageed, M., Diab, M., and Kübler, S. (2013). Asma: A system for automatic segmentation and morpho-syntactic disambiguation of modern standard arabic. In *Proceedings of the International Conference Recent Advances in Natural Language Processing RANLP 2013*, pages 1–8.

Abdul-Mageed, M., Diab, M., and Kübler, S. (2014a). Samar: Subjectivity and sentiment analysis for arabic social media. *Computer Speech & Language*, 28(1):20–37.

Abdul-Mageed, M., Diab, M., and Kübler, S. (2014b). Samar: Subjectivity and sentiment analysis for arabic social media. *Computer Speech & Language*, 28(1):20–37.

Abdul-Mageed, M., AlHuzli, H., and Duaa'Abu Elhija, M. D. (2016). Dina: A multidialect dataset for arabic emotion analysis. In *The 2nd Workshop on Arabic Corpora and Processing Tools*, page 29.

Abdul-Mageed, M. (2019). Modeling arabic subjectivity and sentiment in lexical space. *Information Processing & Management*, 56(2):291–307.

Abdulla, N., Mahyoub, N., Shehab, M., and Al-Ayyoub, M. (2013). Arabic sentiment analysis: Corpus-based and lexicon-based. In *Proceedings of The IEEE conference on Applied Electrical Engineering and Computing Technologies (AEECT)*.

Abumalloh, R. A., Al-Sarhan, H. M., Ibrahim, O., and Abu-Ulbeh, W. (2016). Arabic part-of-speech tagging. *Journal of Soft Computing and Decision Support Systems*, 3(2):45–52.

Al-Ayyoub, M., Khamaiseh, A. A., Jararweh, Y., and Al-Kabi, M. N. (2019). A comprehensive survey of arabic sentiment analysis. *Information Processing & Management*, 56(2):320–342.

Al-Moslmi, T., Albared, M., Al-Shabi, A., Omar, N., and Abdullah, S. (2018). Arabic senti-lexicon: Constructing publicly available language resources for arabic sentiment analysis. *Journal of Information Science*, 44(3):345–362.

Al Sallab, A., Hajj, H., Badaro, G., Baly, R., El Hajj, W., and Shaban, K. B. (2015). Deep learning models for sentiment analysis in arabic. In *Proceedings of the second workshop on Arabic natural language processing*, pages 9–17.

Al-Smadi, M., Talafha, B., Al-Ayyoub, M., and Jararweh, Y. (2019). Using long short-term memory deep neural networks for aspect-based sentiment analysis of arabic reviews. *International Journal of Machine Learning and Cybernetics*, 10(8):2163–2175.

Alhuzali, H., Abdul-Mageed, M., and Ungar, L. (2018). Enabling deep learning of emotion with first-person seed expressions. In *Proceedings of the Second Workshop on Computational Modeling of People's Opinions, Personality, and Emotions in Social Media*, pages 25–35.

Alomari, K. M., ElSherif, H. M., and Shaalan, K. (2017). Arabic tweets sentimental analysis using machine learning. In *International Conference on Industrial, Engineering and Other Applications of Applied Intelligent Systems*, pages 602–610. Springer.

Alshehri, A., Nagoudi, E. M. B., and Abdul-Mageed, M. (2020). Understanding and detecting dangerous speech in social media. In *The 4th Workshop on Open-Source Arabic Corpora and Processing Tools (OSACT4), LREC*.

Aly, M. and Atiya, A. (2013). Labr: A large scale arabic book reviews dataset. In *Proceedings of the 51st Annual Meeting of the Association for Computational Linguistics (Volume 2: Short Papers)*, volume 2, pages 494–498.

Baly, R., Khaddaj, A., Hajj, H., El-Hajj, W., and Shaban, K. B. (2019). Arsentd-lev: A multi-topic corpus for target-based sentiment analysis in arabic levantine tweets. *arXiv preprint arXiv:1906.01830*.

Bouamor, H., Habash, N., Salameh, M., Zaghouani, W., Rambow, O., Abdulrahim, D., Obeid, O., Khalifa, S., Eryani, F., Erdmann, A., et al. (2018). The madar arabic dialect corpus and lexicon. In *Proceedings of the Eleventh International Conference on Language Resources and Evaluation (LREC-2018)*.

Bouamor, H., Hassan, S., and Habash, N. (2019a). The madar shared task on arabic fine-grained dialect identification. In *Proceedings of the Fourth Arabic Natural Language Processing Workshop (WANLP19), Florence, Italy*.

Bouamor, H., Hassan, S., and Habash, N. (2019b). The MADAR Shared Task on Arabic Fine-Grained Dialect Identification. In *Proceedings of the Fourth Arabic Natural Language Processing Workshop (WANLP19)*, Florence, Italy.

Buckwalter, T. (2002). Buckwalter arabic morphological analyzer version 1.0. *Linguistic Data Consortium, University of Pennsylvania*.

Cotterell, R. and Callison-Burch, C. (2014). A multi-dialect, multi-genre corpus of informal written arabic. In *LREC*, pages 241–245.

Devlin, J., Chang, M.-W., Lee, K., and Toutanova, K. (2018). Bert: Pre-training of deep bidirectional transformers for language understanding. *arXiv preprint arXiv:1810.04805*.

Diab, M., Hacioglu, K., and Jurafsky, D. (2004). Automatic tagging of arabic text: From raw text to base phrase chunks. In *Proceedings of HLT-NAACL 2004: Short papers*, pages 149–152. Association for Computational Linguistics.

Elfardy, H. and Diab, M. T. (2013). Sentence level dialect identification in arabic. In *ACL (2)*, pages 456–461.

Elmadany, A., Zhang, C., Abdul-Mageed, M., and Hashemi, A. (2020). Leveraging affective bidirectional transformers for offensive language detection. In *The 4th Workshop on Open-Source Arabic Corpora and Processing Tools (OSACT4), LREC*.

ElSahar, H. and El-Beltagy, S. R. (2015). Building large arabic multi-domain resources for sentiment analysis. In *International Conference on Intelligent Text Processing and Computational Linguistics*, pages 23–34. Springer.

Farha, I. A. and Magdy, W. (2019). Mazajak: An online arabic sentiment analyser. In *Proceedings of the Fourth Arabic Natural Language Processing Workshop*, pages 192–198.

Ghanem, B., Karoui, J., Benamara, F., Moriceau, V., and Rosso, P. (2019). Idat@fire2019: Overview of the track on irony detection in arabic tweets. In *Mehta P., Rosso P., Majumder P., Mitra M. (Eds.) Working Notes of the Forum for Information Retrieval Evaluation (FIRE 2019). CEUR Workshop Proceedings. In: CEUR-WS.org, Kolkata, India, December 12-15*.

Karoui, J., Zitoune, F. B., and Moriceau, V. (2017). Soukhria: Towards an irony detection system for arabic in social media. *Procedia Computer Science*, 117:161–168.

Kiritchenko, S., Mohammad, S., and Salameh, M. (2016). Semeval-2016 task 7: Determining sentiment intensity of english and arabic phrases. In *Proceedings of the 10th international workshop on semantic evaluation (SEMEVAL-2016)*, pages 42–51.

Maamouri, M., Bies, A., Buckwalter, T., and Mekki, W. (2004). The penn arabic treebank: Building a large-scale annotated arabic corpus. In *NEMLAR conference on Arabic language resources and tools*, volume 27, pages 466–467. Cairo.

Mohammad, S., Bravo-Marquez, F., Salameh, M., and Kiritchenko, S. (2018). Semeval-2018 task 1: Affect in tweets. In *Proceedings of The 12th International Workshop on Semantic Evaluation*, pages 1–17.

Nabil, M., Aly, M., and Atiya, A. (2015). Astd: Arabic sentiment tweets dataset. In *Proceedings of the 2015 Conference on Empirical Methods in Natural Language Processing*, pages 2515–2519.

Pasha, A., Al-Badrashiny, M., Diab, M. T., El Kholy, A., Eskander, R., Habash, N., Pooleery, M., Rambow, O., and Roth, R. (2014). Madamira: A fast, comprehensive tool for morphological analysis and disambiguation of arabic. In *LREC*, volume 14, pages 1094–1101.

Pavlinek, M. and Podgorelec, V. (2017). Text classification method based on self-training and lda topic models. *Expert Systems with Applications*, 80:83–93.

Rangel, F., Rosso, P., Charfi, A., Zaghouani, W., Ghanem, B., and Sánchez-Junquera, J. (2019). Overview of the track on author profiling and deception detection in arabic. In *Mehta P., Rosso P., Majumder P., Mitra M. (Eds.) Working Notes of the Forum for Information Retrieval Evaluation (FIRE 2019). CEUR Workshop Proceedings. In: CEUR-WS.org, Kolkata, India, December 12-15.*

Rosenthal, S., Farra, N., and Nakov, P. (2017). Semeval-2017 task 4: Sentiment analysis in twitter. In *Proceedings of the 11th international workshop on semantic evaluation (SemEval-2017)*, pages 502–518.

Salameh, M., Mohammad, S., and Kiritchenko, S. (2015). Sentiment after translation: A case-study on arabic social media posts. In *Proceedings of the 2015 conference of the North American chapter of the association for computational linguistics: Human language technologies*, pages 767–777.

Triguero, I., García, S., and Herrera, F. (2015). Self-labeled techniques for semi-supervised learning: taxonomy, software and empirical study. *Knowledge and Information Systems*, 42(2):245–284, Feb.

Vaswani, A., Shazeer, N., Parmar, N., Uszkoreit, J., Jones, L., Gomez, A. N., Kaiser, Ł., and Polosukhin, I. (2017). Attention is all you need. In *Advances in Neural Information Processing Systems*, pages 6000–6010.

Zaghouani, W. and Charfi, A. (2018). Arap-tweet: A large multi-dialect twitter corpus for gender, age and language variety identification. In *Proceedings of the Eleventh International Conference on Language Resources and Evaluation (LREC-2018)*.

Zaidan, O. F. and Callison-Burch, C. (2011). The arabic online commentary dataset: an annotated dataset of informal arabic with high dialectal content. In *Proceedings of the 49th Annual Meeting of the Association for Computational Linguistics: Human Language Technologies: short papers-Volume 2*, pages 37–41. Association for Computational Linguistics.

Zaidan, O. F. and Callison-Burch, C. (2014). Arabic dialect identification. *Computational Linguistics*, 40(1):171–202.

Zhang, C. and Abdul-Mageed, M. (2019a). Multi-task bidirectional transformer representations for irony detection. In *The 11th meeting of the Forum for Information Retrieval Evaluation 2019*.

Zhang, C. and Abdul-Mageed, M. (2019b). No army, no navy: Bert semi-supervised learning of arabic dialects. In *Proceedings of the Fourth Arabic Natural Language Processing Workshop*, pages 279–284.

Proceedings of the 4th Workshop on Open-Source Arabic Corpora and Processing Tools, pages 24–31
with a Shared Task on Offensive Language Detection.
Language Resources and Evaluation Conference (LREC 2020), Marseille, 11–16 May 2020
© European Language Resources Association (ELRA), licensed under CC-BY-NC

Building a Corpus of Qatari Arabic Expressions

Sara Al-Mulla, Wajdi Zaghouani
Hamad Bin Khalifa University
salmulla@mail.hbku.edu.qa ; wzaghouani@hbku.edu.qa

Abstract

The current Arabic natural language processing resources are mainly build to address the Modern Standard Arabic (MSA), while we witnessed some scattered efforts to build resources for various Arabic dialects such as the Levantine and the Egyptian dialects. We observed a lack of resources for Gulf Arabic and especially the Qatari variety. In this paper, we present the first Qatari idioms and expression corpus of 1000 entries. The corpus was created from on-line and printed sources in addition to transcribed recorded interviews. The corpus covers various Qatari traditional expressions and idioms. To this end, audio recordings were collected from interviews and an online survey questionnaire was conducted to validate our data. This corpus aims to help advance the dialectal Arabic Speech and Natural Language Processing tools and applications for the Qatari dialect.

Keywords: Qatari Dialect, Lexical Resources, Multiword Expressions, Corpus Annotation

1.   Introduction

Language and nationalism are strongly connected. In the 1950s, a revival movement called Pan-Arabism or Arabism founded by Jurji Zaydan, encouraged the unification of the Arabs who extend from North Africa, West Asia, and the Atlantic Ocean to the Arabian Sea. Arabism aims to strengthen Arab countries' alliances against outside forces. This had an implication which resulted in adopting the Standard Arabic as the unified official language of the Arabic countries instead of the dialectical Arabic (Rubin, 1991). This led to the production of numerous studies about the Mordern Standard Arabic (MSA) in different countries.

On the other hand, there is a lack of studies focusing on the pecularities of the numerous Arabic dialectal varieties such as the Qatari Gulf dialect.

The Qatari dialect contains many expressions borrowed from other languages such as Turkish, Farsi, Hindi and English. Furthermore, another factor that is believed to have impacted the Qatari dialect is the country's globalization. This has made from English to be the first used language in different sectors of the country; hence, it may put the local dialect and especially the traditional words at risk of being lost in the short future if there aren't any preservation attempts yet to face the problem.

Currently, Qatari traditional expressions are available in limited resources, mainly in the oral form such as traditional TV shows, interviews, and some printed books. Several Qatari idioms and expression are no longer used by the new generation and the only way to document such expression is by conducting suryeys and interviews with the older generation in Qatar and create a digital historical archive of such expressions. Furthermore, with the rapid development in Qatar, Doha became an international city where the Arabic language became less used when compared to English. In fact, Al-Attiyah (2013) revealed that there is a high probability of vocabulary loss from the Qatari dialect, especially the traditional expressions and idioms. Furthermore, Dialectal Arabic is typically not used on official platforms such as media, education, and others. As mentioned by Bouamor et al. (2018), while the MSA is the commonly used Arabic variety in public and official events, such as culture, media, and education in the middle east. But the MSA is not used by any speaker of Arabic in his or her everyday interactions.

Dialectal Arabic become a hot topic recently and building dialectal linguistic resources are needed to improve the current situation of Dialectal Arabic processing and applications such as dialectal Machine Translation application covering a large number of Arabic dialects given that each region has its own Arabic dialect, such as Egyptian, Gulf, Yemeni, or sub-regionally (e.g., Tunisian, Algerian, Lebanese, Syrian, Jordanian, Kuwaiti, Qatari). Moreover, the Dialectal Arabic (DA) differs from region to region and more precisely from city to city in each region phonologically, lexically, and morphologically.

Given this context and the lack of resources dedicated to the Qatari Arabic, we created a pilot corpus of 1000 Qatari traditional expressions and idioms[1] from various sources. The expressions collected are single word or Multiword Expressions (MWEs). The intitial version of corpus is made freely available for the research community. The corpus was collected from transcribed natural spoken recordings and written dialect material collected from various online and written sources. In the next sections, we will present the related work and the corpus collection methodology, the survey questionnaire design, and the corpus details.

---

[1] In this paper, the term expression refer to single words as to Multiword Expressions (MWEs)

2. Related Work

Recent years have witnessed a surge in the availability of corpora and resources for the Arabic Natural Language Processing, the Modern Standard Arabic (MSA) variety has received most of the attention as presented in the surveys of Rosso (2018) and Zaghouani (2014). There are many parallel and monolingual data collected and annotated such as the Arabic Treebank (Maamouri et al., 2010) and the Arabic Propbank as in Palmer et al. (2008), Diab et al. (2008) and Zaghouani et al (2012). Other corpora focused on building an error annotated corpus or an Arabic diacritized corpus such as in Bouamor et al. (2015) and Zaghouani et al. (2014). Moreover, we observed a growing interest in collecting and processing Arabic user-generated content from social media sources as in the projects discussed in (Rangel et al., 2019a; Rangel et al., 2019b; Atanasova et al., 2018; Barron-Cedeno et al. (2018).

Recently, the dialectal Arabic has attracted a considerable amount of research given the availability of social media data such as the MADAR project Bouamor et al. (2018) and Habash et al. (2018) and the ARAP-Tweet project (Zaghouani et al. 2018). Khalifa et al. (2016) built a large scale Gulf Arabic lexicon covering various Gulf dialects while Laoudi et al. (2018) created a Morrocan Arabic lexicon of words and idioms. On the other hand, Carmen Berlinches (2019) focused on building a Syrian Arabic idioms corpus.

Regarding the Gulf dialects, there are multiple studies conducted by Al-Fahad (2013) who published three books about the traditional Kuwaiti expressions and sayings.

Moreover, the Lahajat website lists the dialectal Arabic of various Gulf States and other Arabic regions. Similarly, Al-Badawi created the Alhewar Almotamadin website which includes different Arabic words taken from Persia, India, Turkey, and the West (English) created by Al-Badawi (2013).

Furthermore, there are several studies related to Qatar. For instance, Professor AlMuhannadi's (2006) study examined traditional Qatari idioms and their equivalent English idioms. Similarly, Al-Malki (2005) wrote a book about Qatari idioms with the purpose of use and meanings.

Also, another Qatari author Al-Malki (2015) published a book about camels and expressions relevant to different types of camels. His other book, published in (2005), investigated the pearl diving industry (tools and manes of pearls) and the related expressions. Moreover, Al-Kuwari (2014) published an extensive study about marine life in Qatar as well as the GCC region, in general.

Another Qatari contribution comes from AlNaama (2012) who documented the stories, expressions, and events that took place during the Oil discovery era. Recently, Georgetown University in Qatar created the "Qatari phrasebook"; a smartphone application that includes 1,500 traditional Qatari words and phrases and explains the meaning of each in English.

The pilot experiment described in this paper focused only on the Qatari dialects given the lack of dedicated electronic resources for the Qatari dialect.

3. Corpus Description

To build our corpus and given the lack of resources of relied on several scattered online sources listing some Qatari idioms and expressions and also some printed books.

Moreover, we conducted, recorded and transcribed several interviews to enrich our corpus. We used multiple primary and secondary sources to increase the corpus coverage and the credibility of the acquired data (Liaquat, 2016). Finally, to validate and annotate our data into semantic categories, we used a crowdsourcing approach based on volunteers who filled a survey questionnaire to validate our corpus.

3.1 Corpus Collection and Annotation

The created corpus consists of 1000 colloquial Qatari traditional expressions (single and multi-word expressions). The corpus was mainly collected from various sources such as five printed books, online articles, and eight online sources such as the Mojam[2], the AlArab newspaper lexicon[3], ElBadi message board[4], the AlHewar website[5] and the Mufradat online lexicon[6].

We automatically collected all the entries from the online sources above and a performed a manual cleaning process to remove the duplicates and the non relevant entries. Once, we are done with data cleaning process, we compiled around 600 expressions from those sources and we added 400 expressions from the transcribed recorded interviews.

As explained in Burnard (2004) "data about data" or metadata is essential to be provided for a corpus since it makes the corpus more useful. In our corpus, metadata annotation information has been added to each entry. First of all, the corpus entries were organized by 11 metadata themes or categories as described below:

1) Category or Theme that groups the expressions into different buckets and these words share a common characteristic, such as Kitchenware related items are objects that can be found only at

---

[2] https://en.mo3jam.com/dialect/Qatari
[3] https://bit.ly/3dFhNrw
[4] http://elbadi.ahlamontada.net/t72-topic
[5] http://www.ahewar.org/debat/show.art.asp?aid=360683&r=0

[6] http://www.hostingangle.com/mufrdat/415/%D9%85%D8%A7-%D9%85%D8%B9%D9%86%D9%89-%D8%A7%D9%84%D9%82%D9%84%D8%A7%D9%81%D8%9F

the kitchen and probably used for cooking purposes.

2) The Word or the traditional expression in Arabic.

3) The Meaning in Standard Arabic (MSA); the Arabic translation is required as many of the expressions are time bounded and aren't used currently.

4) The English Translation.

5) The Borrowing status; this column indicates if the traditional expression is borrowed from another language, such as English or western, Persian, Indian, or Turkish.

6) The Part of speech (POS) [7]; which determines whether the word is a noun, verb, adjective or a pronoun...

7) Word forms (inflection), this column identifies the other word forms such as the verbs inflected in the various tenses and nouns inflected in the plural.

8) Example of a sentence that contains the traditional expression

9) Pronunciation of the traditional expression.

10) Synonyms; in this column, all the synonyms of the traditional expression are listed.

11) The reference column identifies the source from which the traditional expression is obtained.

The expressions categorized as borrowing were categorized separately into four main categories that represent the countries or regions from which it was borrowed to the Qatari language and these categories are: Indian, Turkish, Persian, and Western. The reason for choosing those four source countries or regions of borrowing specifically is due to the fact that the majority of the Qatari loaned words came from these languages considering the quantity of the loaned words.

The themes that were added to the metadata of the corpus are Kitchenware, House equipment, Gold, Marine life, Adjective, Occasions, Verb, Food, Clothes, Traditional Game, Occupation, Personal items, Plant, Device, Medical, Hairstyle, Transportation, Education, Old currency, Animal, Family, Shop, Building, Oil, and Gas. The full listing of the corpus themes is listed in table 5 of the Appendix 1 following the references. The above metadata will be extremly useful to study the Qatari dialects as in most of the the corpus linguistics studies, linguists usually rely on the corpus metadata to answer important research

questions as explained by (Burnard, 2004) "without metadata, the investigator has no way of answering such questions. Without metadata, the investigator has nothing but disconnected words of unknowable provenance or authenticity".
Indeed, corpus linguistics is an empirical science, and the identification of patterns of linguistic behavior is the goal of the researcher through inspecting, studying, and analyzing the targeted aspect of the language.

3.2   The Recorded Interviews

Braber and Davies (2016) identified the advantages of the recorded interviews by discussing the relationship between the reminiscence, narrative, and identity. It helps us link the personal to the social and historical, setting a speaker's use of language and dialect within a wider cultural context (Braber & Davies, 2016)

In order to increase the coverage of our corpus, we conducted eitgh interviews. The targeteded population are Qatari citizens with an age range of 40-80 years old, and both genders were considered. We used a snowball sampling approach to recruit our participants, in which one participant is interviewed from the targeted population and based on the interviewee's suggestion for other applicable participants, the next interviewee is selected for the study (Babbie, 2010).

The recorded interviews are considered a useful research approach as it will provide more information than intended, which can result in more accurate analysis and outcomes (Babbie, 2010). This data was recorded and transcribed from the interviews forms the basis of this experiment. The interviews were given a list of topics and we explicitly asked them not to be limited to the provided topics. This approach made them generate a larger set of Qatari expressions and idioms as they narrated some traditional Qatari stories behind the expressions.

Accordingly, the recorded oral information supported the creation, categorization, and the analysis of the corpus. Additionally, the audio recordings helped in maintaining the proper pronunciation of the traditional expressions. The participants also explained the meaning of these expressions, while others mentioned examples of the borrowed expressions. When we interviewed our speakers and we gave them some technical guidelines to ensure high recording quality and recording best practices such as recording in a quiet environment. We used an external microphone and to maintain a fixed distance from the microphone while speaking. The audio recording was anonymized and stored in an MP3 format.

3.3   The Data Validation Survey Questionnaire

To validate and verify the data collected in our corpus, a survey questionnaire was designed and conducted to verify

---

[7] We used MADAMIRA Part of Speech tag set (Pasha et al. 2014)

a sample of the collected expressions and asses the understanding on the idioms and expressions collected by the general population. An online survey questionnaire was created using Google forms and distributed to several Qatari participants. The age range of the survey participants ranged from 18 until 40 years old, and both genders answered the survey. Some participants helped in recruiting more participants from their family and friends circle using the snowball sampling methodology that was considered for approaching the targeted subjects. In total, 50 participants answered the survey and helped validate the corpus as ilusstrated in table 3.

The survey questionnaire included two different sections, in which the first section consisted of 10 different questions about 10 various Qatari traditional expressions. The second section consisted of two questions and these questions were about grouping 26 Qatari traditional expressions into several groups using a crowdsourcing approach to annotate the data. The 36 expressions were mentioned in multiple sources as traditional expressions and currently, most of these words are rarely used in colloquial communication. The survey questionnaire was conducted using the Arabic language as the targeted subjects are Qataris. Furthermore, as Buchanan & Hvizdak (2009) revealed that the survey questionnaire is one of the commonly used research tools in the social sciences researches.

3.4 Corpus Download

The corpus is made freely available for research purposes as per the Creative Commons license using the URL in the footnote.[8]

3.5 Corpus Illustration

In this section, we illustrate a sample of data collected from the survey questionnaire. In table 1 and table 2, we provide sample entries from the first and the second section of the survey questionnaire. In Table 4 of Appendix 1, we listed a sample of the Corpus Entries for the various corpus themes.

While, the second section of the survey questionnaire is about loaned expressions, in which the participant has to select the correct origin from which the expression was borrowed.

	Expression	Meaning
1	دربيل *Darbeel*	Telescope
2	تجوري *Teejory*	Locker
3	دختر *Dakhtar*	Doctor
4	دريشة *Deresha*	Window
5	قرطاس *Qertas*	Paper
6	طاسه *Tasah*	Container
7	ديرم *Dayram*	lipstick
8	دفتر *Daftar*	Notebook
9	بيذيان *Bethyan*	Eggplant
10	برندة *Baranda*	Ground floor balcony

Table 1: The outcomes of the survey questionnaire's second section

Arabic sentence	English translation	Percentage of answers
"اللي عطاكم في جفير يعطينا في قرطله" ..ما معنى كلمة (قرطله)؟ *Lly atakum fi jafeer ya'atyna fi qartalh" ..ma ma'naa kalimat (qartalh)?*	Who gives you in *jafeer* (a container made of Palm fronds with two handles) gives us in *qartalh* (a container made of Palm fronds with two handles, which is smaller than the *jafeer*)	39.3% chose the right definition. 25% chose I don't know The rest chose one of the three wrong answers.
"هالصبي جمبازي" ..ما معنى كلمة (جمبازي)؟ *" Hal essbuyi jumbazy" .. ma ma'naa kulimut (jumbuzy)?*	This boy is *jumbazy* (fraud)	83.9% chose the right definition. 1 participant chose I don't know
"تعد قلعة الزبارة من القلاع التاريخية الشهيرة" ..ما معنى كلمة (الزبارة)؟ *"tua'add qala'at alzibarah min alqyila'a alttarikhiyah alshaira" .. ma ma'naa kalimat (alzibarah)?*	*Alzibarah* (The high place of the desert land) Fortress is one of the famous historical castles	35.7% chose the right definition. 30.5% chose I don't know
" اشزين بسايل بنتج"..ما معنى كلمة (بسايل)؟ *"eshzeen besaiyl bintich".. ma ma'naa kalimat (besaiyl)?*	How beautiful is your daughter's *besaiyl* (hair)	87.5% chose the right definition. 3 participants (5.4%) chose I don't know.

Table 2: The outcomes of the survey questionnaire's first section

---

[8] https://data.world/saraalmulla/qatari-heritage-expressions

No. of participants	Age	Ave. Age	Correct answers
6	18-22	20	16
9	23-26	24.5	59
8	27-30	28.5	40
8	31-34	32.5	42
1	35-38	36.5	7
18	39 and above	39	129

Table 3: The survey questionnaire participants Age groups

4. Conclusion

We created a corpus of Qatari expressions and idioms and we made it available on the Data World repository. The corpus consists of 1000 Qatari traditional expressions grouped into different themes and every word is linked to a theme and the user can go directly and filter the corpus based on the preferred theme in order to display all the related expressions listed with their detailed information. Also, the themes have hyper links to the glossary of themes' descriptions.

Soon, we plan to release the audio files and the transcription files as well.

We would like to mention that the small size of the participants in the interviews is due to the fact that several potential participants declined the interviews as they were uncomfortable with this method. This has resulted in having a limited sample; i.e. only 8 participants were involved in the study. Furthermore, the process of audio transcription was time-consuming. We believe that the data collected in this initial pilot experiement is still small and a larger dataset with more interviews would be needed to have a more representative corpus.

This research has several future directions, thus, in the future, more expressions will be added using different methodologies to increase the corpus coverage. Likewise, audio recordings will be released to help address the lack dialectal Arabic speech data.

5. References

Al-Fahad, G. (2013). The Encyclopedia of Words Gone with Days . Kuwait.

Al-Badawi, K. (2013). Turkish words exotic to the Arabic language. Retrieved from Civilized dialogue: http://www.m.ahewar.org/s.asp?aid=360711&r=0&cid=0&u=&i=6452&q=

Al-Kuwari, R. (2014). The dictionary of Pearl diving and marine life terms in the Gulf. Doha: Katara Cultural Village.

Al-Malki, A. (2015). Camels in Qatar. Doha: Dar for Qatari books (Qatari books' house).

Al-Malki, K. (2005). Brief explanation of the Qatari parables. Doha: Al Majlis Al watani lethaqafa walfounon walturath.

AlMuhannadi, M. (2006). A guide to the idioms of Qatari Arabic with reference to English idioms. Doha: Dar Al kutub AlQataria.

Al-Attiyah, H. (2013, 5 27). Reviving the Local Dialect in Qatar: An Issue of Linguistic Concern or Identity Politics? Retrieved from Arab Center for Research and PolicyStudies: https://www.dohainstitute.org/en/ResearchAndStudies/Pages/Reviving_the_Local_Dialect_in_Qatar_An_Issue_of_Linguistic_Concern_or_Identity_Politics.aspx

AlNaama, N. (2012). Torath Al'ajdad. Retrieved from AlArab.Newspaper: https://www.alarab.qa/story/209946/%D8%AA%D8%B1%D8%A7%D8%AB-%D8%A7%D9%84%A3%D8%AC%D8%AF%D8%A7%D8%AF

Atanasova Pepa, Alberto Barron-Cedeno, Tamer Elsayed, Reem Suwaileh, Wajdi Zaghouani, Spas Kyuchukov, Giovanni Da San Martino, Preslav Nakov (2018). Overview of the CLEF-2018 CheckThat! Lab on automatic identification and verification of political claims. Task 1: Check-worthiness. CLEF 2018 Working Notes. Working Notes of CLEF 2018 - Conference and Labs of the Evaluation Forum

Babbie, E. (2010). The practice of social research. Belmont: Wadsworth, Cengage Learning.

Barrón-Cedeño Alberto, Tamer Elsayed, Reem Suwaileh, Lluís Màrquez, Pepa Atanasova, Wajdi Zaghouani, Spas Kyuchukov, Giovanni Da San Martino and Preslav Nakov (2018). Overview of the CLEF-2018 CheckThat! Lab on automatic identification and verification of political claims. Task 2: Factuality. CLEF 2018 Working Notes. Working Notes of CLEF 2018 - Conference and Labs of the Evaluation Forum

Bouamor, H., Habash, N., Salameh, M., Zaghouani, W., Rambow, O., Abdulrahim, D., Obeid, O., Khalifa, S., Eryani, F., Erdmann, A., et al. (2018). The MADAR arabic dialect corpus and lexicon. In Proceedings of the Eleventh International Conference on Language Resources and Evaluation (LREC 2018).

Bouamor, H., Zaghouani, W., Diab, M., Obeid, O., Oflazer,

K., Ghoneim, M., and Hawwari, A. (2015). A pilot study on arabic multi-genre corpus diacritization. In Proceedings of the Second Workshop on Arabic Natural Language Processing, pages 80–88.

Bouamor Houda, Nizar Habash, Mohammad Salameh, Wajdi Zaghouani, Owen Rambow, Dana Abdulrahim, Ossama Obeid, Salam Khalifa, Fadhl Eryani, Alexander Erdmann, Kemal Oflazer(2018). The MADAR Arabic Dialect Corpus and Lexicon. In Proceedings of The International Conference on Language Resources and Evaluation, Miyazaki, Japan .

Braber , N., & Davies, D. (2016). Using and creating oral history in dialect research. Oral History, 44(1), 98-107. Carmen Berlinches Ramos, . "Idioms in Syrian Arabic: A First Approach towards a Lexico-Semantic and Grammatical Analysis." Zeitschrift für Arabische Linguistik 70 (2019): 17-43.

Buchanan , E., & Hvizdak, E. (2009). Online Survey Tools: Ethical and Methodological Concerns of Human Research Ethics Committees. Journal of Empirical Research on Human Research Ethics: An International Journal, 4(2), 37-48.

Burnard, L. (2004). Developing Linguistic Corpora: a Guide to Good Practice -Metadata for corpus work. Retrieved from ahds: Literature, Languages, and Linguistics: https://ota.ox.ac.uk/documents/creating/dlc/chapter3.htm

Diab Mona , Aous Mansouri, Martha Palmer, Olga Babko-Malaya, Wajdi Zaghouani, Ann Bies, Mohammed Maamouri. 2008) A Pilot Arabic Propbank. In Proceedings of the Sixth International Conference on Language Resources and Evaluation (LREC'08)

Habash (2010). Arabic Natural Language Processing. Morgan & Claypool Publishers.

Habash, N., Khalifa, S., Eryani, F., Rambow, O., Abdulrahim, D., Erdmann, A., Faraj, R., Zaghouani, W., Bouamor, H., Zalmout, N., Hassan, S., Shargi, F. A., Alkhereyf, S., Abdulkareem, B., Eskander, R., Salameh, M., and Saddiki, H. (2018). Unified Guidelines and Resources for Arabic Dialect Orthography. In Proceedings of the International Conference on Language Resources and Evaluation (LREC 2018), Miyazaki, Japan

Khalifa Salam, Nizar Habash, Dana Abdulrahim, Sara Hassan (2016) A Large Scale Corpus of Gulf Arabic. In Proceedings of the Tenth International Conference on Language Resources and Evaluation (LREC'16)

Laoudi, Jamal, Claire Bonial, Lucia Donatelli, Stephen Tratz, and Clare Voss. "Towards a Computational Lexicon for Moroccan Darija: Words, Idioms, and Constructions." In Proceedings of the Joint Workshop on Linguistic Annotation, Multiword Expressions and Constructions (LAW-MWE-CxG-2018), pp. 74-85. 2018.

Liaquat, S. Q. (2016). Freedom of Expression in Pakistan: A myth or a reality. (R. f. http://0-www.jstor.org.library.qnl.qa/stable/resrep02846.4, Trans.) Sustainable Development Policy Institute.

Maamouri, M., Bies, A., Kulick, S., Zaghouani, W., Graff, D., and Ciul, M. (2010). From speech to trees: Applying treebank annotation to Arabic broadcast news. In Proceedings of the Nine International Conference on Language Resources and Evaluation (LREC 2010).

Pasha, A., Al-Badrashiny, M., Kholy, A. E., Eskander, R., Diab, M., Habash, N., Pooleery, M., Rambow, O., and Roth, R. (2014). MADAMIRA: A Fast, Comprehensive Tool for Morphological Analysis and Disambiguation of Arabic. In In Proceedings of LREC, Reykjavik, Iceland

Palmer Martha , Olga Babko-Malaya, Ann Bies, Mona Diab, Mohamed Maamouri, Aous Mansouri, Wajdi Zaghouani. (2008) A Pilot Arabic Propbank. In Proceedings of the Sixth International Conference on Language Resources and Evaluation (LREC'08)

Rangel, F., Rosso, P., Charfi, A., and Zaghouani, W. (2019a). Detecting deceptive tweets in arabic for cybersecurity. In 2019 IEEE International Conference on Intelligence and Security Informatics (ISI), pages 86–91. IEEE.

Rangel, F., Rosso, P., Charfi, A., Zaghouani, W., Ghanem, B., and Snchez-Junquera, J. (2019b). Overview of the Track on Author Profiling and Deception Detection in Arabic. In Working Notes of the Forum for Information Retrieval Evaluation (FIRE'19). CEUR Workshop Proceedings. In: CEUR-WS. org, Kolkata, India

Rosso, P., Rangel, F., Far´ıas, I. H., Cagnina, L., Zaghouani, W., and Charfi, A. (2018). A survey on author profiling, deception, and irony detection for the Arabic language. Language and Linguistics Compass, 12(4):e12275

Rubin, B. (1991). Pan-Arab Nationalism: The Ideological Dream as Compelling Force. Journal of Contemporary History, 26(3/4), 535-551.

Zaghouani, W. (2014). Critical Survey of the Freely Available Arabic Corpora. In Proceedings of the Nine International Conference on Language Resources and Evaluation (LREC'14), OSACT Workshop, Reykjavik, Iceland, May. European Language Resources Association (ELRA).

Zaghouani Wajdi , Abdelati Hawwari, Mona Diab (2012). A pilot Propbank annotation for quranic Arabic. In Proceedings of the NAACL-HLT 2012 Workshop on Computational Linguistics for Literature.

Zaghouani, W., Mohit, B., Habash, N., Obeid, O., Tomeh,., Rozovskaya, A., Farra, N., Alkuhlani, S., and Oflazer, K. (2014). Large scale arabic error annotation: Guidelines

Zaghouani, W. and Charfi, A. (2018). Arap-tweet: A large multi-dialect twitter corpus for gender, age and language variety identification. arXiv preprint arXiv:1808.07674.

Appendix 1

No.	Theme	Description
1.	Adjective	This theme includes adjectives that describe a person, object, or situation using traditional expressions, such as annoying (Sindara)
2.	Animal	This theme includes animals' traditional names, the majority of these names still exist, such as camels' different names (Mathaya)
3.	Body Parts	This theme includes the human's body parts' colloquial Qatari traditional names, such as mouth (Halj)
4.	Building	This theme includes expressions that describe Qatar's old building, construction, infrastructure, or any construction related items, such as street (Rastah).
5.	Transportation	This theme includes colloquial Qatari expressions that are related to automobiles, boats and the related spare parts and accessories, such as Tire (Tiyer)
6.	Clothes	This theme includes the names of the Qatari traditional clothes for both men and women, such as the black Abaya of women.
7.	Device	This theme includes expressions describing electronic devices that were used in the past, such as telescope (Darbeel)
8.	Education	This theme includes expressions related to education, school's building, and stationary in old Qatar, such as notebook (Daftar)
9.	Family	This theme includes expressions that describe different kinships in the Qatari family since the old days, such as mother (Youmah)
10.	Food	This theme includes the Qatari traditional food items, that mostly exist until now, such as the crispy crepe bread (Regag)
11.	Gold	This theme includes the different names of various Qatari traditional styles of gold. as different styles of necklaces have different names, such as (Meaznat) which is a choker that is a close-fitting necklace worn around the neck
12.	Hairstyle	This theme includes the different names of the various old Qatari hairstyles for men and women, such as braid (Achfaa)
13.	House equipment	This theme includes any object that can be found at the old Qatari houses, such as furniture (Afish)
14.	Kitchenware	This theme includes the expressions related to the old Qatari kitchen items such as stirring spoon (Millas)
15.	Marine life	This theme includes the various expressions related to the sea creatures, sea activities, and tools used in performing the different activities in the sea, such as king fish (Chanad)
16.	Medical	This theme includes the expressions related to diseases, medical treatments, and medical equipment that used in the past, such as: Hospital (Aspitar)
17.	Nature	This theme includes the names of natural phenomena, such as storm(Daloob)
18.	Noun	This theme includes expressions that refer to old names of objects, such as: part of something (Hessa)
19.	Occasions	This theme includes the names of various traditional Qatari occasions, such as: mid Ramadan's celebration (Garangaoo)
20.	Occupation	This theme includes the names of the various old occupations that mostly doesn't exist anymore, such as water supplier (AlKendry)
21.	Oil and Gas	This theme includes the expressions that are related to Oil and Gas tasks and tools such as Rig (Rik)
22.	Old currency	This theme includes the old Qatari currencies, such as Rupees (Rubyah)

23.	Personal items	This theme includes names of personal beauty items and accessories that were used or worn in the past by the Qataris, such as glasses (Kashma)
24.	Plant	This theme includes the old names of the plants in Qatar
25.	Question	This theme includes the expressions the are related to questions using the colloquial Qatari traditional words such as How? (Eshloan?)
26.	Shop	This theme includes the old names of the diverse shops in Qatar, such as Laundry (Dobee)
27.	Traditional game	This theme includes the names of traditional games in Qatar, such as hide and seek (kheshasha)
28.	Verb	This theme includes the expressions that are related to verbs known in the past, such as wait (Thayad)

Table 4. Description of themes in the corpus of Qatari traditional expressions

Category	Word	English Meaning	Standard Arabic Translation	Word origin	Inflection (forms)	Synonym	Example (sentence) from reliable source
Animals	متوه Matoh	Parrot	ببغاء	-	-		أبي أشتري متوه بتوه
	يربوع yarbou	Rodent	جربوع	-	يرابيع		اليربوع يعيش في الصحراء
Household	كرفاية kerfayah	Bed	سرير	-	كرفايتي، كرفايتهم،		وين كرفايتي
	سبير spare	Spare	البديل/ القطعة الاحتياطية	English	-	-	ضاع مفتاحي ابي السبير
Kitchen/ Food	علي ولم Aliwalam	Potato	بطاطس	English	-		حطي في الاكل علي ولم
Personal items	كشمة Kashma	Glasses	النظارة	-	-		بشتري كشمة
Professions	كهربجي Kahrabchi	Electrician	الكهربائي		-	-	الكهربجي قاعد يصلح
Appearance	بسايل Besayl	Hair	شعر	-	-	-	حلات البنت ببسايلها
Adjective	سندارة Sindara	annoying	المزعج	-	سندرني	-	ولدج سندرني

Table 5. A Sample of the Corpus Entries of various themes

Proceedings of the 4th Workshop on Open-Source Arabic Corpora and Processing Tools, pages 32–39
with a Shared Task on Offensive Language Detection.
Language Resources and Evaluation Conference (LREC 2020), Marseille, 11–16 May 2020
© European Language Resources Association (ELRA), licensed under CC-BY-NC

From Arabic Sentiment Analysis to Sarcasm Detection:
The ArSarcasm Dataset

Ibrahim Abu-Farha[1] and Walid Magdy[1,2]
[1] School of Informatics, The University of Edinburgh
Edinburgh, United Kingdom
[2] The Alan Turing Institute
London, United Kingdom
i.abufarha@ed.ac.uk, wmagdy@inf.ed.ac.uk

Abstract

Sarcasm is one of the main challenges for sentiment analysis systems. Its complexity comes from the expression of opinion using implicit indirect phrasing. In this paper, we present ArSarcasm, an Arabic sarcasm detection dataset, which was created through the reannotation of available Arabic sentiment analysis datasets. The dataset contains 10,547 tweets, 16% of which are sarcastic. In addition to sarcasm the data was annotated for sentiment and dialects. Our analysis shows the highly subjective nature of these tasks, which is demonstrated by the shift in sentiment labels based on annotators' biases. Experiments show the degradation of state-of-the-art sentiment analysers when faced with sarcastic content. Finally, we train a deep learning model for sarcasm detection using BiLSTM. The model achieves an F1-score of 0.46, which shows the challenging nature of the task, and should act as a basic baseline for future research on our dataset.

Keywords: Arabic, sarcasm detection, sentiment analysis

1 Introduction

Work on subjective language analysis, has been prominent in the literature during the last two decades. A major theme that dominated the area is the work on sentiment analysis (SA). According to (Liu, 2012), SA is a process where we extract and analyse the emotional polarity in a given piece of text. Large amount of work focused on classifying the text into its sentiment class, which varies based on the granularity. SA is one of the research areas within the larger natural language processing (NLP) field. The interest in SA research was embarked by the advent of user-driven platforms such as social media websites. Research on SA started with the early work of (Pang et al., 2002), where they analysed the sentiment in movie reviews. Since then, the work has developed and spanned different topics and fields such as social media analysis, computational social science and others. Most of the work is focused on English, whereas Arabic did not receive much attention until after 2010. The work on Arabic SA was kicked off by (Abdul-Mageed et al., 2011), but it still lacks behind the progress in English. This can be attributed to the many challenges of Arabic language; including the large variety in dialects (Habash, 2010; Darwish et al., 2014) and the complex morphology of the language (Abdul-Mageed et al., 2011).

As the work on SA systems developed, researchers started analysing the intricacies of such systems in order understand their performance and where they fail. There are many challenges when doing SA, such as negation handling, domain dependence, lack of world knowledge and sarcasm (Hussein, 2018). Sarcasm can be defined as a form of verbal irony that is intended to express contempt or ridicule (Joshi et al., 2017). Sarcasm is correlated with expressing the opinion in an indirect way, where the intended meaning is different from the literal one (Wilson, 2006). Additionally, sarcasm is highly context-dependent, as it al-

ways takes part between parties where shared knowledge exist. Usually, a speaker will not use sarcasm unless he/she thinks that it will be understood as so (Joshi et al., 2017). Sarcasm detection is a crucial task for SA. The reason for this is that a sarcastic utterance usually carries a negative implicit sentiment, while it is expressed using positive expressions. This contradiction between the surface sentiment and the intended one creates a complex challenge for SA systems (Bouazizi and Ohtsuki, 2016).

There has been lots of work on English sarcasm detection, those include datasets such as the works of (Abercrombie and Hovy, 2016; Barbieri et al., 2014a; Barbieri et al., 2014b; Filatova, 2012; Ghosh et al., 2015; Joshi et al., 2016) and detection systems such as (Rajadesingan et al., 2015; Joshi et al., 2015; Amir et al., 2016).

Work on Arabic sarcasm is yet to follow. Up to our knowledge, work on Arabic sarcasm is limited to the work of (Karoui et al., 2017), a shared task on irony detection (Ghanem et al., 2019) along with the participants' submissions and a dialectal sarcasm dataset by (Abbes et al., 2020). Currently, there is no publicly available dataset for Arabic sarcasm detection. The data in (Karoui et al., 2017) is not publicly available and most of the tweets provided in (Ghanem et al., 2019) were deleted.

In this paper, we present ArSarcasm dataset, a new Arabic sarcasm detection dataset. The dataset was created using previously available Arabic SA datasets and adds sarcasm and dialect labels to them. The dataset contains 10,547 tweets, 1,682 (16%) of which are sarcastic. In addition, we analyse annotators' subjectivity regarding sentiment annotation, hoping to promote finding better procedures for collecting and annotating new datasets. The analysis shows that annotators' biases could be reflected on the annotation. Moreover, we provide an analysis of the performance of SA systems on sarcastic content. Finally, our BiLSTM based model , which serves as a baseline for this dataset, achieves an F1-score of 0.46 on the sarcastic class, which indicates that sarcasm detection is a challenging task.

ArSarcasm is publicly available for research purposes, and it can be downloaded for free[1].

2 Background

2.1 Sarcasm and Irony Detection

The literature has a large amount of work on sarcasm and irony detection, which vary from collecting datasets to building detection systems. However, researchers and linguists cannot yet agree on a specific definition of what is considered to be sarcasm. According to (Grice et al., 1975) sarcasm is a form of figurative language where the literal meaning of words is not intended, and the opposite interpretation of the utterance is the intended one. Gibbs Jr et al. (1994) define sarcasm as a bitter and caustic from of irony. According to Merriam Webster's dictionary [2], sarcasm is "a sharp and often satirical or ironic utterance designed to cut or give pain", while irony is defined as " the use of words to express something other than and especially the opposite of the literal meaning". These definitions are quite close to each other, yet each of them gives a different definition of sarcasm. While most of the literature assumes that sarcasm is a form of irony, Justo et al. (2014) argues that it is not necessarily ironic. Thus, sarcasm is always confused with other forms of figurative language such as metaphor, irony, humour and satire.

One of the early works on English sarcasm/irony detection is the work of (Davidov et al., 2010), where the authors created a dataset from Twitter using specific hashtags such as #sarcasm and #not, which indicate sarcasm. This way of data collection is called distant supervision, where data is collected based on some specific content that it bears. Distant supervision is the most common approach to collect sarcasm data from Twitter, where the hashtag #sarcasm and others are used. Some other works that utilised distant supervision to create Twitter datasets include (Barbieri et al., 2014a; Bamman and Smith, 2015; Bouazizi and Ohtsuki, 2016; Ptáček et al., 2014). Davidov et al. (2010) mention that the use of the #sarcasm hashtag is possible but not reliable, and they used it as a search anchor. In addition, such hashtags can be useful in the cases of subtle sarcasm which might not be easily understood. Khodak et al. (2018) proposed a dataset collected from Reddit. They used a similar distant supervision approach, but they relied on "/s" marker which indicates sarcasm.

The other way to create a dataset is through manual labelling. This is done by collecting a large amount of data and asking annotators to manually label it. Works that relied on this approach include (Riloff et al., 2013; Van Hee et al., 2018). According to (Oprea and Magdy, 2019a), this approach of creating datasets captures only the sarcasm that the annotators could perceive and misses the intended sarcasm. Intended sarcasm is when the text is considered to be sarcastic by its author. In their work, they experimented with the benefits of the context in detecting perceived and intended sarcasm. In another work (Oprea and

Magdy, 2019b), the authors propose a new dataset that captures intended sarcasm. They collected their data using an online survey, where they asked the participants to provide sarcastic and non-sarcastic tweets. They also asked them to provide an explanation for the sarcastic text and how would they convey the same idea in a direct way.

The work on Arabic sarcasm is scarce and limited to few attempts. It is also worth mentioning that researchers on Arabic inherited the aforementioned confusion about sarcasm definition. The earliest work on Arabic sarcasm/irony is (Karoui et al., 2017), where the authors created a corpus of Arabic tweets, which they collected using a set of political keywords. They filtered sarcastic content using distant supervision, where they used the Arabic equivalent of #sarcasm such as #سخرية, #مسخرة, #تهكم and #استهزاء. The result was a set of 5,479 tweets distributed as follows: 1,733 ironic tweets and 3,746 non-ironic. However, this corpus is not publicly available. Ghanem et al. (2019) organised a shared task competition for Arabic irony detection. They collected their data using distant supervision and used similar Arabic hashtags. In addition, they manually annotated a subset of tweets, which were sampled from ironic and non-ironic sets. The dataset provided in the shared task contained 5,030 tweets with almost 50% of them being ironic. It is worth mentioning that at the time of writing this paper around 1,300 tweets were still available. Finally, Abbes et al. (2020) proposed a dialectal Arabic irony corpus, which was also collected from Twitter.

2.2 Arabic Sentiment Analysis

In contrast to the recent attention coming to irony and sarcasm detection, Arabic SA has been under the researchers' radar for a while. There is a reasonable amount of Arabic SA resources that include corpora, lexicons and datasets.

Early work on Arabic such as (Abdul-Mageed et al., 2011; Abbasi et al., 2008), focused on modern standard Arabic (MSA). Later, attention started moving to dialects such as the work of (Mourad and Darwish, 2013), where the authors introduced an expandable Arabic sentiment lexicon along with a corpus of tweets. El-Beltagy (2016) introduced a lexicon, which contains around 6000 sentiment terms that are taken from the Egyptian dialect and MSA. The Arabic Sentiment Tweets Dataset (ASTD) (Nabil et al., 2015) contains 10,006 tweets mainly in the Egyptian dialect. It is distributed over 4 classes: positive (799), negative (1,684), neutral (832) or objective (6,691). The tweets were collected over the period between 2013 and 2015, based on the most trending topics at that time.

Elmadany et al. (2018) introduced ArSAS dataset, which is annotated for Arabic speech-act and sentiment analysis. The dataset consists of around 21K tweets, that cover multiple topics. The data was manually annotated using CrowdFlower[3] crowd-sourcing platform. The annotation scheme for the sentiment analysis task was 4-way sentiment classification, as each of the tweets is labelled with one of the following: positive (4,543), negative (7,840), neutral (7,279), or mixed (1,302). Badaro et al. (2014) introduced ArSenL, an Arabic sentiment lexicon. The lexicon was built

---

[1]ArSarcasm is available at:
https://github.com/iabufarha/ArSarcasm
[2]https://www.merriam-webster.com

[3]Currently known as Figure-Eight

using different resources such as Arabic WordNet and English sentiment WordNet. In SemEval 2016, Arabic was included in the sentiment analysis task for multiple languages (Kiritchenko et al., 2016), where they introduced a small dataset of 1,366 tweets. In 2017, Arabic was also a part of SemEval with a larger dataset of 9,455 Arabic tweets annotated with 3 labels: positive, negative or neutral (Rosenthal et al., 2017). Other datasets and lexicons were proposed in the works of (Ibrahim et al., 2015; Refaee and Rieser, 2014; Aly and Atiya, 2013; Mahyoub et al., 2014).

3 Proposed Dataset

In this work, we present ArSarcasm, a new dataset for Arabic sarcasm detection. The dataset consists of a combination of Arabic SA datasets, where we reannotated them for sarcasm. In addition to that, we also provide labelling for the dialect and sentiment.

3.1 Resources

In this work, we relied on a set of well-known Arabic SA datasets. The reason for this choice is that sarcasm is highly subjective and always mentioned as one of the main reasons that degrades sentiment analysers' performance. The datasets we are using are SemEval's 2017 (Rosenthal et al., 2017) and ASTD (Nabil et al., 2015) datasets. ASTD dataset consists of 10,006 tweets labelled as shown in Table 1. The dataset contains tweets that date back to the period between 2013 and 2015. The tweets are mostly in Egyptian dialect and they were annotated using Amazon's Mechanical Turk. In our work, since we are aiming to annotate for sarcasm, we decided to eliminate the objective class and we took our sample from the other subjective classes.

Class	Count
Positive	799
Negative	1,684
Neutral	832
Objective	6,691
Total	10,006

Table 1: ASTD statistics.

The other dataset we are using is the one provided in SemEval's 2017 task for Arabic SA (Rosenthal et al., 2017). This dataset consists of 10,126 tweets distributed over different sets as shown in Table 2. The data was annotated using CrowdFlower[4] crowd-sourcing platform. The new dataset contains 10,543 tweets, most of which were taken from SemEval's dataset.

Set	Positive	Negative	Neutral	Total
Training	743	1,142	1,470	3,355
Validation	222	128	321	671
Testing	1,514	2,222	2,364	6,100
Total	2,479	3,492	4,155	10,126

Table 2: SemEval 2017 Task 4-A dataset statistics.

---

[4]Currently Figure-Eight.

3.2 Annotation

For the annotation process, we used Figure-Eight[5] crowd-sourcing platform. Our main objective was to annotate the data for **sarcasm** detection, but due to the challenges imposed by dialectal variations, we decided to add the annotation for **dialects**. We also include a new annotation for **sentiment** labels in order to have a glimpse of the variability and subjectivity between different annotators. Thus, the annotators were asked to provide three labels for each tweet as the following:

- **Sarcasm:** sarcastic or non-sarcastic.

- **Sentiment:** positive, negative or neutral.

- **Dialect:** Egyptian, Gulf, Levantine, Maghrebi or Modern Standard Arabic (MSA).

To keep the sentiment annotation process consistent, we used the same guidelines that were used to annotate SemEval's dataset. Regarding sarcasm, we define it as *an utterance that is used to express ridicule, where the intended meaning is different from the apparent one.*

Only annotators who have Arabic language in their profiles and come from an Arab country were allowed to participate. Each tweet was annotated by at least three different annotators. The quality of annotation was monitored using a set of 100 hidden test questions that appear randomly during the task, each of those question has the correct label for sentiment, sarcasm and dialect. If the performance of an annotator in these test questions dropped below 80%, this annotator is eliminated and all the labels he provided are also ignored. Agreement among annotators was 80.7% for sentiment, 89.3% for sarcasm and 86.7% for dialects.

4 Statistics and Analysis

4.1 Dataset Statistics

The new dataset contains 10,547 tweets, 8,075 of them were taken from SemEval's dataset while the rest (2,472 tweets) were taken from ASTD. Each of the tweets has three labels for sarcasm, sentiment and dialect. Table 3 shows the statistics of the new dataset, where we can see that 16% of the data is sarcastic (1,682 tweets). The new annotation shows that most of the data is either in MSA or the Egyptian dialect, while there are few examples of the Maghrebi dialect. Figure 1 shows the ratio of sarcasm in the tweets belonging to each dialect. Maghrebi dialect has the largest percentage, but this is an outlier due to the small number of Maghrebi tweets (only 32 tweets). Thus, sarcasm is more prominent in the Egyptian dialect with 34% of the Egyptian tweets being sarcastic . Also, from the table, it is noticeable that the Egyptian dialect comprises most of the sarcastic tweets (799 tweets, 47.5% of the sarcastic tweets). Table 4 provides examples of sarcastic tweets from different dialects.

4.2 Sentiment in Sarcasm

Figure 2 shows the sentiment distribution over the sarcastic tweets. It is clear that most of the sarcastic tweets

---

[5]https://www.figure-eight.com/

Dialect	Non-Sarcastic	Sarcastic	Negative	Neutral	Positive	Total
Egyptian	1,584	799	1,179	733	471	2,383
Gulf	397	122	200	218	101	519
Levantine	433	118	239	178	134	551
Maghrebi	20	12	18	10	4	32
MSA	6,431	631	1,893	4,201	968	7,062
Total	8,865	1,682	3,529	5,340	1,678	10,547

Table 3: Dataset statistics for sarcasm and sentiment over the dialects.

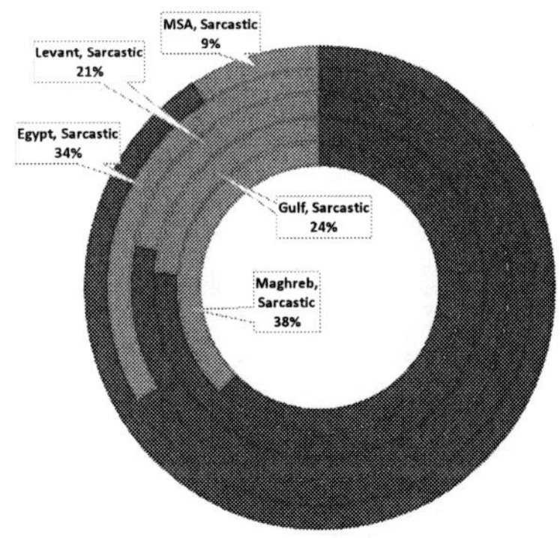

Figure 1: Ratio of sarcasm over the dialects.

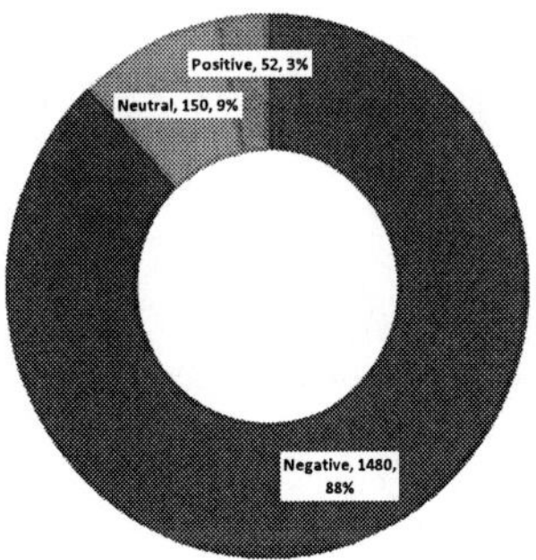

Figure 2: Sentiment distribution over the sarcastic tweets.

have negative sentiment, and this agrees with the definition we adopted, which implies that sarcasm includes making ridicule of someone or something. However, there are some neutral and positive sarcastic tweets, which could be due to the highly subjective nature of sarcasm. In addition, this could be attributed to the fact that some other metaphoric or figurative expressions might fall under the sarcasm definition. An example of that is understatement, where a person describes a good thing using negative terms such as "This was an extremely hard exam". This phenomenon is demonstrated in example 2 in Table 4, where the speaker is bragging about his success in being a presenter, and he mentions that this had happened because his mother wished him to be embarrassed and looked at as a weird person.

Table 4 provides examples of sarcastic tweets from different dialects along with their sentiment. Those examples show some aspects of the sarcasm nature, such as referencing real world items or figures. The examples show how challenging sarcasm can be, as some of them are expressed using positive expressions, yet having negative sentiment and vice versa. This, in turn, makes it extremely challenging for an SA system to analyse such examples, which urges the need for sarcasm detection systems. They also show that sarcasm relies heavily on world knowledge and context, thus incorporating such information is necessary to correctly identify sarcasm.

4.3 Annotation Subjectivity

We also studied the difference between the original and new sentiment labels. Figure 3 shows how the new labels are different from the original ones, labels above the charts are the original ones. It is clear that there is an extreme change

ID	Tweet	Sentiment	Dialect
1	كنت أعتقد أن خدمة غوغل ترجمة سيئة جدا إلى أن جربت بينغ. ملك جمال الترجمة غوغل (I was thinking that Google translate is bad, till I tried Bing. Google is Mr. Translation)	Negative	MSA
2	واضح إن أمي دعت عليا وأنا صغير وقالتلي روح ربنا يفرج عليك خلقو، قام ربنا طلعني مذيع (It is clear that my mother was mad at me and wished that I get embarrassed and looked at by people, Now I am a TV presenter)	Positive	Egyptian
3	بالصيفيات الحلوه محد يقرر ينزلني على لبنان لما وصلت درجه الحراره تحت الصفر امي تقول نفكر نروح لا شكرا (When it is summer, no one suggests going to Lebanon. Now, when it is below zero, my mother considers going there. No, thanks)	Negative	Levantine
4	الناس المؤمنين بالسحر كان لازم نوضحلهم ان هاري بوتر مو فلم وثائقي (We should have explained for those who believe in magic that Harry Potter is not a documentary)	Negative	Gulf

Table 4: Examples of some sarcastic tweets from different dialects.

in the labels. This is empirical proof of the highly subjective nature of sentiment analysis annotation. We can see that in the case of the positive class, more the 50% of the labels has been changed, Table 5 provides examples of these cases. From the table, it is noticeable that these cases can be attributed to different reasons. For example, in the second tweet, the original annotator failed to perceive the sarcasm intended by the author. This can be due to either a misunderstanding of the intentions, or a mismatch between the author's intention and the annotator's preference. The other reason that might have caused the labels to change

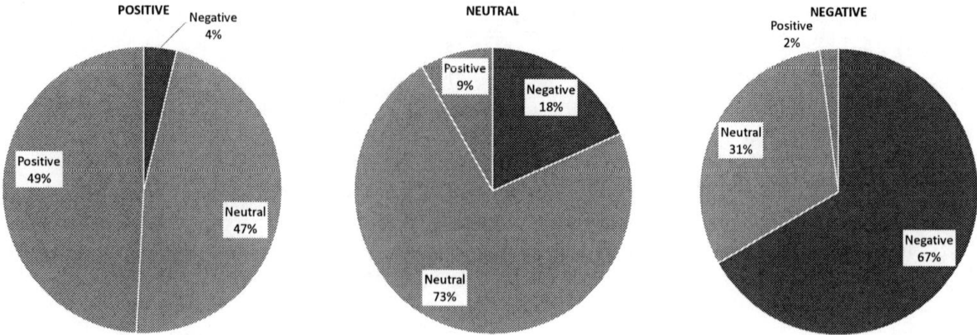

Figure 3: The change in sentiment labels between the original and new annotation. The labels above the charts are the original labels.

is the different perspectives that a text can been looked at from. For example, some annotators might annotate news as neutral, considering the view of the news agency, while others might reflect their own preference. The same thing occurs if the text is about two conflicting parties, where the annotators are likely to take one side. In addition to that, the available Arabic SA datasets are highly political and they contain different dividing topics. Having all of these factors together would result in the high presence of the annotator's biases and personal views.

Moreover, in the case of most sentiment and sarcasm datasets, they were annotated using crowd-sourcing platforms. These platforms provide multiple annotations for each data point, but they do not ensure having the same annotators to annotate all the data. This would provide inconsistent labels for the subjective text, where different conflicting biases are reflected on the assigned label. Thus, having multiple people annotating a dataset would probably give conflicting labels for different related instances within the data. These phenomena impose challenges for sentiment analysis systems, since the boundaries between the labels are not clear.

Based on the previous statistics and examples, we can see that the current annotation schemes and procedures are not robust enough against bias, and they do not ensure the consistency among different annotators. In addition, the current approach of considering sarcasm as binary text classification problem is not precise. Sarcasm is highly related to the context, cultural background, world knowledge and personal traits of its author. We believe that more sophisticated data collection and annotation approaches should be used to have a proper computational representation of sarcasm.

5 Effect of Sarcasm on Sentiment Analysis

To better understand how sarcasm can be disruptive for SA systems, we conducted an experiment on the newly annotated data. This was done through comparing the performance of an available SA system on both sarcastic and non-sarcastic tweets. In this experiment, we used Mazajak (Abu Farha and Magdy, 2019), state-of-the-art Arabic sentiment analyser. In order to have an informative comparison, we separated the dataset into two sets, sarcastic

ID	Tweet	Original label	New label
1	جوجل تنافس أبل وسامسونج بهاتف جديد (Google is competing Apple and Samsung with a new phone)	Positive	Neutral
2	مبروك عليك ويندوز ١٠ ـ ربنا يخلهولللللك (Congratulations on Windows 10, God keeeeep it for you)	Positive	Negative
3	اخس مشغلين اغنيه جستن بيبر (Shame, they are playing a Justin Bieber song)	Neutral	Negative
4	سيتم الرد علي حضرتك في اقرب وقت يا فندم. (Sir, we will respond to you soon)	Neutral	Positive
5	سمعة أبل على المحك.. مشكلة حقيقية في آيفون ٧ (Apple's reputation is on the line ... A real problem in iPhone 7)	Negative	Neutral
6	طقس كاذب يقولو ثلوج ويطلع حر (deceitful weather, they say it will snow and it is warm)	Negative	Positive

Table 5: Examples of some tweet that have its labels changed.

(1,682) and non-sarcastic (8,865). The performance was compared using the original and new sentiment labels. Table 6 shows the achieved macro F1-score. It is clear that there is a gap between the performance on sarcastic and non-sarcastic. Mazajak achieved F1-scores of 0.43 (new labels) and 0.44 (original labels) on sarcastic tweets, and F1-scores of 0.64 (new labels) and 0.61 (original labels) on the non-sarcastic ones.

Although Mazajak was trained on samples from the same dataset, the results on the sarcastic tweets are much lower than those on the non-sarcastic ones. The low performance on the sarcastic tweets indicates that SA systems rely mostly on the surface sentiment expressed by the words. This, in turn, means that sarcasm, which is an indirect implicit expression tool, is a major challenge for SA systems.

Set	F-score (new)	F-score (original)
Sarcastic	0.43	0.44
Non-Sarcastic	0.64	0.61

Table 6: Mazajak's performance on sarcastic and non-sarcastic tweets. The references are the original and the new sentiment labels.

6 Sarcasm Detection Baseline System

In this section, we conduct an experiment to set a baseline system for the new dataset. We tested a deep learning model, which consists of a bidirectional long short-term memory (BiLSTM) followed by a fully connected layer. We used the hyper-paremeters shown in Table 7. For text representation, we utilised the embeddings provided by (Abu Farha and Magdy, 2019).

#LSTM cells	128
Recurrent dropout	0.2
Dropout	0.2
#Hidden units	64
Activation	ReLU
Optimiser	Adam
Learning rate	0.0001
Batch size	512

Table 7: Hyper-parameters used for BiLSTM model.

The data was divided using an 80/20 split to create training and testing sets. Table 8 shows the results achieved by the model on the sarcastic class. As shown, the system detected sarcasm with precision 62%, but quite low recall of only 38%, which demonstrates that it is not straightforward to spot sarcasm. The overall F1-score is 0.46, which empirically proves that sarcasm detection is a challenging task that requires additional investigation. An example of that is the use of contextual information alongside the text itself, which proved to be effective in English sarcasm detection (Oprea and Magdy, 2019a).

Metric	Result
Precision	0.62
Recall	0.38
F1-score	0.46

Table 8: Baseline results on the sarcastic class.

From the previous experiment, we conclude that sarcasm is a challenging task, and it relies heavily on the context, world knowledge and cultural background. Thus, having better performance or good detection systems relies heavily on how these aspects are incorporated into the training and preparation of these systems (Oprea and Magdy, 2019b).

7 Conclusion and Future Work

Sarcasm is an important aspect of any language. It includes expressing ideas, opinions and emotions in an indirect implicit way. This nature of implicitness makes sarcasm problematic for SA systems which mostly rely on the surface meaning/features.

In this work, we presented ArSarcasm, a new Arabic sarcasm dataset. The dataset was created through the re-annotation of available Arabic sentiment datasets. The new dataset contains sarcasm, sentiment and dialect labels. Analysis shows that sarcasm is highly prominent in sentiment datasets with 16% of them being sarcastic. We also show the high subjective nature of such datasets, which was demonstrated by the change in sentiment labels in the new annotation. The experiments show the gap between SA systems' performance on non-sarcastic tweets compared to sarcastic tweets, which urges the need to study such phenomena. Finally, our initial experiments on sarcasm detection show that it is a challenging task.

We believe that this dataset is a starting point in the direction of full study of sarcasm and figurative language in Arabic. However, due to the highly subjective nature of sarcasm, its reliance on world knowledge, cultural background and the perspectives of the communication parties, we believe that the data collection procedure should incorporate more signals about these information. In the future, we hope to prepare a new dataset that incorporates more textual information. We also hope to study and analyse the differences and similarities among sarcastic expressions used by Arabic speakers in different countries.

Acknowledgements

This work was supported by the D&S Programme of The Alan Turing Institute under the EPSRC grant EP/N510129/1.

8 References

Abbasi, A., Chen, H., and Salem, A. (2008). Sentiment analysis in multiple languages: Feature selection for opinion classification in web forums. *ACM Transactions on Information Systems (TOIS)*, 26(3):1–34.

Abbes, I., Zaghouani, W., and El-Hardlo, O. (2020). Daict: A dialectal arabic irony corpus extracted from twitter. *LREC 2020*.

Abdul-Mageed, M., Diab, M. T., and Korayem, M. (2011). Subjectivity and sentiment analysis of modern standard arabic. In *Proceedings of the 49th Annual Meeting of the Association for Computational Linguistics: Human Language Technologies: Short Papers - Volume 2*, HLT '11, pages 587–591, Stroudsburg, PA, USA. Association for Computational Linguistics.

Abercrombie, G. and Hovy, D. (2016). Putting sarcasm detection into context: The effects of class imbalance and manual labelling on supervised machine classification of twitter conversations. In *Proceedings of the ACL 2016 Student Research Workshop*, pages 107–113.

Abu Farha, I. and Magdy, W. (2019). Mazajak: An online Arabic sentiment analyser. In *Proceedings of the Fourth Arabic Natural Language Processing Workshop*, pages 192–198, Florence, Italy, August. Association for Computational Linguistics.

Aly, M. and Atiya, A. (2013). Labr: A large scale arabic book reviews dataset. In *Proceedings of the 51st Annual Meeting of the Association for Computational Linguistics (Volume 2: Short Papers)*, pages 494–498.

Amir, S., Wallace, B. C., Lyu, H., Carvalho, P., and Silva, M. J. (2016). Modelling context with user embeddings for sarcasm detection in social media. In *Proceedings of The 20th SIGNLL Conference on Computational Natural Language Learning*, pages 167–177, Berlin, Germany, August. Association for Computational Linguistics.

Badaro, G., Baly, R., Hajj, H., Habash, N., and El-Hajj, W. (2014). A large scale arabic sentiment lexicon for arabic opinion mining. In *Proceedings of the EMNLP 2014 workshop on arabic natural language processing (ANLP)*, pages 165–173.

Bamman, D. and Smith, N. A. (2015). Contextualized sarcasm detection on twitter. In *Ninth International AAAI Conference on Web and Social Media*.

Barbieri, F., Ronzano, F., and Saggion, H. (2014a). Italian irony detection in twitter: a first approach. In *The First Italian Conference on Computational Linguistics CLiC-it*, page 28.

Barbieri, F., Saggion, H., and Ronzano, F. (2014b). Modelling sarcasm in twitter, a novel approach. In *Proceedings of the 5th Workshop on Computational Approaches to Subjectivity, Sentiment and Social Media Analysis*, pages 50–58.

Bouazizi, M. and Ohtsuki, T. O. (2016). A pattern-based approach for sarcasm detection on twitter. *IEEE Access*, 4:5477–5488.

Darwish, K., Magdy, W., et al. (2014). Arabic information retrieval. *Foundations and Trends® in Information Retrieval*, 7(4):239–342.

Davidov, D., Tsur, O., and Rappoport, A. (2010). Semi-supervised recognition of sarcastic sentences in twitter and amazon. In *Proceedings of the fourteenth conference on computational natural language learning*, pages 107–116. Association for Computational Linguistics.

El-Beltagy, S. R. (2016). Nileulex: A phrase and word level sentiment lexicon for egyptian and modern standard arabic. In *LREC*.

Elmadany, A. A., Mubarak, H., and Magdy, W. (2018). Arsas: An arabic speech-act and sentiment corpus of tweets. In *OSACT 3: The 3rd Workshop on Open-Source Arabic Corpora and Processing Tools*, page 20.

Filatova, E. (2012). Irony and sarcasm: Corpus generation and analysis using crowdsourcing. In *Lrec*, pages 392–398. Citeseer.

Ghanem, B., Karoui, J., Benamara, F., Moriceau, V., and Rosso, P. (2019). Idat at fire2019: Overview of the track on irony detection in arabic tweets. In *Proceedings of the 11th Forum for Information Retrieval Evaluation*, pages 10–13.

Ghosh, D., Guo, W., and Muresan, S. (2015). Sarcastic or not: Word embeddings to predict the literal or sarcastic meaning of words. In *proceedings of the 2015 conference on empirical methods in natural language processing*, pages 1003–1012.

Gibbs Jr, R. W., Gibbs, R. W., and Gibbs, J. (1994). *The poetics of mind: Figurative thought, language, and understanding*. Cambridge University Press.

Grice, H. P., Cole, P., and Morgan, J. L. (1975). Syntax and semantics.

Habash, N. Y. (2010). Introduction to arabic natural language processing. *Synthesis Lectures on Human Language Technologies*, 3(1):1–187.

Hussein, D. M. E.-D. M. (2018). A survey on sentiment analysis challenges. *Journal of King Saud University - Engineering Sciences*, 30(4):330 – 338.

Ibrahim, H. S., Abdou, S. M., and Gheith, M. (2015). Mika: A tagged corpus for modern standard arabic and colloquial sentiment analysis. In *2015 IEEE 2nd International Conference on Recent Trends in Information Systems (ReTIS)*, pages 353–358. IEEE.

Joshi, A., Sharma, V., and Bhattacharyya, P. (2015). Harnessing context incongruity for sarcasm detection. In *Proceedings of the 53rd Annual Meeting of the Association for Computational Linguistics and the 7th International Joint Conference on Natural Language Processing (Volume 2: Short Papers)*, pages 757–762.

Joshi, A., Tripathi, V., Bhattacharyya, P., and Carman, M. (2016). Harnessing sequence labeling for sarcasm detection in dialogue from tv series 'friends'. In *Proceedings of The 20th SIGNLL Conference on Computational Natural Language Learning*, pages 146–155.

Joshi, A., Bhattacharyya, P., and Carman, M. J. (2017). Automatic sarcasm detection: A survey. *ACM Computing Surveys (CSUR)*, 50(5):73.

Justo, R., Corcoran, T., Lukin, S. M., Walker, M., and Torres, M. I. (2014). Extracting relevant knowledge for the detection of sarcasm and nastiness in the social web. *Knowledge-Based Systems*, 69:124–133.

Karoui, J., Zitoune, F. B., and Moriceau, V. (2017). Soukhria: Towards an irony detection system for arabic in social media. *Procedia Computer Science*, 117:161–168.

Khodak, M., Saunshi, N., and Vodrahalli, K. (2018). A large self-annotated corpus for sarcasm. In *Proceedings of the Eleventh International Conference on Language Resources and Evaluation (LREC 2018)*, Miyazaki, Japan, May. European Language Resources Association (ELRA).

Kiritchenko, S., Mohammad, S., and Salameh, M. (2016). Semeval-2016 task 7: Determining sentiment intensity of english and arabic phrases. In *Proceedings of the 10th international workshop on semantic evaluation (SEMEVAL-2016)*, pages 42–51.

Liu, B. (2012). Sentiment Analysis and Opinion Mining. *Synthesis Lectures on Human Language Technologies*, 5(1):1–167.

Mahyoub, F. H., Siddiqui, M. A., and Dahab, M. Y. (2014). Building an arabic sentiment lexicon using semi-supervised learning. *Journal of King Saud University - Computer and Information Sciences*, 26(4):417 – 424. Special Issue on Arabic NLP.

Mourad, A. and Darwish, K. (2013). Subjectivity and sentiment analysis of modern standard arabic and arabic microblogs. In *Proceedings of the 4th workshop on computational approaches to subjectivity, sentiment and social media analysis*, pages 55–64.

Nabil, M., Aly, M., and Atiya, A. (2015). Astd: Arabic sentiment tweets dataset. In *Proceedings of the 2015 Conference on Empirical Methods in Natural Language Processing*, pages 2515–2519.

Oprea, S. and Magdy, W. (2019a). Exploring author context for detecting intended vs perceived sarcasm. In *Proceedings of the 57th Annual Meeting of the Association for Computational Linguistics*, pages 2854–2859, Florence, Italy, July. Association for Computational Linguistics.

Oprea, S. and Magdy, W. (2019b). isarcasm: A dataset of intended sarcasm. *arXiv preprint arXiv:1911.03123*.

Pang, B., Lee, L., and Vaithyanathan, S. (2002). Thumbs up?: sentiment classification using machine learning techniques. In *Proceedings of the ACL-02 conference on Empirical methods in natural language processing-Volume 10*, pages 79–86. Association for Computational Linguistics.

Ptáček, T., Habernal, I., and Hong, J. (2014). Sarcasm detection on czech and english twitter. In *Proceedings of COLING 2014, the 25th International Conference on Computational Linguistics: Technical Papers*, pages 213–223.

Rajadesingan, A., Zafarani, R., and Liu, H. (2015). Sarcasm detection on twitter: A behavioral modeling approach. In *Proceedings of the Eighth ACM International Conference on Web Search and Data Mining*, pages 97–106. ACM.

Refaee, E. and Rieser, V. (2014). An arabic twitter corpus for subjectivity and sentiment analysis. In *LREC*, pages 2268–2273.

Riloff, E., Qadir, A., Surve, P., De Silva, L., Gilbert, N., and Huang, R. (2013). Sarcasm as contrast between a positive sentiment and negative situation. In *Proceedings of the 2013 Conference on Empirical Methods in Natural Language Processing*, pages 704–714.

Rosenthal, S., Farra, N., and Nakov, P. (2017). SemEval-2017 task 4: Sentiment analysis in Twitter. In *Proceedings of the 11th International Workshop on Semantic Evaluation*, SemEval '17, Vancouver, Canada, August. Association for Computational Linguistics.

Van Hee, C., Lefever, E., and Hoste, V. (2018). Semeval-2018 task 3: Irony detection in english tweets. In *Proceedings of The 12th International Workshop on Semantic Evaluation*, pages 39–50.

Wilson, D. (2006). The pragmatics of verbal irony: Echo or pretence? *Lingua*, 116(10):1722.

Proceedings of the 4th Workshop on Open-Source Arabic Corpora and Processing Tools, pages 40–47
with a Shared Task on Offensive Language Detection.
Language Resources and Evaluation Conference (LREC 2020), Marseille, 11–16 May 2020
© European Language Resources Association (ELRA), licensed under CC-BY-NC

Understanding and Detecting Dangerous Speech in Social Media

Ali Alshehri[1†], El Moatez Billah Nagoudi[2†] , Muhammad Abdul-Mageed[2]
[1] SUNY at Buffalo
[2] Natural Langauge Processing Lab, The University of British Columbia
alimoham@buffalo.edu, {moatez.nagoudi,muhammad.mageeed}@ubc.ca

Abstract

Social media communication has become a significant part of daily activity in modern societies. For this reason, ensuring safety in social media platforms is a necessity. Use of dangerous language such as physical threats in online environments is a somewhat rare, yet remains highly important. Although several works have been performed on the related issue of detecting offensive and hateful language, dangerous speech has not previously been treated in any significant way. Motivated by these observations, we report our efforts to build a labeled dataset for dangerous speech. We also exploit our dataset to develop highly effective models to detect dangerous content. Our best model performs at 59.60% macro F_1, significantly outperforming a competitive baseline.

1. Introduction

The proliferation of social media makes it necessary to ensure online safety. Unfortunately, offensive, hateful, aggressive, etc., language continues to be used online and put the well-being of millions of people at stake. In some cases, it has been reported that online incidents have caused not only mental and psychological trouble to some users but have indeed forced some to deactivate their accounts or, in extreme cases, even commit suicides (Hinduja and Patchin, 2010). Previous work has focused on detecting various types of negative online behavior, but not necessarily dangerous speech. In this work, our goal is to bridge this gap by investigating dangerous content. More specifically, we focus on direct threats in Arabic Twitter. A threat can be defined as "a statement of an intention to inflict pain, injury, damage, or other hostile action on someone in retribution for something done or not done."[1] This definition highlights two main aspects: (1) the speaker's intention of committing an act, which (2) he/she believes to be unfavorable to the addressee (Fraser, 1998). We especially direct our primary attention to threats of physical harm. We build a new dataset for training machine learning classifiers to detect dangerous speech. Clearly, resulting models can be beneficial in protecting online users and communities alike.

The fact that social media users can create fake accounts on online platforms makes it possible for such users to employ hostile and dangerous language without worrying about facing effective social nor legal consequences. This continues to put the responsibility on platforms such as Facebook and Twitter to maintain safe environments for their users. These networks have related guidelines and invest in fighting negative and dangerous content. Twitter, for example, prohibits any form of violence including threats of physical harm and promotion of terrorism. [2] However, due to the vast volume of communication on these platforms, it is not easy to detect harmful content manually. Our work aims at developing automated models to help alleviate this problem in the context of dangerous speech.

Our focus on Arabic is motivated by the wide use of social media in the Arab world (Lenze, 2017). Relatively recent estimates indicate that there are over $11M$ monthly active users as of March 2017, posting over $27M$ tweets each day (Salem, 2017). An Arabic country such as Saudi Arabia has the highest Twitter penetration level worldwide, with 37% (Iqbal, 2019). The Arabic language also presents interesting challenges primarily due to the dialectical variations cutting across all its linguistic levels: phonetic, phonological, morphological, semantic and syntactic (Farghaly and Shaalan, 2009). Our work caters for dialectal variations in that we collect data using multi-dialectal seeds (Section 3.3.). Overall, we make the following contributions:

1) We manually curate a multi-dialectal dictionary of *physical harm threats* that can be used to collect data for training dangerous language models.

2) We use our lexicon to collect a large dataset of threatening speech from Arabic Twitter, and manually annotate a subset of the data for dangerous speech. *Our datasets are freely available online.*[5]

3) We investigate and characterize threatening speech in Arabic Twitter.

4) We train effective models for detecting dangerous speech in Arabic.

The remainder of the paper is organized as follows: In Section 2., we review related literature. Building dangerous lexica used to collect our datasets is discussed in Section 3.3.. We describe our annotation in Section 4.1.. We present our models in Section 5., and conclude in Section 6..

2. Related work

Detection of offensive language in natural languages has recently attracted the interest of multiple researchers. However, the space of abusive language is vast and has its own nuances. Waseem et al. (2017) classify abusive

---

† Both authors contributed equally.
[1] `https://en.oxforddictionaries.com/definition/threat`
[2] `https://help.twitter.com/en/rules-and-policies/twitter-rules`

language along two dimensions: *directness* (the level to which it is directed to a specific person or organization or not) and *explicitness* (the degree to which it is explicit). Jay and Janschewitz (2008) categorize offensive language to three categories: *Vulgar, Pornographic,* and *Hateful.* The Hateful category includes offensive language such as threats as well as language pertaining to class, race, or religion, among others. In the literature, these concepts are sometimes confused or even ignored altogether. In the following, we explore some of the relevant work on each of these themes.

Offensive Language. The terms *offensive language* and *abusive language* are commonly used interchangeably. They are cover terms that usually include all types of undesirable language such as *hateful, racist, obscene,* and *dangerous* speech. We review some work looking at these types of language here, with no specific focus on any of its forms. GermEval 2018 is a shared task on the Identification of Offensive Language in German proposed by Wiegand et al. (2018). Their dataset consists of $8,500$ annotated tweets with two labels, "offensive" and "non-offensive". Another relevant shared task is the OffensEval (Zampieri et al., 2019), which focuses on identifying and categorizing offensive language in social media. Very recently, an Arabic offensive language shared task is included in the 4th Workshop on Open-Source Arabic Corpora and Processing Tools (OSACT4). [3]

Hate Speech. Hate speech is a type of language that is biased, hostile, and malicious targeting a person or a group of people because of some of their actual or perceived innate characteristics (Gitari et al., 2015). This type of harmful language received the most attention in the literature. Burnap and Williams (2014) investigate the manifestation and diffusion of hate speech and antagonistic content in Twitter in relation to situations that could be classified as 'trigger' events for hate crimes. Their dataset consists of $450K$ tweets collected during a two weeks window in the immediate aftermath of Drummer Lee Rigby's murder in Woolwich, UK. In Waseem (2016), issues of annotation reliability are discussed. Authors examine whether the expertise level of annotators (e.g expert or amateur) and/or the type of information provided to the annotators, can improve the classification of hate speech. For this purpose, they extend the dataset of (Waseem and Hovy, 2016) with a set of about $7K$ tweets annotated by two types of CrowdFlower users: expert and amateur. They find that hate speech detection models trained on expert annotations outperform those trained on amateur annotations. *This suggests that hate speech can be implicit and thus harder to detect by humans and machines alike.* Another work by (Davidson et al., 2017) builds a hate speech lexicon based on a list of words and phrases provided by *Hatebase.org.* Using Twitter API, they crawled a set of $85M$ tweets containing terms from the lexicon. Most recent works on detecting hate on Twitter are done as part of a

SemEval2019 competition, HatEval (Òscar Garibo, 2019). This shared task addresses the problem of multilingual detection of hate speech against immigrants and women in Twitter.

Obscene Language. Obscene speech includes vulgar and pornographic speech. A few research papers have looked at this kind of speech in social media (Singh et al., 2016; Mubarak et al., 2017; Alshehri et al., 2018). Mubarak et al. (2017) present an automated method to create and expand a list of obscene words, for the purpose of detecting obscene language. Abozinadah (2015) build a dataset of over $1M$ tweets comprising the most recent 50 tweets of 255 users who has participated in swearing hashtags as well as the most recent 50 tweets of users in their network. As feature input to their classifiers, the authors extracted basic statistical measures from each tweet and reported 96% accuracy of adult content detection. Alshehri et al. (2018) build a dataset of adult content in Arabic twitter and their distributors. The work identifies geographical distribution of targets of adult content and develops models for detecting spreaders of such content.Alshehri et al. (2018) report 79% accuracy on detecting adult content.

Racism and Sexism. Kwok and Wang (2013) create a balanced dataset comprising $24,582$ of 'racist' and 'non-racist' tweets. Waseem and Hovy (2016) collect a set of $136K$ hate tweets based on a list of common terms and slurs pertaining ethnic minorities, gender, sexuality, and religion. Afterwards, a random set of $16K$ tweets are selected and manually annotated with three labels: 'racist', 'sexist', or "neither". Gambäck and Sikdar (2017) introduce a deep-learning-based Twitter hate speech text classification model. Using data from Waseem and Hovy (2016) with about $6.5K$ tweets, the model classifies tweets into four categories: 'sexist', 'racist', 'both sexist and racist', and 'neither'. Clarke and Grieve (2017), using the same list, explore differences among racist and sexist tweets along three dimensions: *interactiveness, antagonism,* and *attitude* and find an overall significant difference between them.

Dangerous Language. Little work has been dedicated to detection and classification of dangerous language and threats. They are usually part of work on abusive and hate speech. This is to say that dangerous language has only been indirectly investigated within the NLP community. However, there is some research that is not necessarily computational in nature. For example, Gales (2011) investigates the correlation between interpersonal stance and the realization of threats by analyzing a corpus of 470 authentic threats. Ultimately, the goal of Gale's work is to help predict violence before it occurs. Hardaker and McGlashan (2016), on the other hand, investigates the language surrounding threats of rape on Twitter. In their corpus, the authors find that women were the prime target of rape threats. In the rest of this paper, we explore the space and language of threats in Arabic Twitter. We now describe our lexicon and datasets.

Verb	Dialect	English	Verb	Dialect	English	Verb	Dialect	English
أباد	G,M,R	exterminate	رض	G,M	contuse	فجر	all	blow up
أتل	E,L	kill	* سطر	E,G	mark	فشق	G,L	split
* أدى	E,G	give	سلخ	all	skin	*فقع	E,G,L,R	burst
أعدم	all	execute	سلق	E,G,R	boil	*فك	E,G,L	disentangle
أفنى	G,M,R	exterminate	شج	M	slash	قتل	all	kill
أهلك	G,M,R	destroy	شرب **	E,G,L,R	drink	قرح	E	sound
إغتال	G,L,M,R	assassinate	شق	E,G,L,R	rip off	قسم	all	divide
إغتصب	all	rape	شوه	E,G,L,R	distort	قصف	G,R	smash
* إقتلع	G,L,R	pluck	صرم	G	cut off	قصم	G,M	smash
بطش	E,L,M	assault	صفق	G,L	slap	قضى	E,G,L,M	eliminate
جرح	all	wound	صلخ	G,L	skin	قطع	all	cut
جزر	G	cut off	ضرب	all	hit	قلع	E,G,L,R	pluck
جلد	all	whip	طخ	E,G	shoot	كسر	all	break
حرق	all	burn	طعن	all	stab	لخ	G	hit
حطم	E,L,M,R	smash	طير	E,G,L,R	make fly	محا **	E,G,L,R	erase
دك	E,G,L	demolish	عذب	E,G,M,R	torture	محق	M	destroy
دهك	G	run over	عزب	E	torture	نحر	E,G,M,R	slaughter
ذبح	all	slaughter	عقر	E,G	kill	نسف	E,G,M,R	blast
رجم	E,G,M,R	stone	فتك	E,G,L,M	destroy	هشم	G,L,R	smash

Table 1: Our list of dangerous verbs. All= all dialects. E= Egyptian. G= Gulf. L= Levantine. M= MSA. R= Maghrebi. * = metaphorical. ** = used idiomatically.

3. Dangerous Lexica and Dataset

3.1. Dangerous Language

We define dangerous language as *a statement of an intention to inflict physical pain, injury, or damage on someone in retribution for something done or not*. This definition excludes threats that do not reflect physical harm on the side of the receiver end of the threat. The definition also excludes *tongue in cheek* whose real intention is to tease. An example of this later category is a threat made in the context of sports where it is common among fans to tease one another using metaphorical, string language (see Example # 6 in Section 3.3.).

3.2. Dangerous Lexica

We came up with a list of 57 verbs in their basic form that can be used literally or metaphorically to indicate physical harm (see table 1). This list is by no means exhaustive, although we did our best to expand it as much as possible. As such, the list covers the frequent verbs used in the threatening domain in Arabic. [4] These verbs are used in one or more of the following varieties: Egyptian, Gulf, Levantine, Maghrebi, and MSA (see table 2 for more details). Most of these verbs (n=50 out of 57) literally indicate physical harm. Examples are طعن (*'to stap'*)

and سلخ (*'to de-skin'*). The rest are used (sometimes metaphorically) to indicate threatening, such as اقتلع (*'to pluck'*) and سطر (*'to mark'*) usually with a body part such as وجه (*'face'*) or رأس (*'head'*). Finally, some of the verbs are used idiomatically, such as شرب من دم (*'to drink someone's blood'*) and محا من على وش الارض (*'to erase/eliminate from the face of the earth'*). Multiword expressions in our seed list can be found in Table 3.

Dialect	# of verbs
MSA	30
Gulf	50
Egyptian	39
Maghrebi	34
Levantine	34
All (unique)	57

Table 2: Distribution of threat verbs across Arabic dialects.

To be able to collect data, we used our manually curated list to construct threat phrases indicating physical harm such as اقتلك (*'I kill you'*) and يكسره (*'He breaks him/it'*). That is, each phrase consists of a physical harm verb, a singular or plural first or third person subject, and a plural or singular second or third person object. This gives us the following pattern:

1st/3rd (SG / PL) + threat verb + 2nd/3rd (SG / PL)

---

[4] The concept of frequency here is based on native speaker knowledge of the language. The list was developed by the 3 authors, all of whom are native speakers of Arabic with multi-dialectal fluency.

Some of the phrases only differ on the basis of spelling due to dialectical variations. For example, the body part وجه ('face') can be spelled as وجيهكم or وجوهكم in the plural form depending on the dialect. Another example is the verb قتل ('kill'), which can also be spelled as اتل in Egyptian and some other Arabic dialects. Manual search of some of the seed tokens in twitter suggests that patterns involving 3rd person subject are almost always not threats. The following are two illustrating examples of this non-threatening use:

1) ميسي إذا لم يسجل فإنه يقتل فرحة بعض البشر
   'If he doesn't score, Messi kills happiness in some people'

2) ما يكسر الخاطر ... سوى شخص غالي
   'Only a dear friend can break one's heart'

Thus, we decided to limit our list of phrases to 'direct' dangerous threats, which are phrases involving a singular or plural first person subject and singular or plural second person object as follows:

1st (SG/PL) + threat verb + 2nd (SG/PL)

Examples of these direct threats include نغتصبك ('We rape you') and احرقكم ('I burn you'). Less dangerous threats such as اجرحكم ("We hurt you (all)") and أدفك ('I push you') are also not considered. Our motivation for not including these latter phrases even though they involve direct threats is that they indicate less danger and (more crucially) are more likely to be used metaphorically in Arabic. This resulted in a set of 286 direct and dangerous phrases, which constitute our list of 'dangerous' seeds. We make the list of 286 direct threats phrases available to the research community. [5]

3.3. Dataset

We use the constructed 'dangerous' seed list to search Twitter using the REST API for two weeks resulting in a dataset of $2.8M$ tweets involving 'direct' threats as shown in Table 4. We then extract *user ids* from all users who contributed the REST API data ($n = 399K$ users) and crawled their timelines ($n = 705M$ tweets). We then acquire $107.5M$ tweets from the timelines, each of which carry one or more items from our 'dangerous' seed list. Combining these two datasets (the REST API dataset and dataset based on the timelines) results in a dataset consisting of $110.3M$ tweets as shown in Table 4. In this work, we focus on exploiting the REST API dataset exclusively, leaving the rest of the data to future research.

4. Data Annotation

4.1. Annotation

We first randomly sample $1K$ tweets from our REST API dataset.[5] Two of the authors annotated each tweet for being a threat ('dangerous') or not ('safe'). This sample annotation resulted in a Kappa (κ) score of 0.57, which is fair

---

[5] https://github.com/UBC-NLP/ara_ dangspeech.

according to Landis and Koch's scale (Landis and Koch, 1977). The two annotators then held several discussion sessions to improve their mutual understanding of the problem and define some instructions as to how to label the data. We also added another random sample of $4K$ tweets (for a total size of $5K$) to the annotation pool. After extensive revisions of the disagreement cases by the two annotators, the κ score for the whole dataset ($5K$) was found to be at 0.90. The annotated dataset has a total of $1,375$ tweets in the 'dangerous' class and $3,636$ in the 'non-dangerous' class. Our overall agreed-upon instructions for annotations include the following:

- Textual threats combined with pleasant emojis such as 😊 and ♥ are not dangerous, as opposed to threat combined with less pleasant emojis such as 🔪🔫. Thus, tweet 3 below should be coded as 'safe' while tweet 4 should be tagged as 'dangerous'.

  3) 😊 المنطق يقول أنا باقتلك user@
     'It goes with logic that I kill you 😊'

  4) 🔪 قدامي بس لا اطعنك user@ user@ user@
     'Move forward [in front of me] or else I stab you 🔪'

- Mitigated threats with question marks or epistemic modals are dangerous unless they are combined with positive language or emojis such as Example 5 below. Note that the word *Touha* in Example 5 is an informal, friendly form for Arabic names such as *FatHi* or *MamdouH*.

  5) 😊 انا بفكر اقتلك يا توحه user@
     'I am thinking of killing you, Touha 😊'

- Threats related to sports are not dangerous. That is because it is common to use verbs like نحر ("slaughter") and اغتصب ("rape") among fans of rival teams to describe wins and losses, as in the following example.

  6) حلاته نغتصبكم على ارضكم وبين جمهوركم user@
     'It's actually better that we 'rape' you in your stadium, among your fans'

- Ambiguous threats such as threats consisting of one word (as in Example 7 below) should be coded as 'dangerous':

  7) اقتلكوا
     'I kill you'

Below, we show examples of tweets that were annotated as 'dangerous':

8) @user @user
   ودي احرقك و ارميك للكلاب
   'I wish to burn you and throw you to dogs'

Seed	English	Seed	English
أشرب من دمك	I drink from your blood	امحيك من على وش الارض	I erase you from the face of the earth
أشرب دمك	I drink your blood	امحيكم من على وش الارض	I erase you all from the face of the earth
أشرب من دمكم	I drink your blood all	نشرب من دمك	We drink from your blood
أشوه وجهك	I disfigure your face	نشرب دمك	We drink your blood
اطير راسك	I cut your head	نشرب من دمكم	We drink your blood all
اطير روسكم	I cut your head all	نطير راسك	I cut your head
الفجر راسك	I blow up your head	نطير روسكم	I cut your head all
افقع وجهك	I burst your face	نفجر راسك	We blow up your head
افقع وجوهكم	I hit your face all	نفقع وجهك	We hit your face
افك وجهك	I disentangle your face	نقضي عليك	We finish you
اقضي عليك	I finish you	نقضي عليكم	We finish you all
اقضي عليكم	I finish you all	نمحيك من على وش الارض	I erase you from the face of the earth
اكسر وجهك	I break your face	نمحيكم من على وش الارض	We erase you all from the face of the earth

Table 3: Multiword expressions in our seed list.

Dataset	# of tweets
REST API	$2.8M$
Timelines	$107.5M$
ALL	$110.3M$

Table 4: Breakdown of our 'dangerous' dataset.

	Safe	Dangerous	Total
Safe	3,570	52	3,622
Dangerous	70	1319	1,389
Total	3,640	1,371	5,011

Table 5: Annotator Agreement of 5011-tweet sample.

Measure	Value
Avg. # timeline tweets	2,313
Avg. # dangerous tweets / user	3.97
St. dev.	3.64
25th percentile	1
50th percentile	4
75th percentile	6
Minimum	1
Maximum	23

Table 6: Descriptive statistics of the timeline data of 1,370 users who contributed tweets classified as 'dangerous' in our annotated dataset.

9) @user ماتكلمنيش ب الطريقة دي لحسن اقوم اضربك
قال اربع نسوة قال 😡

'Don't talk to me in this way, or else I hit you! Talking of (marrying) four women!'

10) @user @user سوف تبدا الحرب ورب العرش العظيم سوف
نحرقكم حرق انتم يالمخنثيين يا خنزير العرب يا خاونه

'The war will begin. By God, we will burn you down, you fags, you pigs, you traitors'

11) @user الحمار دايم حمار ماستفدتوا من الدرس هاذا لازم
نضربكم على قفاكم زي الجهال انتوا بشر ولاحيونات

'A donkey will always be a donkey. You didn't learn the lesson. We have to hit you on the back of you heads like kids. Are you humans or animals?'

12) @user عطيني كروكي بيتكم واجي اشرحك مو بس اقتلك
'Give me your address so I can come to you, and not only kill you but also dissect you'

Seed	English	Emoji
اذبحك	I slaughter you	😵
اقتلك	I kill you	🖤
اغتصبك	I rape you	🐱
اضربك	I hit you	👊
اعذبك	I torture you	😣
اديك	I hit/give you	❤
اجلدك	I lash you	😞
اطعنك	I stab you	👇
اجرحك	I hurt you	✏
احرقك	I burn you	🔥

Table 7: Top 10 most frequent 'dangerous' seeds and emojis in our REST API dataset.

4.2. Data Analysis

The fact that 'dangerous' tweets are not frequent in the dataset suggests that *this phenomenon of dangerous speech is relatively rare in the Twitter domain*. To further investigate the commonality of such a phenomenon, we extract

Models	Datasets	Precision	Recall	Acc	F_1
Baseline	–	50.00	29.33	58.66	36.97
BERT	Dangerous	58.42	**60.10**	74.27	58.98
BERT	Dangerous + Offensive	53.80	53.44	66.11	53.52
BERT-Emotion	Dangerous	**60.06**	59.24	**77.97**	**59.60**
BERT-Emotion	Dangerous + Offensive	54.50	53.99	66.84	54.11

Table 8: Results from our models on TEST.

the timelines of the authors of tweets in the dangerous class in the annotated dataset. Table 6 shows some descriptive statistics of the occurrence of dangerous seeds in their time-lines. We can see from Table 6 that timelines contain on average $2,313$ tweets for each user, and there are on average 3.97 tweets in each timeline containing a dangerous seed token. This represents $\sim 0.17\%$ of the tweets for each user. The average number of dangerous tweets is higher ($n = 6$) for users in the $75th$ percentile as opposed to $n = 1$ in the $25th$ percentile.

To further understand dangerous language, we also analyze all the $5,011$ tweets from our annotated dataset. We identify a number of patterns in the data, cutting across both the 'dangerous' and 'safe' classes. We explain each of these patterns next.

Conditional threats: One common threatening pattern involves conditional statements where the consequent involves a physical threat by the speaker toward the addressee, and the antecedent is a conditional phrase involving deterrence of an action that can possibly be carried out by the addressee or someone else. The following are two examples:

13) @user اذ بحك اذا تسوين شى
   'I slaughter you if you (F) do anything'

14) @user اذا انتقل سوف اطعنك طعناً مبرحاً امام الملآ
   'If he transfers, I will stab you hardly in front of the crowds'

It is clear from Examples 13 and 14 that the threats are directed to a twitter user mentioned in the tweet. So these tweets are potentially part of ongoing conversations between the person who posted the tweet and the user mentioned in the body of the tweet. As Table 9 shows, $\sim 71.2\%$ of tweets in our annotated dataset (across the 'dangerous' and 'safe' classes) contain mentions of other Twitter users. This percentage is higher within the dangerous class (%= 78).

Threats accompanied with commands: Another common pattern involves a command accompanying the threat as in Example 15 below. These kinds of threats are more common in the dangerous than the safe class.

15) @user اقول انقلعي لا افقع وجهك
   'I say get out before I hit your face'

Threats accompanied with questions: Another less common pattern is threats in the form of questions. This kind of

Phenomena	Freq.	Percentage (non-dangerous)	Percentage (dangerous class)
Mentions	3673	72.8%	78%
Questions	100	2.8%	5%
Emoji	2,010	45.5%	36%
Conditional	742	15.8%	11.4%
Body parts	378	6.6%	11.3%
Hahaha	355	9.9%	1.1%

Table 9: The frequency of some textual phenomena in our Annotated data.

threats occurs in about 5% of our dangerous data as compared to 2.8% in the safe class. Unlike the examples above, the reason behind most of the 'question' threats is not particularly clear as they tend to be short, sometimes of one word. Interpretation of these threats requires more context, beyond the level of the tweet itself. Examples 16-18 illustrate this category.

16) ممكن اقتلك من الم الحبر؟
   'can i kill you by the pen'

17) @user ينفع اغتصبك؟
   'Does it work if I rape you?'

18) @user اذ بحك؟
   'I slaughter you?'

Threat accompanied by modality: Some threats carry *deontic modality* where modals such as 'would', 'probably', 'may' are employed. *Epistemic modality* are also found in some data points. Similar to the question types above, these tweets (Examples 19-21 below) are less threatening than Examples 13-18 above.

19) @user جعلني اغتصبك
   'May I rape you?!' (**deontic modality**)

20) @user ودي اذ بحك
   'I would like to kill you' (**deontic modality**)

21) @user شكلي رح اقتلك مع صحبتك
   'I am probably going to kill you with your friends' (**epistemic modality**)

Metaphorical threats: Many of the tweets involve metaphorical use of the phrases in our annotated data. The target domain of the majority of these metaphorical uses is either sports or relationships. Words such as 'kill', 'rape', and 'slaughter' are used to indicate 'wining' in sport or 'burn' to mean 'pain' or 'longing' in romantic relationships. Examples 23-24 illustrate these cases:

20) احب قول لاخواني المانشستراويه بكره راح نغتصبكم فلا داعي للذعر والضجر وانمااستمتعوا
'I would like to tell my Manchester (football club) fans that we will rape them tomorrow'

21) س احرقك عشقا واطفئك غراما
'I will burn you with love and put off (the fire on you) with affection'

Emojis: Another interesting phenomenon (see Table 9) is the frequent use of emojis, which are found in about 40% of the annotated dataset. This is not surprising as it helps participants mitigate (and hence better disambiguate the nature of) their threats. Table 7 shows the top most frequent emojis used in our REST API data. It is evident that most of the used emojis do not indicate friendliness, but rather have a threatening nature. This is also true of using expressive interjections such as *hahaha*, which is more common in the non-dangerous than the dangerous class. Additionally, as mentioned above, some expressions involve use of 'body parts' such as *eyes, head, face, nose,* etc.. These are found to occur significantly higher in the 'dangerous' class.

Conversational context: Finally, Table 7 also shows the top 10 most frequent seeds in our REST API dataset. All of these seeds involve a first singular person subject and a singular second person object, which indicate that many of these tweets containing dangerous seeds are part of one-to-one conversations on Twitter.

5. Deep Learning Models

Dangerous speech data. We use our $5,011$ annotated tweet dataset for training deep learning models on dangerous speech. The dataset comprises $3,570$ 'safe' tweets and $1,389$ 'dangerous' tweets. We first remove all the seeds in our lexicon since these were used in collecting the data. We then keep only tweets with at least two words, obtaining $4,445$ tweets with $3,225$ 'safe' labels and $1,220$ 'dangerous' tweet (see Table 10). We split this dataset into 80% training, 10% development, and 10% test.

Offensive speech data. In one of our settings, we also use the offensive dataset released via the Offensive Shared Task 2020.[6] This offensive content dataset consists of 8000 tweets ($1,590$ 'offensive' and $6,410$ 'non-offensive'). We use the offensive class data to augment our train split. Hence, we evaluate only on our test split where tweets are restricted to our dangerous gold tweets in the annotated dataset. We run this experiment as a way to test the utility of exploiting offensive tweets for enhancing dangerous language representation based on the assumption that dangerous speech is a subset of offensive language. However,

as we see in Table 8, this measure did not result in any improvements on top of our dangerous models. In fact, it leads to model deterioration.

	Train	Dev	Test
#Safe	$2,727$	244	254
#Dangerous	852	189	179
Total	$3,579$	433	433

Table 10: Distribution of dangerous and safe classes in our annotated dataset after normalization by removing seeds and one-word tweets.

Models. For the purpose of training deep learning models for detecting dangerous speech, we exploit the Bidirectional Encoder Representations from Transformers (BERT) (Devlin et al., 2018) model. For all our models, we use the BERT-Base Multilingual Cased (Multi-Cased) model.[7] It is trained on Wikipedia for 104 languages (including Arabic) with 12 layers, 12 attention heads, 768 hidden units each and 110M parameters. Additionally, we further fine-tune an off-the-shelf trained BERT Emotion (BERT-EMO) from AraNet (Abdul-Mageed et al., 2019) on our dangerous speech task. BERT-EMO is trained with Google's BERT-Base Multilingual Cased model on 8 emotion classes exploiting Arabic Twitter data. We train all BERT models for 20 epochs with a batch size of 32, maximum sequence size of 50 tokens and learning rate up to $2e^{-5}$. We identify best results on the development set, and report final results on the blind test set. As our baseline, we use the majority class in our training split. Note that since our dataset is not balanced, the majority class baseline is competitive (63.97% macro F_1 score). Also, importantly, due to the imbalance in class distribution, the macro F_1 score (the harmonic mean of precision and recall) is our metric of choice as it is more balanced than accuracy.

Results & Discussion. As Table 8 shows, the results demonstrate that all the models outperform the baseline and succeed in detecting the dangerous speech with F_1 scores between 53.42% and 59.60%. We also observe that training on the offensive dataset did not improve the results. On the contrary, augmenting training data with the offensive task tweets cause deterioration to 53.52% F_1 for BERT and 54.11% F_1 for BERT-Emotion.

The best model for detecting dangerous tweets is BERT-Emotion when fine-tuned on our gold dangerous dataset. It obtains an accuracy level of 77.97% and F_1 score of 59.60%. We note that *both* accuracy and F_1 are *significantly higher then the the baseline*. As mentioned earlier, since our dataset is highly imbalanced, F_1, rather than accuracy, should be used as the metric of choice for evaluation. As such, our models are significantly better than our baseline.

---

[6] http://edinburghnlp.inf.ed.ac.uk/workshops/OSACT4/

[7] https://github.com/google-research/bert/blob/master/multilingual.md

6. Conclusion

We have described our efforts to collect and manually label a dangerous speech dataset from a range of Arabic varieties. Our work shows that dangerous speech is rare online, thus making it difficult to find data for training machine learning classifiers. However, we were able to collect and annotate a sizeable dataset. To accelerate research, we will make our data available upon request. Another contribution we made is developing a number of models exploiting our data. Our best models are effective, and can be deployed for detecting the rare, yet highly serious, phenomenon of dangerous speech. For future work, we plan to further explore contexts of use of dangerous language in social media. We also plan to explore other deep learning methods on the task.

7. Bibliographical References

Abdul-Mageed, M., Zhang, C., Hashemi, A., and Nagoudi, E. M. B. (2019). Aranet: A deep learning toolkit for arabic social media. *arXiv preprint arXiv:1912.13072*.

Abozinadah, A., M. A. a. J. J. (2015). Detection of abusive accounts with arabic tweets. *International Journal of Knowledge Engineering*, Vol. 1, No. 2.

Alshehri, A., Nagoudi, A., Hassan, A., and Abdul-Mageed, M. (2018). Think before your click: Data and models for adult content in arabic twitter. *The 2nd Text Analytics for Cybersecurity and Online Safety (TA-COS-2018), LREC*.

Burnap, P. and Williams, M. L. (2014). Hate speech, machine classification and statistical modelling of information flows on twitter: Interpretation and communication for policy decision making.

Clarke, I. and Grieve, J. (2017). Dimensions of abusive language on twitter. Association for Computational Linguistics.

Davidson, T., Warmsley, D., Macy, M., and Weber, I. (2017). Automated hate speech detection and the problem of offensive language. *arXiv preprint arXiv:1703.04009*.

Devlin, J., Chang, M.-W., Lee, K., and Toutanova, K. (2018). Bert: Pre-training of deep bidirectional transformers for language understanding. *arXiv preprint arXiv:1810.04805*.

Farghaly, A. and Shaalan, K. (2009). Arabic natural language processing: Challenges and solutions. *ACM Transactions on Asian Language Information Processing (TALIP)*, 8(4):1–22.

Fraser, B. (1998). Threatening revisited. *Forensic linguistics*, 5(2).

Gales, T. (2011). Identifying interpersonal stance in threatening discourse: An appraisal analysis. *Discourse Studies*, 13(1):27–46.

Gambäck, B. and Sikdar, U. K. (2017). Using convolutional neural networks to classify hate-speech. In *Proceedings of the First Workshop on Abusive Language Online*, pages 85–90.

Gitari, N. D., Zuping, Z., Damien, H., and Long, J. (2015). A lexicon-based approach for hate speech detection. *International Journal of Multimedia and Ubiquitous Engineering*, 10(4):215–230.

Hardaker, C. and McGlashan, M. (2016). 'real men don't hate women': Twitter rape threats and group identity. *Journal of Pragmatics*, 91:80 – 93.

Hinduja, S. and Patchin, J. W. (2010). Bullying, cyberbullying, and suicide. *Archives of suicide research*, 14(3):206–221.

Iqbal, M. (2019). Twitter revenue and usage statistics in 2019. November.

Jay, T. and Janschewitz, K. (2008). The pragmatics of swearing. *Journal of Politeness Research. Language, Behaviour, Culture*, 4(2):267–288.

Kwok, I. and Wang, Y. (2013). Locate the hate: Detecting tweets against blacks. In *AAAI*.

Landis, J. R. and Koch, G. G. (1977). The measurement of observer agreement for categorical data. *Biometrics*, 33(1):159–174.

Lenze, N. (2017). Social media in the arab world: Communication and public opinion in the gulf states. *European Journal of Communication*, 32(1):77–79.

Mubarak, H., Darwish, K., and Magdy, W. (2017). Abusive language detection on arabic social media. In *Proceedings of the First Workshop on Abusive Language Online*, pages 52–56.

Òscar Garibo, i. O. (2019). Multilingual detection of hate speech against immigrants and women in twitter at semeval-2019 task 5: Frequency analysis interpolation for hate in speech detection. In *Proceedings of the 13th International Workshop on Semantic Evaluation*, pages 460–463.

Salem, F. (2017). The arab social media report 2017: Social media and the internet of things: Towards data-driven policymaking in the arab world. Vol. 7.

Singh, M., Bansal, D., and Sofat, S. (2016). Behavioral analysis and classification of spammers distributing pornographic content in social media. *Social Network Analysis and Mining*, 6(1):41, Jun.

Waseem, Z. and Hovy, D. (2016). Hateful symbols or hateful people? predictive features for hate speech detection on twitter. In *Proceedings of the NAACL student research workshop*, pages 88–93.

Waseem, Z., Davidson, T., Warmsley, D., and Weber, I. (2017). Understanding abuse: A typology of abusive language detection subtasks. *CoRR*, abs/1705.09899.

Waseem, Z. (2016). Are you a racist or am i seeing things? annotator influence on hate speech detection on twitter. In *Proceedings of the first workshop on NLP and computational social science*, pages 138–142.

Wiegand, M., Siegel, M., and Ruppenhofer, J. (2018). Overview of the germeval 2018 shared task on the identification of offensive language.

Zampieri, M., Malmasi, S., Nakov, P., Rosenthal, S., Farra, N., and Kumar, R. (2019). Semeval-2019 task 6: Identifying and categorizing offensive language in social media (offenseval). *arXiv preprint arXiv:1903.08983*.

Proceedings of the 4th Workshop on Open-Source Arabic Corpora and Processing Tools, pages 48–52
with a Shared Task on Offensive Language Detection.
Language Resources and Evaluation Conference (LREC 2020), Marseille, 11–16 May 2020
© European Language Resources Association (ELRA), licensed under CC-BY-NC

Overview of OSACT4 Arabic Offensive Language Detection Shared Task

Hamdy Mubarak[1], Kareem Darwish[1], Walid Magdy[2], Tamer Elsayed[3], Hend Al-Khalifa[4]

[1] Qatar Computing Research Institute, HKBU, Doha, Qatar
[2] School of Informatics, University of Edinburgh, Edinburgh, UK
[3] Qatar University, Doha, Qatar
[4] Information Technology Department, KSU, Riyadh, KSA
{humbarak, kdarwish}@hbku.edu.qa, wmagdy@inf.ed.ac.uk, telsayed@qu.edu.qa, hendk@ksu.edu.sa

Abstract

This paper provides an overview of the offensive language detection shared task at the 4th workshop on Open-Source Arabic Corpora and Processing Tools (OSACT4). There were two subtasks, namely: Subtask A, involving the detection of offensive language, which contains unacceptable or vulgar content in addition to any kind of explicit or implicit insults or attacks against individuals or groups; and Subtask B, involving the detection of hate speech, which contains insults or threats targeting a group based on their nationality, ethnicity, race, gender, political or sport affiliation, religious belief, or other common characteristics. In total, 40 teams signed up to participate in Subtask A, and 14 of them submitted test runs. For Subtask B, 33 teams signed up to participate and 13 of them submitted runs. We present and analyze all submissions in this paper.

Keywords: OSACT, Arabic Offensive Language, Arabic Hate Speech, Shared Task, CodaLab

1. Introduction

Offensive speech (vulgar or targeted offense), as an expression of heightened polarization or discord in society, has been on the rise. This is due in part to the large adoption of social media platforms that allow for greater polarization. The OSACT4 shared task provides a platform to bring researchers from around the world to tackle the detection of offensive and hate speech in the realm of Arabic social media. The shared task has two subtasks. Subtask A involves detecting offensive language, which contains explicit or implicit insults or attacks against individuals or groups and includes vulgar and inappropriate language. Subtask B is concerned with detecting hate speech, which contains insults or threats targeting specific groups based on their nationality, ethnicity, race, gender, political or sport affiliation, religious belief, or other common characteristics. The goal of the shared task is to aid research on the identification of offensive content and hate speech in Arabic language Twitter posts. The shared task attracted a large number of participants. In all, 40 and 33 teams signed up to Subtasks A and B respectively. From them, 13 teams submitted test runs to both subtasks, and only one team submitted runs to Subtask A. Of those teams, 11 submitted system description papers (Abdellatif and Elgammal, 2020; Abu Farha and Magdy, 2020; Abuzayed and Elsayed, 2020; Alharbi and Lee, 2020; Djandji et al., 2020; Elmadany et al., 2020; Haddad et al., 2020; Saeed et al., 2020; Hassan et al., 2020; Husain, 2020; Keleg et al., 2020).

The highest achieved F1 scores for Subtasks A and B were 90.5 (Accuracy = 93.9, Precision = 90.2, and Recall = 90.9) (Hassan et al., 2020) and 95.2 (Accuracy = 95.9, Precision = 95.2, and Recall = 95.9) (Husain, 2020) respectively.

2. Dataset

Subtasks A and B used the SemEval 2020 Task 12 Arabic offensive language dataset (OffensEval2020, Subtask A), which contains 10,000 tweets that were manually annotated for offensiveness (labels: OFF or NOT_OFF). The subtasks used the same OffensEval2020 training (70% of all tweets), dev (10%), and test (20%) splits.

The tweets were extracted from a set of 660k Arabic tweets containing the vocative particle يا ("yA" – O) from April 15 to May 6, 2019. Based on different random samples of tweets, offensive tweets represented less than 2% of of tweets. However, when considering tweets having one vocative particle, the ratio increased to 5%. This particle is mainly used for directing speech to a person or a group. Moreover, when considering the tweets with two vocative articles, the probability of finding offensive tweets increased to 20%. An example offensive statement is يا مقرف يا جبان للأسف هذه تسمى خسة ("yA mqrf yA jbAn h*h tsmY Ksp" – You disgusting coward. This is called wickedness)[1]. Annotation was performed by a native speaker of Arabic with good understanding of several Arabic dialects. Random samples of 100 tweets (50 offensive and 50 non-offensive) were judged by additional three annotators, and the inter-annotator agreement between them was 0.92 (using Fleiss's Kappa coefficient), which validates the quality of data annotation and indicates that judging the offensiveness of tweets is not difficult in many cases. Offensive tweets containing insults or threats targeting a group based on their nationality, ethnicity, race, gender, political or sport affiliation, religious belief, or other common characteristics, were annotated as Hate Speech (labels: HS or NOT_HS). An example tweet containing hate speech is: الله يقلعكم يالبدو يا مجرمين ("Allh yqlEkm yAlbdw yA mjrmyn" – May Allah remove you O Bedouin. You are

---

[1] We provide Arabic examples, their Buckwalter transliteration, and English translation.

criminals). The distribution of the labels in the dataset is shown in Table 1.

Label	Train	Dev	Test	Total	$\sim$ %
NOT_OFF	5,590	821	1,598	8,009	80%
OFF	1,410	179	402	1,991	20%
NOT_HS	6,639	956	1,899	9,494	95%
HS	361	44	101	506	5%

Table 1: Distribution of labels for Subtasks A and B

Subtask A was concerned with detecting offensive language in general, while Subtask B was concerned with detecting hate speech. Both subtasks used the same train/dev/test splits. For all tweets, some light preprocessing was performed, where user mentions were replaced with @USER, URLs were replaced with URL, and empty lines were replaced with <LF>. The data of Subtask B is more imbalanced than Subtask A data as only 5% of the tweets are labeled as hate speech, while 20% of the tweets are labeled as offensive.

3. Task Settings and Evaluation

Given the strong imbalance between the number of instances in the different classes across Subtasks A and B, we used the macro-averaged F1-score ($\mathcal{F}$) as the official evaluation measure for both subtasks. Macro-averaging gives equal importance to all classes regardless of their size. Other secondary evaluation measures that we used where Precision ($\mathcal{P}$) and Recall ($\mathcal{R}$) on the positive class (offensive or hate speech tweets) as well as the overall Accuracy ($\mathcal{A}$).

Subtasks were hosted on CodaLab platform at the following competition links:

Subtask A: `https://competitions.codalab.org/competitions/22825`
Subtask B: `https://competitions.codalab.org/competitions/22826`

Participants were allowed to submit up to 10 test runs, and they were asked to specify two submissions as their official runs, which would be scored and put on the leaderboard. If official runs are not specified, the latest submissions from each team were considered as official. We gave teams the freedom to describe the differences between their systems in their papers. The idea behind this is to allow teams to examine the effectiveness of different setups on the test set. Macro-average F1 ($\mathcal{F}$) of the first submission is the official score for Subtasks A and B.

We received 43 submissions for Subtask A including 3 failed ones (e.g. incorrect format). For Subtask B, we received 41 submissions including 11 failed ones. Competitions were open from Jan. 21, 2020 until Feb. 19, 2020, and the test sets were available starting on Feb. 13, 2020.

Table 2 lists the names of participating teams and their affiliations.

4. Methods and Results

Most teams performed some data preprocessing, which typically involved character normalization, removal of punctuation, diacritics, repeated letters, and non-Arabic tokens. One team performed extensive preprocessing including normalizing emoticons (translate their English description to Arabic), dialectal to MSA conversion, word category identification (ex. dog, monkey, etc. are mapped to ANIMAL), removal of dialectal stopwords, and hashtag segmentation (Husain, 2020) leading to the best results in Subtask B. As for learning methods, the teams used traditional Machine Learning (ML) techniques, such as SVM and logistic regression, and Deep Neutral Networking (DNN) approaches, such as Convolutional Neural Networks (CNN), Recurrent Neural Networks (RNN) including LSTM, biLSTM, and GRUs with and without attention, and fine tuning of contextual embeddings such as BERT and AraBERT.

The highest ranking submissions used an ensemble of different learning methods that combined both traditional ML and DNN approaches. Most teams used similar setups for both subtasks, and two teams chose to use multitask learning (Abu Farha and Magdy, 2020; Djandji et al., 2020).

Table 3 briefly lists the preprocessing and learning methods used by different teams. Tables 4 and 5 list the results of all the teams for Subtasks A and B ranked by F1-measure ($\mathcal{F}$). Per the rules of the shared task, we judged up to two runs for every team (first submission and second submission). As shown in Tables 4 and 5, first submission from all teams always beat their second submission (column $\mathcal{F}$), meaning that best performing systems on the dev set also performed best on the test set as well.

5. Conclusion

This paper presented an overview of the OSACT4 shared task on offensive language and hate speech detection in the Arabic Twitter sphere. The most successful systems in the shared task performed Arabic specific preprocessing, with the winning system for hate speech detection performing extensive preprocessing, and an ensemble of different machine learning approaches, with the winning system for offensive language detection using an ensemble of SVM trained on character-level n-grams and pretrained embeddings (Mazajak) as well as different DNN setups that use FastText, CNN+RNN, and contextual embeddings (multilingual BERT).

6. References

Abdellatif, M. and Elgammal, A. (2020). Sentiment analysis of imbalanced arabic data using ulmfit. *OSACT*, 4.

Abu Farha, I. and Magdy, W. (2020). Multitask learning for arabic offensive language and hate-speech detection. *OSACT*, 4.

Abuzayed, A. and Elsayed, T. (2020). Quick and simple approach for detecting hate speech in arabic tweets. *OSACT*, 4.

Team	Affiliation	Subtasks
Abeer (Abuzayed and Elsayed, 2020)	Islamic University of Gaza, Palestine	1,2
aialharbi (Alharbi and Lee, 2020)	University of Birmingham, UK	1,2
alisafaya	Koç University, Turkey	1,2
alt (Hassan et al., 2020)	Qatar Computing Research Institute, Qatar	1,2
AMR-KELEG (Keleg et al., 2020)	Faculty of Engineering, Ain Shams University, Egypt	1,2
Bushr (Haddad et al., 2020)	Damascus University, Syria	1,2
elmadany (Elmadany et al., 2020)	University of British Columbia, NLP Lab, Canada	1,2
fatemah (Husain, 2020)	Kuwait University, Dep. of Information Science, Kuwait	1,2
hassaansaeed (Saeed et al., 2020)	University of Antwerpen, Belgium	1,2
iaf7 (Abu Farha and Magdy, 2020)	University of Edinburgh, UK	1,2
mabdellatif (Abdellatif and Elgammal, 2020)	Rutgers University, US	1,2
Marc_Djandji (Djandji et al., 2020)	American University of Beirut. Lebanon	1,2
premjithb	Center for Comp. Engineering and Networking, India	1,2
SAJA	Jordan University of Science and Technology, Jordan	1

Table 2: List of participating teams in Subtasks A and B

Alharbi, A. and Lee, M. (2020). Combining character and word embeddings for the detection of offensive language in arabic. *OSACT*, 4.

Djandji, M., Baly, F., antoun, w., and Hajj, H. (2020). Multi-task learning using arabert for offensive language detection. *OSACT*, 4.

Elmadany, A., Zhang, C., Abdul-Mageed, M., and Hashemi, A. (2020). Leveraging affective bidirectional transformers for offensive language detection. *OSACT*, 4.

Haddad, B., Orabe, Z., Al-Abood, A., and Ghneim, N. (2020). Arabic offensive language detection with attention-based deep neural networks. *OSACT*, 4.

Hassan, S., Samih, Y., Mubarak, H., Abdelali, A., Rashed, A., and Absar Chowdhury, S. (2020). Alt submission for osact shared task on offensive language detection. *OS-ACT*, 4.

Husain, F. (2020). Osact4 shared task on offensive language detection: Intensive preprocessing based approach. *OSACT*, 4.

Keleg, A., El-Beltagy, S. R., and Khalil, M. (2020). Asu_opto at osact4 - offensive language detection for arabic text. *OSACT*, 4.

Saeed, H. H., Calders, T., and Kamiran, F. (2020). Ocast4 shared tasks: Ensembled stacked classification for offensive and hate speech in arabic tweets. *OSACT*, 4.

Team	Preprocessing	Methods
(Abdellatif and Elgammal, 2020)	simple tokenization, replace words below certain threshold with a special token	DNN: ULMFiT – a fine tuned language model based on a 3 layer RNN (LSTM)
(Abu Farha and Magdy, 2020)	character normalization and diacritic, kashida, repeated letter, and non-Arabic character removal	Multitask CNN+BiLSTM with pertained embedding (Mazajak)
(Abuzayed and Elsayed, 2020)	character normalization and diacritic, kashida, repeated letter, and non-Arabic character removal	SVM, Random Forest, XGBoost, Extra Trees, Decision Trees, Gradient Boosting, and LR; DNN: CNN, RNN, CNN+RNN and two different word representations (tf-idf and pre-trained word embeddings (AraVec)
(Alharbi and Lee, 2020)	character normalization and diacritic, kashida, repeated letter, and non-Arabic character removal. Also split بـ ("yA")	LR and XGBoost; DNN: RNN using Mazajak, Aravec, and subword FastText embeddings
(Djandji et al., 2020)	removal of non-Arabic characters, segmentation of words using Farasa segmenter, and splitting of hashtags	fine tuning of contextual embeddings (AraBERT)
(Elmadany et al., 2020)	numbers, usernames, hashtags, and hyperlinks replacement with NUM, USER, HASH, and URL respectively; character normalization; and diacritic removal	fine tuned multilingual BERT-based affective models
(Haddad et al., 2020)	removed non-Arabic words, diacritization, punctuation, emoticons, stopwords, and repeated characters	convolutional neural network (CNN) and bidirectional recurrent neural network with GRU units (Bi-GRU) models with and without attention
(Saeed et al., 2020)	letter normalization, repeated letter removal, and word splitting	DNN: CNN and RNN using contextual embeddings (multilingual BERT) and non-contextual embeddings (Aravec, FastText, word2vec) with an ensemble classifier that combines all outputs using SVM, RF, NB, etc.
(Hassan et al., 2020)	diacritic, kashida, repeated letter, and non-Arabic character removal	ensemble of SVM (character n-grams) and pre-trained embeddings (Mazajak) and DNN: FastText (subword), CNN+RNN, and contextual embeddings (multilingual BERT)
(Husain, 2020)	Intensive preprocessing: normalizing emoticons, dialectal to MSA conversion, word category identification (ex. animals), letter normalization, stopword removal, and hashtag segmentation	SVM (character n-grams)
(Keleg et al., 2020)	word segmentation	LR; DNN: CNN (with Aravec), RNN, and contextual embeddings (multilingual BERT and AraBert)

Table 3: Different methods used by different teams. LR: Logistic Regression; SVM: Support Vector Machines; NB: Naive Bayes; DNN: Deep Neural Network; CNN: Convolutional Neural Network; RNN: Recurrent Neural Network

Team	First Submission				Second Submission			
	$\mathcal{F}$	$\mathcal{A}$	$\mathcal{P}$	$\mathcal{R}$	$\mathcal{F}$	$\mathcal{A}$	$\mathcal{P}$	$\mathcal{R}$
(Hassan et al., 2020)	**90.5**	**93.9**	90.2	**90.8**	89.4	93.4	90.5	88.3
(Djandji et al., 2020)	90.0	93.7	**90.7**	89.4	88.5	93.1	91.9	85.9
(Husain, 2020)	89.8	90.2	89.9	90.2	88.6	89.1	88.6	89.1
(Keleg et al., 2020)	89.6	93.5	90.5	88.7	85.6	90.9	86.2	85.0
(Abu Farha and Magdy, 2020)	87.8	92.4	88.8	86.8	87.8	92.3	88.5	87.1
(Saeed et al., 2020)	87.4	92.4	90.3	85.1	87.8	92.8	91.5	85.1
(Alharbi and Lee, 2020)	86.8	92.1	89.6	84.7	85.7	91.2	87.7	84.1
(Haddad et al., 2020)	85.9	91.5	88.6	83.8	84.6	90.0	84.1	85.2
alisafaya	84.2	90.8	88.4	81.4	81.9	89.5	86.1	79.1
(Abuzayed and Elsayed, 2020)	83.3	89.7	84.7	82.1	82.6	89.9	86.8	79.8
(Elmadany et al., 2020)	82.9	89.4	84.1	81.8	79.3	87.8	82.5	77.1
(Abdellatif and Elgammal, 2020)	77.4	86.2	78.9	76.2	77.4	86.2	78.9	76.2
SAJA	76.2	86.4	80.5	73.6				
premjithb	72.6	81.8	71.9	73.3	72.6	81.8	71.9	73.3

Table 4: Subtask A results

Team	First Submission				Second Submission			
	$\mathcal{F}$	$\mathcal{A}$	$\mathcal{P}$	$\mathcal{R}$	$\mathcal{F}$	$\mathcal{A}$	$\mathcal{P}$	$\mathcal{R}$
(Husain, 2020)	**95.2**	95.9	**95.2**	**95.9**	94.4	95.4	94.3	95.4
(Djandji et al., 2020)	82.3	**96.7**	82.8	81.8	80.7	96.5	82.6	78.9
(Keleg et al., 2020)	80.7	96.5	82.1	79.4				
(Hassan et al., 2020)	80.6	96.6	83.8	78.1	75.5	96.4	86.4	70.0
(Saeed et al., 2020)	79.9	96.5	83.4	77.1	77.7	96.6	86.9	72.4
(Abu Farha and Magdy, 2020)	76.1	96.0	80.2	73.0	74.3	95.8	79.1	71.1
(Haddad et al., 2020)	75.0	95.3	75.5	74.6	74.8	95.2	74.7	74.9
(Alharbi and Lee, 2020)	74.2	96.3	86.4	68.5	48.7	95.0	47.5	50.0
(Elmadany et al., 2020)	70.5	95.2	75.2	67.5	67.7	95.6	80.3	63.0
alisafaya	70.4	95.8	81.6	65.4	69.9	94.9	72.7	67.8
(Abuzayed and Elsayed, 2020)	69.4	95.1	74.0	66.5	64.9	94.8	71.6	61.6
premjithb	63.2	92.3	62.2	64.5				
(Abdellatif and Elgammal, 2020)	58.5	95.1	75.0	55.7	58.5	95.1	75.0	55.7

Table 5: Subtask B results

Proceedings of the 4th Workshop on Open-Source Arabic Corpora and Processing Tools, pages 53–60
with a Shared Task on Offensive Language Detection.
Language Resources and Evaluation Conference (LREC 2020), Marseille, 11–16 May 2020
© European Language Resources Association (ELRA), licensed under CC-BY-NC

OSACT4 Shared Task on Offensive Language Detection: Intensive Preprocessing-Based Approach

Fatemah Husain

Kuwait University, Department of Information Science, State of Kuwait

f.husain@ku.edu.kw

Abstract

The preprocessing phase is one of the key phases within the text classification pipeline. This study aims at investigating the impact of the preprocessing phase on text classification, specifically on offensive language and hate speech classification for Arabic text. The Arabic language used in social media is informal and written using Arabic dialects, which makes the text classification task very complex. Preprocessing helps in dimensionality reduction and removing useless content. We apply intensive preprocessing techniques to the dataset before processing it further and feeding it into the classification model. An intensive preprocessing-based approach demonstrates its significant impact on offensive language detection and hate speech detection shared tasks of the fourth workshop on Open-Source Arabic Corpora and Corpora Processing Tools (OSACT). Our team wins the third place (3rd) in the Sub-Task A Offensive Language Detection division and wins the first place (1st) in the Sub-Task B Hate Speech Detection division, with an F1 score of 89% and 95%, respectively, by providing the state-of-the-art performance in terms of F1, accuracy, recall, and precision for Arabic hate speech detection.

Keywords: offensive language, hate speech, text classification

1. Introduction

Online offensive language detection is one of the most challenging text classification tasks to accomplish due to the ambiguity and informality of the language used in social media platforms. So far, online offensive language detection has been applied to various languages, such as English (Kwok and Wang, 2013; Davidson et al., 2017; Nobata et al., 2016; Pitsilis, Ramampiaro, Langseth, 2018), German (Kent, 2018; Wiedemann et al., 2018), Urdu (Mustafa et al., 2017), Turkish (Özel et al., 2017), Hindi (Bohra et al., 2018; Kapoor et al., 2018), Danish (Derczynski, 2019), and Arabic (Abozinadah, Mbaziira, and Jones, 2015; Mubarak, Darwish, and Magdy, 2017; Alakrot, Murray, and Nikolov, 2018; Mohaouchane, Mourhir, and Nikolov, 2019). Regardless of the text language, a standard text classification pipeline consists of preprocessing, feature extraction, feature selection, and classification model. The preprocessing phase is the one that is the most distinguishable phase among the others based on the text language. Each language contains unique structures and rules, which need to be addressed using unique methods. We develop an intensive preprocessing-based classification model for Arabic offensive language detection. Among the participants of the fourth workshop on Open-Source Arabic Corpora and Corpora Processing Tools (OSACT) throughout the shared tasks, our team wins third place in Sub-Task A Offensive Language Detection division and wins first place in Sub-Task B Hate Speech Detection division.

Text that contains some form of abusive behavior, exhibiting actions with the intention of harming others, is known as offensive language. This abusive behavior could lead to disturbances, disrespect, harm, insults, and anger, thus affecting the harmony of conversations. Wiedemann et al. (2018) describe offensive language as "threats and discrimination against people, swear words or blunt insults" (p.1). Hate speech, aggressive content, cyberbullying, and toxic comments are all different forms of offensive content (Schmidt & Wiegand, 2017). Figure 1 shows an example of an offensive tweet.

Figure 1: Example for an offensive tweet.

Hate speech is one of the most common forms of offensive language. A text that is targeted towards a group of people with the intent to cause harm, violence, or social chaos is known as hate speech (Derczynski, 2019). Davidson et al. (2017) define hate speech as "a language that is used to express hatred towards a targeted group or is intended to be derogatory, to humiliate, or to insult the members of the group" (p.1). Figure 2 illustrates an example of a hate speech tweet.

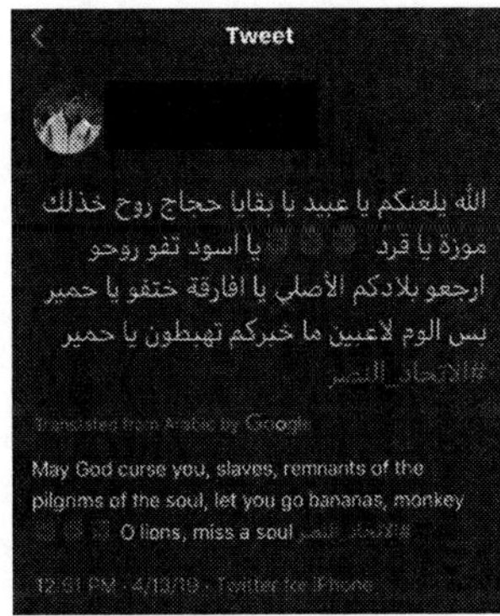

Figure 2: Example for a hate speech tweet.

Developing classification models, which can automatically detect offensive language and hate speech, is a very challenging task due to the following factors: a) the informality of the language used in posts from social media shows posts are usually written using symbols, short forms, and slang that are difficult to semantically process and understand by algorithms; b) the variation and the diversity of the Arabic language dialects and forms; and c) the small sample size of offensive samples; for example, in the dataset used in this study, only 5% of the tweets are labeled as hate speech and 19% of the tweets are labeled as offensive. We apply multiple preprocessing techniques to address the challenges of Arabic offensive language detection. The preprocessing techniques include conversion of emoticons and emoji, conversion of hashtags, normalizing different forms of Arabic letters, normalizing Arabic dialects to Modern Standard Arabic (MSA), normalizing words by categorization, and basic cleaning processes. These intensive preprocessing techniques report valuable influence on the system performance. We train a Support Vector Machine (SVM)-based classifier using character-based count vectorizer (2-5 characters). Results report an F1 score of 89.82% for the offensive language detection model and 95.16% for the hate speech detection model.

In the rest of this paper, we organize the content as follows: Section 2 discusses related work of Arabic offensive language detection on social media, Section 3 introduces data description, details of preprocessing, and the methodology of our models, and experimental results are discussed in Section 4. We also present the conclusion of our work at the end of the paper.

2.   Related Work

There are multiple studies investigating offensive Arabic tweets to identify abusive Twitter accounts (Abozinadah, Mbaziira, & Jones, 2015; Abozinadah & Jones, 2017; Abozinadah, 2017). Abozinadah, Mbaziira, and Jones (2015) construct an initial dataset starting with 500 Twitter accounts based on a set of Arabic swear words. Then, they check the most recent 50 tweets, profile pictures, and hashtags for each of these 500 Twitter accounts in order to reach a dataset of 350,000 Twitter accounts and 1,300,000 tweets with balanced classes; half were labelled abusive while the other half were labelled as non-abusive. Next, they use three types of features, including profile-based features, tweet-based features, and social graph features to train three classifiers: Naive Bayes (NB), SVM, and Decision Tree (J48). The results show that the NB-based classifier outperforms the other classifiers when used with 100 features and 10 tweets for each account with an accuracy score of 85% (Abozinadah, Mbaziira, & Jones, 2015; Abozinadah, 2017).

Another approach for detecting offensive language was adopted by Mubarak, Darwish, and Magdy (2017) for the purpose of detecting vulgar and pornographic obscene speech in Arabic social media by applying a simple obscene phrases list-based approach. They use a Twitter dataset consisting of 175 million tweets to extract a list of seed words for obscene phrases through manual assessment. Then, they utilize the list to construct 3 sub-lists of obscene words, phrases, and hashtags using multiple measurements, such as the Log Odds Ratio (LOR) for unigrams and bigrams. Intrinsic and extrinsic evaluations were used to evaluate these lists. The intrinsic evaluation consists of manual coding for a list of 100 words that are randomly selected from each list to be marked as either obscene or not. The extrinsic evaluation consists of recall, precision, and F1 measures using a dataset that they developed for the purpose of this evaluation. They then select 10 Egyptian Twitter users from the top controversial users. After that, they extract 100 tweets with at least 10 replies for each user. The final dataset has 100 original tweets and 1,000 replies tweets. Each tweet along with its replies were submitted to CrowdFlower to become coded by three annotators from Egypt using three classes: obscene, offensive, and clean; the inter-annotator agreement is 84%. As a result, they develop a linear match model for each labeled tweet; for example, if a match with a phrase from the list occurs, then, it will then predict a label of obscenity to that tweet. The results among all lists show a highest F1 score of 60%, which demonstrate that a list-based approach is very limited and not a good choice for an obscene detection system.

Arabic language has also been studied also by Alakrot, Murray, and Nikolov (2018a, 2018b) for automatic detection of offensive language. They construct a dataset from YouTube comments based on selecting channels that have controversial videos about celebrities. Their final dataset includes 167,549 comments posted by 84,354 users, and 87,388 replies posted by 24,039 users from 150 YouTube videos (Alakrot, Murray, & Nikolov, 2018a). Two labels were used for the classes: positive to label offensive comments and negative to label ones that are not offensive (Alakrot, Murray, & Nikolov, 2018a). They train an SVM-based classifier using two features: character n-gram (n= 1-5) and word-level features. The results show the best performance when using the SVM-based classifier with 10-fold cross validation and word-level features with 90.05% of an accuracy score (Alakrot, Murray, & Nikolov, 2018b).

Mohaouchane, Mourhir, and Nikolov (2019) explore multiple deep learning models to classify offensive Arabic language for YouTube comments using the same dataset developed by Alakrot, Murray, and Nikolov (2018a). They create 300-dimension word embedding using AraVec, which is an Arabic word embedding tool, trained on Twitter dataset and skip-gram model. Four deep learning models were evaluated for classifying offensive comments, including Convolutional Neural Network (CNN), Bidirectional Long Short-Term Memory (Bi-LSTM), Bi-LSTM with an attention mechanism, and a combined model of CNN and LSTM. The results demonstrate an overall better performance for CNN with a highest accuracy score of 87.84%, a precision score of 86.10%, and an F1 score of 84.05%, while the combined CNN-LSTM model shows a better recall score of 83.46% (Mohaouchane, Mourhir, & Nikolov, 2019).

To our knowledge, the only Arabic hate speech detection studies are the studies of Albadi, Kurdi, and Mishra (2018, 2019) and the study of Chowdhury et al. (2019), which investigate religious hate speech in Arabic language for Twitter data, both using the same dataset. Albadi, Kurdi, and Mishra (2018) develop a logistic regression-based model and an SVM-based model using a character n-gram feature (n= 1 to 4), and a Gated Recurrent Unit (GRU) based on the Recurrent Neural Network (RNN) with the Twitter Continuous Bag-of-Word (CBOW) 300-dimension embedding model provided by AraVec, batches of size 32, and Adam as the optimizer. Their findings have indicated that for some religious minorities in the Middle East — Jews, Atheists, and Shia— almost half of the tweets that were mentioning these minorities were referring to them within a hate speech content (Albadi, Kurdi, & Mishra, 2018). Furthermore, results report best performance when using the GRU-based model with an F1 score of 77% (Albadi, Kurdi, & Mishra, 2018). Albadi, Kurdi, and Mishra (2019) enhance the same GRU-based model with additional temporal, users, and content features in another study, then report the state-of-the-art performance in terms of a recall score of 84%. Chowdhury et al (2019) extend previous studies done by Albadi, Kurdi, and Mishra (2018, 2019) to investigate the effects of community interactions and social representations in detecting religious hate speech in the Arabic Twitter sphere. They use multiple features, including word embedding, node embedding, sentence representation, and character n-gram features (n = 1 - 4). Several classification models were explored using multiple combinations of features, such as GRU, logistic regression, SVM, LSTM, Bi-LSTM, CNN and Bi-GRU in addition to combining multiple models, using self-attention mechanisms, and using Node2Vec criteria. Therefore, results have shown a high accuracy score of 81% that was obtained by the model containing a combination of Bi-GRU, CNN, and NODE2VEC. While displaying the best F1 score, recall and precision were recorded by the model that combined LSTM, CNN and NODE2VEC: 89%, 78%, and 86% respectively.

Previous studies focus on features extraction and classification model, while we focus more on text preprocessing. The preprocessing steps we follow in this study are not identical to any of the preprocessing steps of the previous studies.

3. Dataset and Methodology

3.1 Dataset Description

The shared task of the fourth workshop on Open-Source Arabic Corpora and Corpora Processing Tools (OSACT) in Language Resources and Evaluation Conference (LREC) 2020 provides Twitter dataset for offensive language detection in Arabic language. The main goal of this shared task is to identify and categorize Arabic offensive language in Twitter. The organizers collect tweets through Twitter API and annotate them hierarchically regarding offensive language and offense type. The task is divided into two sub-tasks: a) detecting if a post is offensive or not offensive; and b) identifying offensive content type of an offensive post as hate speech or not hate speech.

The provider of the dataset performs some preprocessing to ensure the privacy of users. Twitter user mentions were substituted by "@USER", URLs had simply been substituted by "URL", and empty lines were replaced by "<LF>".

The shared task issues the dataset in three different parts, training dataset, development dataset and testing dataset. The summary of datasets distribution is presented in Table

1. Training dataset and development dataset are provided with their actual labeled, while the testing dataset consists of 2,000 unlabeled tweets for competition evaluation purposes. The training dataset consists of 6,839 tweets with 1,371 offensive tweets and 350 hate speech tweets. The development dataset consists of 1,000 tweets with 179 offensive tweets and 44 hate speech tweets.

Labels	Training	Development	Testing
Not Offensive	5,590	821	*
Offensive	1,410	179	*
Not Hate Speech	6,639	956	*
Hate Speech	361	44	*
Total Tweets	7,000	1,000	2,000

Table 1: Datasets distribution (* not available)

We explore multiple characteristics of the dataset including most frequent emoji, emoticons, and words. The most frequent emoticons and emoji are very similar in both classes. Table 2 and Table 3 show the top 5 most frequent emoji and emoticons for both not offensive and offensive classes, respectively. Most frequent words are also very similar in both classes. Figure 3 and Figure 4 show the most frequent words for both not offensive class and offensive class, respectively.

Emoji	%	Emoticon	%
😂	18%	:<	44%
❤	12%	:)	23%
🖤	5%	:(	16%
🤍	5%	;D	6%
♥	4%	:D	6%

Table 2: The top 5 most frequent emoji and emoticons for not offensive tweets

Emoji	%	Emoticon	%
😂	38.87%	;D	40%
😭	8.52%	:<	33.33%
❤	3.83%	:(	13.33%
😒	3.74%	:)	6.67%
🖤	2.43%	d:	6.67%

Table 3: The top 5 most frequent emoji and emoticons for offensive tweets

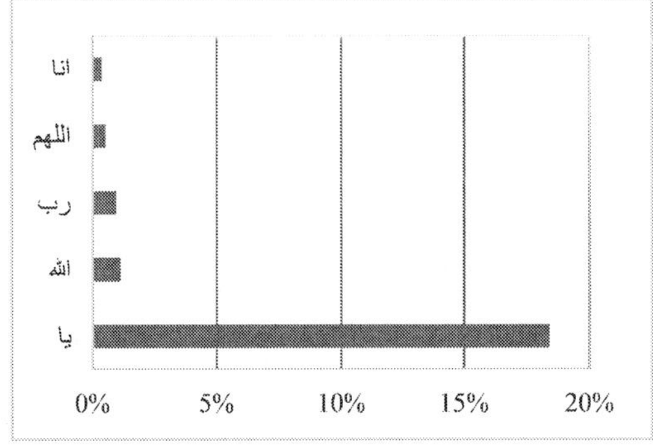

Figure 3: Most frequent 5 words in not offensive tweets

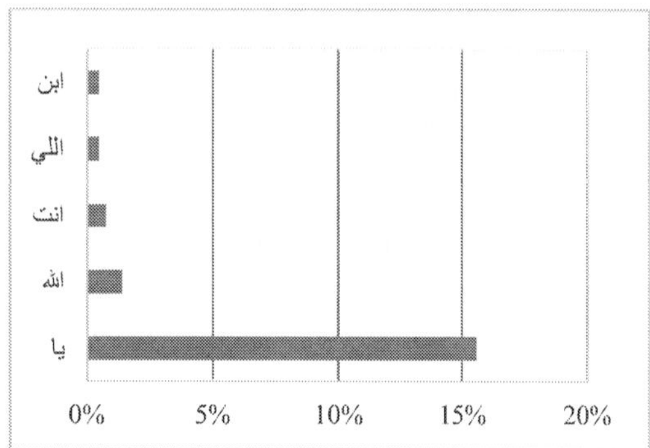

Figure 4: Most frequent 5 words in offensive tweets

3.2 Preprocessing

3.2.1 Emoji and Emoticon Conversion

Emoji and emoticons are often used to convey feelings and attitude, which is very valuable to the task of offensive detection. Knowing some contextual information about the author of the post can provide insight into the textual content of the post. Moreover, a previous study converts an emoji to a textual label, and uses it to provide sentimental features to train a classifier for aggression detection, thus reporting better performance than the other model that does not consider emoji conversion (Orasan, 2018). Thus, we consider converting emoji and emoticons to an Arabic textual label that describe the content of them. To have a more robust system that can scale and cover more emoji and emoticons, we then extract the entire set of emoji defined by Unicode.org (Unicode Organization, n.d.). Beautifulsoup4 4.8.2, a Python package for parsing HTML and XML documents, was used to scrape the emoji list available at the Unicode Organization website. We extract the Unicode and name of each emoji using Beutifulsoup4. The emoji list contains 1,374 emoji. The Unicode Organization website provides textual descriptions for each emoji written in English. We extract these textual descriptions, then, we use Translate 1.0.7 python package to translate them into Arabic language. Thus, during preprocessing of the data, each emoji is converted to its Arabic description. For example, 😉 is replaced by " وجه يغمز مع لسان" . In addition, we manually construct an emoticons list that includes a total of 140 emoticons with their textual descriptions in Arabic language. For example, ":-X" is replaced by " معقود اللسان". Next, we analyze the description phrase as a regular textual phrase in tweets so that it could maintain its semantic meaning after removing the original emoji and emoticon.

3.2.2 Arabic Dialects Normalization

The Arabic dialects have various forms, based on geography and social class (Habash, 2010). Arabic dialects are the Arabic languages that have often been used in user-generated contents such as Twitter. Habash (2010) categorizes the Arabic dialects into seven dialects: Gulf, Egyptian, Iraqi, North African, Yemenite, Levantine, and Maltese Arabic, which is not always considered one of the Arabic dialects. It is very crucial to consider the variations among different dialects when detecting offensive

language, as some words that have exactly the same pronunciation and spelling might have different meanings. For example, the word "عافية - Afiah" means health in Gulf, Egyptian, Iraqi, and Levantine dialects ; however, it also means fire in Moroccan Arabic. We try to solve the variation in dialects by a dimensionality reduction approach. We reduce the dimensionality of the data by normalizing the variation of dialects for a set of nouns to be converted from dialectal Arabic to MSA. For example, the variations of the word boy, "رجل", "زلمة", and "زول" are converted to "ولد". The set of nouns is manually constructed based on manual insepction for a sample of the dataset and based on our own experience as native Arabic speakers.

3.2.3 Words Categorization

Normalizing and reducing the dimensionality can improve the performance of the model. From our manual inspection for a sample of tweets from the dataset, we notice that it is very common to mention name of animals among the hate speech tweets. Thus, we manually create a list of the most common animal names used in different Arabic dialects, such as "كلب - dog", "خنزير - pig", "حية - snake". The list considers the variation in dialects in animal names, such as the word cat in MSA is "Qetta/قطة", while in Egyptian it is "Otta/ أطة", in Levantine it is "Bisse/بسة", in Gulf it is "Qatwa/قطوة", in Moroccan it is "Qetta/قطة", in Iraqi it is "Bazzuna/بزونة", and in Yamani it is "demah/دمة". In addition to the variation in dialects, the list includes variations of the same animal names, such as the female name, male name, plural name. Thus, for the word cat, we include singular female name "Qetta/قطة", singular male name "Qett/قط", two female name "Qettatan/قطتان", two male name "Qettan/قطان", and plural name "Qettat/قطط". The list contains a total of 335 lexicons. All animal names that are listed and occurred in the dataset were converted to the word animal in Arabic "حيوان". Accordingly, all animal names that are included in tweets are reduced to only one word.

3.2.4 Letters Normalization

Arabic letters can be written in various format depending on the location of the letter within the word. We normalize Alif (أ,إ,آ to ا), Alif Maqsura (ي,ئ to ى), and Ta Marbouta (ة to ه). Letters that were repeated more than two times within a word were reduced to two times only.

3.2.5 Hashtag Segmentation

Hashtags are commonly used in Twitter to highlight important phrases within the tweet. Thus, it is very important to consider hashtags during the preprocessing phase to convert hashtags into a meaningful format. We remove the "#" symbol and replace "_" by a space. For example, the hashtag "#الهلال_التعاون" is converted to "الهلال التعاون", which is easier for the system to understand and process.

3.2.6 Miscellaneous

Tweets were filtered to remove numbers, kashida, HTML tags, more than one space, three or more repetitions of any character, and some symbols or terms (e.g., " _", "", "\"", "s", "...", "!", "?", "I", "@USER", "USER", "URL", ".", ";", ":", "/", "\\", " ", "#", "@", "$", "&", ")", "(", "\"). We borrow the list of Arabic stopwords defined by Alrefaie

(2016), which contains 750 stopwords. Furthermore, we remove diacritics that were used in tweets containing text from the holy Qur'an or poetry.

3.2.7 Upsampling

As can be noticed from Table 1, the classes are highly imbalanced, with only 5% hate speech tweets and 19% offensive tweets. we try to solve the problem with the imbalanced distribution of classes by using up-sampling. The original training dataset has 7,000 tweets with a first label hierarchy of 1,410 offensive tweets and 5,590 not offensive tweets. After up-sampling, the number of tweets for each class, offensive tweets and not offensive tweets, becomes 5,590. The second label hierarchy is sharply imbalanced, the original training dataset consists of 361 hate speech tweets and 6639 not hate speech tweet. After up-sampling, the number of tweets for each class, hate speech tweets and not hate speech tweets, becomes 6,639. We use resample function from Python scikit-learn library to implement upsampling. Table 4 illustrates example of tweets before preprocessing and after preprocessing.

Tweet Before Cleaning	Tweet After Cleaning
يا عمرررررررري يا بو شعر ثاير ♥♥♥♥ 😄😄😄😄	يا عمررى يا بو شعر ثاير وجه البكاء بصوت عال وجه البكاء بصوت عال وجه البكاء بصوت عال وجه البكاء بصوت عال قلب اصفر قلب اصفر قلب اصفر قلب اصفر
@USER: يا شعب يا انانيه بطلو انصرافي ويلا على صفوف عيشكم وبنزينكم	بطلو انانيه يا شعب يا انصرافى ويلا صفوف عيشكم وبنزينكم
RT @USER: ما كان ممكن تبدأ بيه بدل ما تخسر تبديل يا حمار يابن الحمار يا غبييبي	ممكن تبدا بيه بدل تخسر تبدل يا حيوان يابن حيوان يا غبى

Table 4: Examples of tweets before preprocessing and after preprocessing

3.3 Feature Extraction

We use two features in training the models, which consists of character-based count vectorizer and TF-IDF vectorizer, both with 2 to 5 characters. Previous studies highlight the importance of using character-based features over word-based features for offensive language detection because it is a language independent feature that can work with misspelling errors or obfuscating offensive words, which are commonly practiced on social media posts (Bohra et al., 2018; Nobata et al., 2016). Both features are implemented using Python scikit-learn library.

3.4 Methodology

3.4.1 Preliminary Models

We explore the effect of each preprocessing technique on the performance of the model before applying them to the final models. Previous studies on offensive language detection report high performance when using an SVM-based classifier (Abozinadah and Jones, 2017; Schmidt and Wiegand, 2017; Albadi, Kurdi, and Mishra, 2018). The SVM classifier focuses on maximizing the margin, the distance of the closest points to the hyperplane that separate between instances of classes using a linear function (Goodfellow, Bengio, and Courville, 2016). Thus, we

decide to be in-line with the findings from earlier studies and use the linear SVM-based classifier in this step trained using the first label hierarchy of the dataset; offensive or not offensive, for the purpose of this exploration task. We did not use the testing dataset during this step. The training dataset used to train the models and the development dataset used to evaluate the models. During this preliminary modeling phase, two main goals were targeted. The first goal is to identify if count vectorizer outperforms TF-IDF vectorizer or not. To accomplish this goal, we trained two SVM-based models using the raw dataset without performing any preprocessing technique, one model applies the count vectorizer and the other one applies the TF-IDF vectorizer. Results are shown in Table 5. The TF-IDF vectorizer is 2% better than the count vectorizer in precision score. However, having a comprehensive measurement that consider multiple factors in evaluating the model is very important. The dataset is highly imbalanced, so we consider F1 score in evaluating the performance rather than accuracy. The accuracy score is often gives misleading results in similar situation with imbalanced dataset. F1 score is the harmonic mean for recall and precision. The count vectorizer outperforms the TF-IDF vectorizer by 2% in F1 score. This finding is consistent with Wiedeman et al. (2018) finding, which reports the unsuitability of TF-IDF vectorizer over twitter datasets because tweets are very short, making it not an optimal source for IDF estimations. Thus, we consider adopting the count vectorizer as the feature for the rest of the models.

Feature	Precision	Recall	F1	Accuracy
Count Vectorizer	85%	76%	79%	89%
TF-IDF Vectorizer	87%	74%	77%	88%

Table 5: Performance results for preliminary models based on features

The second goal of this preliminary modeling phase is to evaluate each preprocessing technique separately and measure their effects on the performance. Table 6 presents the results from the preliminary preprocessing exploration models. Only two preprocessing techniques were merged; hashtags segmentation and miscellaneous cleaning processes due to their relatedness and similarity in term of platform specific attributes. Preliminary results illustrate the contribution of each preprocessing technique to the performance of the model; however, we also expect to have different results when used on larger dataset and when used for hate speech detection. The results report the highest contribution in term of F1 score to letters normalization, followed by dialect normalization and word categorization, then, emoji and emoticon conversion, miscellaneous cleaning and hashtag segmentation, and finally, upsampling. The results demonstrate some issues with the upsampling technique, it reduces F1 score from 79%, as it shown in Table 5, to 71%. Consequently, we decide to apply all the preprocessing techniques except upsampling for the main models.

Preprocessing	Precision	Recall	F1	Accuracy
Emoji and Emoticon	83%	78%	80%	89%
Dialects Normalization	**85%**	80%	82%	**90%**
Word Categorization	84%	80%	82%	**90%**
Letters Normalization	**85%**	**81%**	**83%**	**90%**
Miscellaneous and Hashtags Segmentation	82%	76%	79%	89%
Upsampling	69%	75%	71%	80%

Table 6: Preliminary performance evaluation results from each preprocessing technique on offensive detection

3.4.2 Baseline Models

The baseline models include two linear SVM-based models, both trained on dataset without any sort of preprocessing technique and using a count vectorizer with 2 to 5 characters. The first baseline model classifies tweets to either Offensive (OFF) or Not Offensive (NOT_OFF), while the second one classifies tweets to either Hate Speech (HS) or Not Hate Speech (NOT_HS). To assess our goal in investigating the effect of preprocessing on offensive detection and hate speech detection, we use the same feature and classifier for baseline models and main models. All Models are implemented using Python scikit-learn library.

3.4.3 Sub-Task A Model : Offensive Language Detection

The main model for offensive language detection, which classifies tweets to either offensive (OFF) or not offensive (NOT_OFF), is a Linear SVM-based classifier. The model is trained on full preprocessed tweets that have been preprocessed using all techniques mentioned earlier; conversion of emoticons and emoji, conversion of hashtags, normalizing different forms of Arabic letters, normalizing Arabic dialects to MSA, normalizing words by categorization, and other miscellaneous cleaning processes. As we mentioned earlier, the feature used in training the model is the character-based count vectorizer with 2 to 5 characters. The model is implemented using Python scikit-learn library.

3.4.4 Sub-Task B Model : Hate Speech Detection

The same exact model of Sub-Task A is used for Sub-Task B, including the same preprocessing and feature extraction techniques. However, the model classifies tweets to either hate speech (HS) or not hate speech (NOT_HS).

4. Experiment Results

Table 7 shows the results of performance evaluation for the baseline model and the main model for offensive language detection task, and Table 8 shows the results for hate speech detection task. The baseline models were evaluated using the development dataset while the main models were evaluated using the testing dataset through the shared task competition evaluators. The dataset is highly imbalanced, thus, the accuracy score might not be very informative to evaluate the performance. The F1 score increased from 79% for the baseline model before preprocessing to 89% after preprocessing for Sub-Task A for offensive detection, which was ranked the 3rd place. For Sub-Task B for hate speech detection, F1 score increased sharply from 67% to 95%, which was ranked the 1st place.

The most noticeable point from the tables is that in Sub-Task B results are better than in Sub-Task A, given the fact that the class distribution is more skewed than that of Sub-Task A and the number of training instance is much smaller than Sub-Task A. This interesting point demonstrates how data preprocessing adds value to the performance, even for hate speech class that is very rare.

Model	Precision	Recall	F1	Accuracy
Baseline Model	85%	76%	79%	89%
Main Model	89%	90%	89%	90%

Table 7: Performance evaluation of offensive language detection task

Model	Precision	Recall	F1	Accuracy
Baseline Model	74%	63%	67%	96%
Main Model	95%	95%	95%	95%

Table 8: Performance evaluation of hate speech detection task

5. Conclusion

The preprocessing phase is one of the key phases within the text classification pipeline, including offensive language and hate speech classification. The ambiguity and informality of social media language increase the complexity of achieving high classification performance, particularly for Arabic text that has multiple dialects. Our study shows the competitive results obtained for offensive language detection and hate speech detection by using intensive preprocessing techniques to filter and clean the dataset before feeding it into the rest of the phases for the text classification pipeline. Moreover, results report the significant impacts of preprocessing on a very challenging task, such as the hate speech classification, with very small sample size of 5% from the overall dataset.

In the future, we hope to enhance the available studies of offensive language detection and hate speech detection by investigating our preprocessing techniques using some deep learning models. Another future direction is to use more advanced features in training the model, such as word embedding.

6. Bibliographical References

Abozinadah, E. , Mbaziira, A., and Jones, J. (2015). Detection of Abusive Accounts with Arabic Tweets. *International Journal of Knowledge Engineering*, Vol. 1, No. 2. DOI: 10.7763/IJKE.2015.V1.19

Abozinadah, E. (2017). Detecting Abusive Arabic Language Twitter Accounts Using a Multidimensional Analysis Model.

Abozinadah, E., and Jones, J. (2017). A Statistical Learning Approach to Detect Abusive Twitter Accounts. *Proceedings of the International Conference on Compute and Data Analysis*, 130280, 6–13. https://doi.org/10.1145/3093241.3093281

Alakrot, A., Murray, L., and Nikolov, N. S. (2018a). Dataset Construction for the Detection of Anti-Social Behaviour in Online Communication in Arabic. *Procedia Computer Science*, *142*, 174–181. https://doi.org/https://doi.org/10.1016/j.procs.2018.10.473

Alakrot, A., Murray, L., and Nikolov, N. S. (2018b). Towards Accurate Detection of Offensive Language in Online Communication in Arabic. *Procedia Computer Science*, *142*, 315–320. https://doi.org/https://doi.org/10.1016/j.procs.2018.10.491

Albadi, N., Kurdi, M., and Mishra, S. (2018). Are they Our Brothers? Analysis and Detection of Religious Hate Speech in the Arabic Twittersphere. 2018 IEEE/ACM International Conference on Advances in Social Networks Analysis and Mining (ASONAM), 69–76. https://doi.org/10.1109/ASONAM.2018.8508247

Albadi, N., Kurdi, M., and Mishra, S. (2019). Investigating the effect of combining GRU neural networks with handcrafted features for religious hatred detection on Arabic Twitter space. *Soc. Netw. Anal. Min.*, vol. 9, no. 1, p. 41.

Alrefaie, M. (2016). Arabic-stop-words [Github Repository]. Retrieved on January 24, 2020 from https://github.com/mohataher/arabic-stop-words

Bohra, A., Vijay, D., Singh, V., Akhtar, S. S., & Shrivastava, M. (2018). *A Dataset of Hindi-English Code-Mixed Social Media Text for Hate Speech Detection.* https://doi.org/10.18653/v1/W18-1105

Chowdhury, A., Didolkar, A., Sawhney, R., and Shah, R. (2019). ARHNet - Leveraging Community Interaction for Detection of Religious Hate Speech in Arabic. In Proceedings of the 57th Annual Meeting of the Association for Computational Linguistics: Student Research Workshop. Association for Computational Linguistics, Florence, Italy, 273–280. https://doi.org/10.18653/v1/P19-2038

Davidson, T., Warmsley, D., Macy, M., and Weber, I. (2017). Automated Hate Speech Detection and the Problem of Offensive Language. *AAAI Publications, Eleventh International AAAI Conference on Web and Social Media About offensive content.* arXiv.org.

Retrieved from http://search.proquest.com/docview/2074118430/

Derczynski, L. (2019). Offensive Language and Hate Speech Detection for Danish. *arXiv.org*. Retrieved from http://search.proquest.com/docview/2273023012/

Goodfellow, I., Bengio, B., Courville, A. (2016). Deep Learning. MIT press. Retrieved from http://www.deeplearningbook.org/contents/ml.html

Habash, N. (2010). Introduction to Arabic natural language processing (Vol. 3, pp. 1–185).

Kapoor, R., Kumar, Y., Rajput, K., Shah, R., Kumaraguru, P., & Zimmermann, R. (2018). Mind Your Language: Abuse and Offense Detection for Code-Switched Languages. arXiv.org. Retrieved from http://search.proquest.com/docview/2111970667/

Kent, S. (2018). German Hate Speech Detection on Twitter. *Proceedings of GermEval 2018, 14th Conference on Natural Language Processing (KONVENS 2018)* Vienna, Austria – September 21.

Kwok, I., and Wang, Y. (2013). Locate the Hate: Detecting Tweets Against Blacks. *Proceedings of the Twenty-Seventh AAAI Conference on Artificial Intelligence*, pp.1621-1622

Mohaouchane, H., Mourhir, A., and Nikolov, N. S. (2019). Detecting Offensive Language on Arabic Social Media using Deep Learning, (December). https://doi.org/10.1109/SNAMS.2019.8931839

Mubarak, H., Darwish, K., and Magdy, W. (2017). Abusive Language Detection on Arabic Social Media. Proceedings of the First Workshop on Abusive Language Online. Association for Computational Linguistics (ACL), 2017. pp. 52–56.

Mustafa, R., Nawaz, M., Ferzund, J., Lali, M., Shahzad, B., and ournier-Viger, P. (2017). Early Detection of Controversial Urdu Speeches from Social Media. Data Science and Pattern Recognition, Ubiquitous International, Volume1, Number2. ISSN 2520-4165.

Nobata, C., Tetreault, J., Thomas, A., Mehdad, Y., and Chang, Y. (2016). Abusive language detection in online user content. In *Proceedings of the 25th international conference on world wide web*, pp. 145–153. International World Wide Web Conferences Steering Committee, 2016

Orasan, C. (2018). Aggressive language identification using word embeddings and sentiment features. *Proceedings of the First Workshop on Trolling, Aggression and Cyberbullying.* Association for Computational Linguistics, http://hdl.handle.net/2436/621749

Ozel, S., Sarac, E., Akdemir, S., and Aksu, H. (2017). Detection of cyberbullying on social media messages in Turkish. 2017 International Conference on Computer Science and Engineering (UBMK), 366–370. https://doi.org/10.1109/UBMK.2017.8093411

Pitsilis, G., Ramampiaro, H., and Langseth, H. (2018). Effective hate-speech detection in Twitter data using recurrent neural networks. *Applied Intelligence*, 48(12), pp. 4730–4742. https://doi.org/10.1007/s10489-018-1242-y

Wiedemann, G., Ruppert, E., Jindal, R., and Biemann, C. (2018). *Transfer Learning from LDA to BiLSTM-CNN for Offensive Language Detection in Twitter*.

Proceedings of the 4th Workshop on Open-Source Arabic Corpora and Processing Tools, pages 61–65
with a Shared Task on Offensive Language Detection.
Language Resources and Evaluation Conference (LREC 2020), Marseille, 11–16 May 2020
© European Language Resources Association (ELRA), licensed under CC-BY-NC

ALT Submission for OSACT Shared Task on Offensive Language Detection

Sabit Hassan[1], Younes Samih[1], Hamdy Mubarak[1], Ahmed Abdelali[1]
Ammar Rashed[2], Shammur Chowdhury[1]
[1]Qatar Computing Research Institute, [2] Özyeğin University
{sahassan2, ysamih, hmubarak, aabdelali}@hbku.edu.qa
ammar.rasid@ozu.edu.tr, shchowdhury@hbku.edu.qa

Abstract

In this paper, we describe our efforts at OSACT Shared Task on Offensive Language Detection. The shared task consists of two subtasks: offensive language detection (Subtask A) and hate speech detection (Subtask B). For offensive language detection, a system combination of Support Vector Machines (SVMs) and Deep Neural Networks (DNNs) achieved the best results on development set, which ranked 1st in the official results for Subtask A with F1-score of 90.51% on the test set. For hate speech detection, DNNs were less effective and a system combination of multiple SVMs with different parameters achieved the best results on development set, which ranked 4th in official results for Subtask B with F1-macro score of 80.63% on the test set.

Keywords: Offensive Language Detection, Hate Speech Detection, Arabic Shared Task

1. Introduction

Detecting offensive language or hate speech on social media has gained a lot of interest recently. Use of offensive language and hate speech on social media can be an indication of hate crimes, toxic environment or level of antagonism against individuals or particular groups. Detecting offensive language and hate speech can also help in filtering out inappropriate content for users. Although there is a lot of research on detecting offensive language and hate speech (Agrawal and Awekar, 2018; Djuric et al., 2015; Davidson et al., 2017), work on Arabic offensive language detection is still in its early stages with very few notable works (Mubarak and Darwish, 2019; Mubarak et al., 2017; Albadi et al., 2018, Alakrot et al., 2018). Mubarak and Darwish (2019) report that only 1-2% of the tweets are offensive. The highly skewed distribution of data makes it extremely difficult to build useful datasets and effective systems. OS-ACT4 shared task (Mubarak et al., 2020) presents the problem of detecting offensive language and hate speech in Arabic tweets to the community. The shared task consists of 2 subtasks: offensive language detection (subtask A), and hate speech detection (subtask B).

This paper describes the systems submitted for OSACT4 shared task on Offensive Language Detection by the team ALT. First, we experimented with classical machine learning classifiers such as Support Vector Machines (SVMs) that are trained on character and word-level features. Then, we experimented with Deep Neural Networks (DNNs) and Bidirectional Encoder Representations from Transformers (BERT). SVMs were seen to outperform the DNNs and BERT. Since we expect the different kinds of classifier to make different kinds of errors, we take the most promising and diverse individual classifiers and perform voting to decide the final output. Majority voting on SVMs, DNNs and BERT yielded better results than individual systems for subtask A on the development set. The best results on development set for subtask B were obtained by combining the output of different SVMs and considering an instance to be hate speech if any of the classifiers voted it to be hate speech.

In section 2, we describe the dataset and the tasks, in section 3, we describe our approach and compare results for subtask A, in section 4, we describe our approach and compare results for subtask B and in section 5, we provide conclusion of our work.

2. Dataset and Task Description

In this section, we describe the dataset provided to the participants and the two subtasks.

2.1. Dataset

The dataset for OSACT Shared task consists of 10,000 Arabic tweets that are tagged for offensiveness and hate speech. The 10,000 tweets are split into training, development and testing sets as shown in Table 1.

Train	Dev	Test
7,000	1,000	2,000

Table 1: Training, development and testing data split

The organizers note that the data is highly skewed. Only 19% of the tweets are tagged as offensive and 5% of the tweets are tagged as hate speech. Table 2 shows examples from the training set. If a tweet has offensive language (insults or threats) targeting a group of people based on their origin (nationality, race, or ethnicity), their ideology (religion, political affiliation, etc.), gender or any other common characteristics, this is considered as hate speech, so all hate speech tweets are offensive according to this definition.

2.2. Task Description

The participants were required to produce labels indicating if a tweet is offensive (subtask A) or hate speech (subtask B). Each tweet took one of these labels for subtask A: "OFF" (offensive) or "NOT_OFF" (not offensive), and "HS" (Hate Speech) or "NOT_HS" (not Hate Speech) for subtask B. The full train and development data were made

Tweet	Offensive?	Hate Speech?
فدوه يا بخت فدوه يا زمن واحد منكم يحبيه	NO	NO
يا شيخ المعرضين يا آفاق يا نتن !! ربنا ينتقم منك ...	YES	NO
.يا وقح يا كلب الصهاينة يا عميل الفرس أنت عبد من عبيد نعال الحكام الظلمة	YES	YES

Table 2: Examples from the dataset

available to the participants at the beginning of the shared task. At a later stage, only the tweets from test split were made available to the participants via Codalab. The test labels remained unseen by the participants throughout the shared task. The participants were evaluated on the test labels produced by their systems in a blind test phase on Codalab — without access to the participants' own scores or other participants' scores. As the labels in each subtask are not balanced, the macro-averaged F1 scores were used for official ranking.

3. Subtask A: Offensive Language Detection

In this section, we discuss our approach in Subtask A. First, we describe the preprocessing step. Then, we describe the different models we experimented on and compare results of different models. Lastly, we perform an error analysis to understand the limitations of our models and the dataset.

3.1. Preprocessing Tweets

Preprocessing the tweets is an important step as the data from social media can be quite noisy as they contain a lot of emojis, text in mixed languages, excessive use of punctuation etc. It is important to note that some of our models (described in the next subsection) use pretrained word embeddings as feature. In order to reduce noise and be able to find more words in the embeddings, we perform the following steps for preprocessing the tweets.
Step 1: Remove all words that contain non-Arabic characters.
Step 2: Remove all diacritics.
Step 3: Remove all punctuation.
Step 4: Replace repeated characters with only one.

In our initial experiments, we noticed that the settings listed above produces the best results. Therefore, we keep the same preprocessing settings for all experiments.

3.2. System Descriptions

We experimented on a myriad of classifiers including classical machine learning classifiers such as Support Vector Machines (SVMs), Logistic Regression (LR), Multinomial Naive Bayes (MNB), and deep learning classifiers such as Feed-forward Neural Network (FFNN), Convolutional Neural Network (CNN), Bidirectional Long Short Term Memory (BiLSTM), and Bidirectional Encoder Representations from Transformers (BERT). LR and MNB performed quite poorly, and therefore, excluded from the discussion that follows. The results on development set for rest of the classifiers are discussed next and are summarized in table 3. Note that the values for precision, recall and F1 are macro averaged and F1-macro is the official metric.

3.2.1. SVMs

As the features for SVMs, we transform the tweets into bag-of-n-grams vector weighted with logarithmic term frequencies (tf) multiplied with inverse document frequencies (idf). We created both character and word n-grams this way. We experimented with different ranges of character and word n-grams. We also experimented on using Mazajak embeddings (Abu Farha and Magdy, 2019) as features to SVM. Mazajak embeddings were trained on Twitter data, which matches the domain of data in our task. Therefore, we expect it to be more useful compared to other embeddings that are trained on different domain of data (BERT-Multilingual, for example). From table 3, we can see that the best results were obtained when character $[1, 5]$ gram and word $[1 - 3]$ gram features were combined with pretrained Mazajak word embeddings.

3.2.2. FastText

FastText is an efficient deep-learning based system for learning embeddings and performing text classification (Joulin et al., 2016). Since the task of offensive language detection is a text classification problem, we experimented with FastText, but as we can see from Table 3, FastText was outperformed by other systems.

3.2.3. FFNN

For the FFNN architecture, we use four hidden layers with a different number of units (1000, 500, 500, 100) and a sigmoid activation function in each layer, followed by an softmax output layer. To train the network, we use a batch size of 256, with maximum epochs of 50 and early stopping using a 10% of the training set with similar distribution of the labels. The models are then optimized using rmsprop optimization function. The parameter were initialized with small random numbers, sampled from a uniform distribution. Since other systems outperform FFNN, we have not tuned the architecture for different parameters such as number of hidden units or the learning rates, among others.

3.2.4. CNN-BiLSTM

We use two sets of features for this model. First, we have pretrained word embedding (Mazajak embeddings) features for each word. Second, we use CNN as character-level feature extractor. First layer of the network is used to project the input string to character embeddings, which is then passed through a convolutional layer and max-over-time pooling is applied to obtain fixed length representation of words. Character-level representations have been shown to capture morphology of words (Kim et al., 2015). If we were to use only word level features obtained from pretrained word embeddings, we would lose out information when a word does not appear in the vocabulary of the pre-

No.	Model	Features	Acc.	Prec.	Recall	F1
1	SVM	Word [1-3] Gram	80.1	71.6	82.4	73.7
2		Char [1-5] Gram	91.5	78.9	90.8	83.3
3		Mazajak SG-250	92.2	85.5	90.2	87.6
4		Mazajak SG-100 + char[1-5] + word[1-3]	93	88.3	87.7	88
5		Mazajak SG-250 + char[1-5] + word[1-3]	94.3	89.8	91	90.4
6	FastText		89.5	85.5	75.7	79.4
7	FFNN	Char [1-8] + Word [1-4]	91.9	87.1	84	85.1
8	CNN	Mazajak SG-250	92.1	86.7	86.2	86.5
9	CNN-BiLSTM	Mazajak SG-100	92.9	87.6	88.1	87.8
10	M-BERT		90.1	83	83.7	83.3
11	**Ensemble(4+5+7+8)**		**94.3**	**89.9**	**91.1**	**90.5**

Table 3: Comparison of different systems submitted to subtask A

	Tweet	True Label	Majority Label	Reason
	چايمي خط احمر يا دينيريس يا بنت الاحبة انتي#GameofThrones	OFF	NOT	Out of context
	# غلاق_حسابات_البدون_في_البنوك الحل رصاصه يا فيك يا فيه نقطه اخر السطر .	OFF	NOT	Out of vocab
	يا جبران يا ابن جرجي وقف عند حدّك بقى كتير زوّدتا بطل في شي تسرقو شكّيت على جيبة المواطن الفقير يلي بيفلح كل لنهار ليطلع	NOT	OFF	Ambiguity

Table 4: Error analysis of subtask A

trained embedding. The character-level features obtained this way will provide us with information in such cases.
The character level representation of words are then merged with the word embedding features and passed to the BiL-STM. Then a softmax layer is used for projecting the probability distribution of the target classes. Note that the CNN learns the character-level features jointly with the BiLSTM, minimizing the cross entropy loss. Stochastic Gradient Descent (SGD) optimizer was used during the training.

3.2.5. BERT

Deep contextualized language models such as BERT. (Devlin et al., 2019) have been shown to perform really well in many NLP tasks. We fine-tuned BERT-multilingual (referred to as M-BERT) for offensive language detection. M-BERT is pretrained on Wikipedia text from 104 languages that include Arabic. From Table 3, we can see that M-BERT is outperformed by CNN-BiLSTM. We speculate that this is because the domain of data M-BERT is trained on, Wikipedia text, is quite different from the Twitter data used in the shared task. Articles on Wikipedia are typically written in a formal way and follow the structure and rules of grammar. Text on social media platforms such as Twitter, on the other hand, can be very informal and chaotic.

3.2.6. Ensemble Method

From table 3, we can see that several system are promising and perform quite close to each other. Since these systems are quite diverse (SVMs are quite different from BERT, for example), they are likely to make different types of errors. In order to improve our results, we experiment on combining multiple systems. We took the output of two SVM

classifiers (No.4 and No.5), the CNN-BiLSTM (No.9) and M-BERT (No.10) and performed majority voting to decide on the label for each input. From table 3, we can see that this ensemble method is the best system on the development data and this is the system we submitted for official ranking. The official scores for this system on the test set is shown in table 5.

Official Rank	Acc.	Prec.	Recall	F1
1st	93.85%	90.18%	90.85%	90.51%

Table 5: Official results on subtask A test set

	NOT OFF	OFF
NOT OFF	789	32
OFF	25	154

Table 6: Confusion matrix on subtask A dev set

3.3. Error analysis

To have a better understanding of where our system is failing will help us improve our system in future and understand the limitation of the data. We examine 100 samples from the development data and attempt to identify *where* and *why* our best system (No. 11 from table 3) is failing. Examining the specific tweets provides us with some interesting insights. Table 4 lists examples of errors made by our best performing system. The first entry in

No.	Model	Features	Acc.	Prec.	Recall	F1
1	SVM	Mazajak SG-250 + char[1-5] + word[1-3]	96.2	72	78.2	74.7
2		Char [2-6] Gram	**97.1**	72.5	**88.8**	78.2
3	Bagged SVM	Mazajak SG-250 + char[1-5] + word[1-3]	96.4	68.9	81.3	73.4
4	CNN-BiLSTM	Mazajak SG-100 + CNN Feature Extractor	95.9	76.1	67.5	70.9
5	M-BERT		95.7	72.4	74.9	73
11	**Ensemble(1+2+3)**		96.6	**80**	78.7	**79.3**

Table 7: Comparison of different systems submitted to subtask B

	Tweet	True Label	Majority Label	Reason
	اقطع واخس يا الداعشي يا بو حساب نتن ..	HS	NOT	?
	الله لا يوفقك يا خرا يا برازيلي يا تبن	HS	NOT	?
	بيلعب يا توتنهام يا الستي والاقرب توتنهام وبيفوز وبيلعب النهائي قدام الليفر الاقرب واحتمال كبير يفوز بالبطولة الخامسة اياكس	NOT	HS	?

Table 8: Errors analysis of subtask B

the table contains reference to Game of Thrones. This is offensive only if context of Game of Thrones is taken into account. We cannot expect the classifier to be correct on such instances. The second entry provides us with an example of error that we can tackle in the future. We see that the hashtag غلاق_حسابات_البدون_في_البنوك # is offensive toward immigrants. But it's out of vocabulary for our systems. In the future, we can attempt to parse the hashtags into its constituent words and see if it improves the performance. The third entry in the table is quite interesting. The sentence uses an offensive word, تسرقو, which means "stealing", but the sentence itself is not offensive. It's likely our system picked up the offensive word but failed to take into account the context in which the word was used. In future, we can particularly target resolving issues of ambiguous use of words.

Table 6 shows the confusion matrix of our best system. We can see that the classifier is much more likely to misclassify offensive instance as not offensive compared to misclassifying not offensive instances as offensive. This is to be expected as the data is highly skewed with only 19% of the instances being offensive.

4. Subtask B: Hate Speech Detection

For subtask B, The preprocessing is the same as section 3. In this section, we describe the different models we experimented on for subtask B, present the results for the different models and discuss errors made by the models.

4.1. System Descriptions

Since same tweets are used for both the subtasks, for subtask B, we focused only on those systems that were promising in subtask A. These systems include SVMs, CNN-BiLSTM and M-BERT. The accuracy, precision, recall and F1 score are reported in Table 7. The precision, recall and F1 scores are macro averaged.

4.1.1. SVMs
As the features for SVMs, we use the same features as subtask A. In addition, we also experiment with bagged SVM (5 estimators). The SVMs outperformed CNN-BiLSTM and M-BERT in this subtask as well.

4.1.2. CNN-BiLSTM
We keep the same structure and settings of the CNN-BiLSTM used in subtask A.

4.1.3. M-BERT
Once again, we follow the same methodology as subtask A. The only difference is that the M-BERT is now fine-tuned on hate speech detection.

4.1.4. Ensemble Method
For subtask B, we opt for a slightly different ensemble method. The best ensemble on the development set was obtained by only considering the three SVMs (Nos. 1,2,3 from table 7). We also change the voting mechanism such that it's no longer majority voting. We consider an instance to be hate speech if any of the three SVMs vote it to be hate speech. This voting scheme was outperforming majority voting scheme on the development set. The official result on this ensemble is shown in table 9.

Official Rank	Acc.	Prec.	Recall	F1
4th	96.6%	83.8%	78.1%	80.6%

Table 9: Official results on subtask B test set

	NOT HS	HS
NOT HS	940	16
HS	18	26

Table 10: Confusion matrix on subtask B dev set

4.2. Error analysis

We attempt to perform error analysis similar to subtask A by collecting 100 samples from development set and examining them. Unfortunately, we could not identify any particular reasons for the system to fail. We speculate this to be because of the data for subtask B being *extremely* skewed (with only 5% of the data being hate speech). Table 8 contains examples of errors made by the best system (no. 6 from table 7).

Table 10 shows the confusion matrix of our best system on subtask 2. As expected, because of the extreme imbalance of the data, we can see that the classifier is prone to misclassifying hate speech instances as non hate speech instances.

5. Conclusion and Future Work

To conclude, we experimented heavily with classical machine learning and deep learning approaches to detect if a tweet is offensive or contains hate speech. We achieve state of the art results for offensive language detection by combination of SVMs, CNN-BiLSTM and Multilingual BERT. We achieve competitive results on hate speech detection with a system combination of SVMs. Our error analysis indicates certain types of errors for offensive language detection that can be addressed in future. In future, we aim to explore augmentation of hate speech data to build better systems.

6. Bibliographical References

Abu Farha, I. and Magdy, W. (2019). Mazajak: An online Arabic sentiment analyser. In *Proceedings of the Fourth Arabic Natural Language Processing Workshop*, pages 192–198, Florence, Italy, August. Association for Computational Linguistics.

Agrawal, S. and Awekar, A. (2018). Deep learning for detecting cyberbullying across multiple social media platforms. *CoRR*, abs/1801.06482.

Alakrot, A., Murray, L., and Nikolov, N. S. (2018). Towards accurate detection of offensive language in online communication in arabic. *Procedia Computer Science*, 142:315 – 320. Arabic Computational Linguistics.

Albadi, N., Kurdi, M., and Mishra, S. (2018). Are they our brothers? analysis and detection of religious hate speech in the arabic twittersphere. In *2018 IEEE/ACM International Conference on Advances in Social Networks Analysis and Mining (ASONAM)*, pages 69–76, Aug.

Davidson, T., Warmsley, D., Macy, M. W., and Weber, I. (2017). Automated hate speech detection and the problem of offensive language. *CoRR*, abs/1703.04009.

Devlin, J., Chang, M.-W., Lee, K., and Toutanova, K. (2019). BERT: Pre-training of deep bidirectional transformers for language understanding. In *Proceedings of the 2019 Conference of the North American Chapter of the Association for Computational Linguistics: Human Language Technologies, Volume 1 (Long and Short Papers)*, pages 4171–4186, Minneapolis, Minnesota, June. Association for Computational Linguistics.

Djuric, N., Zhou, J., Morris, R., Grbovic, M., Radosavljevic, V., and Bhamidipati, N. (2015). Hate speech detection with comment embeddings. In *Proceedings of the 24th International Conference on World Wide Web*, WWW '15 Companion, page 29–30, New York, NY, USA. Association for Computing Machinery.

Joulin, A., Grave, E., Bojanowski, P., Douze, M., Jégou, H., and Mikolov, T. (2016). Fasttext.zip: Compressing text classification models. *CoRR*, abs/1612.03651.

Kim, Y., Jernite, Y., Sontag, D. A., and Rush, A. M. (2015). Character-aware neural language models. *CoRR*, abs/1508.06615.

Mubarak, H. and Darwish, K. (2019). Arabic offensive language classification on twitter. In *International Conference on Social Informatics*, pages 269–276. Springer.

Mubarak, H., Darwish, K., and Magdy, W. (2017). Abusive language detection on Arabic social media. In *Proceedings of the First Workshop on Abusive Language Online*, pages 52–56, Vancouver, BC, Canada, August. Association for Computational Linguistics.

Mubarak, H., Darwish, K., Magdy, W., Elsayed, T., and Al-Khalifa, H. (2020). Overview of osact4 arabic offensive language detection shared task. 4.

Proceedings of the 4th Workshop on Open-Source Arabic Corpora and Processing Tools, pages 66–70
with a Shared Task on Offensive Language Detection.
Language Resources and Evaluation Conference (LREC 2020), Marseille, 11–16 May 2020
© European Language Resources Association (ELRA), licensed under CC-BY-NC

ASU_OPTO at OSACT4 - Offensive Language Detection for Arabic text

Amr Keleg [1], Samhaa R. El-Beltagy [2], Mahmoud Khalil [1]
[1] Faculty of Engineering - Ain Shams University, [2] Optomatica
[1] Cairo, [2] Giza
Egypt
amr.keleg@eng.asu.edu.eg, samhaa@computer.org, mahmoud.khalil@eng.asu.edu.eg

Abstract

In the past years, toxic comments and offensive speech are polluting the internet and manual inspection of these comments is becoming a tiresome task to manage. Having a machine learning based model that is able to filter offensive Arabic content is of high need nowadays. In this paper, we describe the model that was submitted to the Shared Task on Offensive Language Detection that is organized by (The 4th Workshop on Open-Source Arabic Corpora and Processing Tools). Our model makes use transformer based model (BERT) to detect offensive content. We came in the fourth place in subtask A (detecting Offensive Speech) and in the third place in subtask B (detecting Hate Speech).

Keywords: Offensive speech, Hate speech, BERT

1. Background and task description

During the past decade, Social media platforms such as Facebook and Twitter have attracted millions of users from the Arab region. These platforms have given people the chance to express their ideas, beliefs and feelings. Unlike real life conversations, people tend to be more aggressive when they are communicating through this virtual online world. The aggression might also reach an extreme case where racist, violent and completely unacceptable words are shared online. Sites are trying to control the spread of these toxic comments by manually moderating and checking the reports that other users are filing. Moreover, Some services provide an automatic way to automatically filter offensive content. For example, Google Search has an option to use "SafeSearch Filters" which is allows filtering out any harmful or violent content before presenting the search results to the user.

All these facts have attracted researchers from all around the world to build different techniques that can be used to automatically detect offensive content. Various definitions and aspects have been used to tackle this task. Having a typology that can be clearly agreed upon by humans is of great importance. Mubarak et al. (2017) have used the term abusive speech to refer offensive text that contains profane content. On other hand, Hate speech (Toxic comments) is often used to refer to offensive text that is targeted towards a certain person or a group of people based on a common trait (race, ethnicity, religion, etc.) (Malmasi and Zampieri, 2017).

The competition is composed of two subtasks. Subtask A aims at differentiating between offensive and non-offensive text irrespective of the type of the offensive text (Hate Speech, Profanity, Cyber-bullying, etc). Substask B focuses on detecting text that contains targeted Hate Speech towards a person or a group of people.

2. Systems description

Lately, Fine-tuning large models using the idea of transfer learning such as: BERT (Devlin et al., 2019) and ULMFiT

(Howard and Ruder, 2018) that are pre-trained on language modeling tasks reaches state-of-the-art results in multiple classification tasks. For this competition, we have focused on Subtask A and tested different models/ architectures keeping in mind that fine-tuning BERT based models should be among the top performing ones. The best performing model for subtask A was then adapted to work on subtask B as well. The following models were developed throughout our experiments[1]:

- Training a basic model using tf-idf (term frequency - inverse document frequency) and logistic regression. The tf-idf generates a sparse representation of the input text using character ngrams in range [1, 9] e.g: Some of the grams of the sentence

  (في غيابك الفرح والنور) are (رغ، غي، غيا، غياب، غيابك، و، وا، وال، والن، والنو، والنور، والنور، ل، لن، لنو، لنور، ن، نو، نون) .

  This sparse feature vector is then fed to the logistic regression model to discriminate between the two classes (offensive and non-offensive). This model represents the baseline model for all other deep learning based architectures.

- Training a 1D Convolutional Layer using word embeddings from Aravec (Mohammad et al., 2017) as a 2D input array. At first, the line-feed token <LF>is replaced by a newline character \n. Then, the sentence is cleaned in the way that is used by the Aravec model. This step includes the removal of diacritics and fixing elongated words (Replacing any sequence of the same character of length two or more by a sequence of length two of the same character). Then, the sentence is tokenized using whitespaces. The tokens are mapped to their respective index in the word2vec model using 0 as the index for any unknown token.

---

[1] The source code for the developed models can be found through: https://github.com/AMR-KELEG/offenseval-2020-ASU_OPTO

The list of ids is then padded by the id 0 such that it has a fixed length of 75 ids. The list is truncated to have the length of 75 in case it had more than 75 tokens. The list of ids is then used to generate the respective word embeddings. The word embeddings are concatenated to form a 2D array of shape(75, 300) where 300 is the size of the word embedding for each token. 100 different 1D convolutional filters are then applied to the 2D array with kernel size of 3 and stride of 1 (e.g: the filter is applied to the word embeddings of all 3-consecutive tokens). A 1D max-pooling layer is then applied with a pool size of 4. Drop-out with probability of 0.5 succeeds the max pooling layer then a Dense layer of 1 neuron with a sigmoid activation function is used to predict the probability that the sentence is offensive or not. The model is trained for 2 epochs with L2 regularization (penalty factor is set to 0.0001). The used cost function is binary cross entropy and it's optimized using Adam (Kingma and Ba, 2014). The initial word vectors will also be fine-tuned during the training process to minimize the cost function.

- Training a Bi-directional LSTM using word embeddings from Aravec. Only the most occurring 300,000 words of the Aravec vocabulary are kept and fine-tuned as part of the model due to the limited GPU memory. After the embedding layer, a bidirectional LSTM layer of 64 cells is used followed by two dense layers of 64 neurons with relu activation function and 1 neuron with a sigmoid activation function.

- Fine-tuning multilingual BERT that is pre-trained on cased text of the top 104 languages with the largest Wikipedias (which includes Arabic). The text is tokenized using a word piece tokenizer (Wu et al., 2016) which is trained on large text in an unsupervised fashion to determine a set of word-pieces that form the words (e.g: the word **unaffable** might be split to (un, ##aff, ##able) according the word-pieces that were generated on training the tokenizer). After tokenizing the input text, the tokens are padded/truncated to the length of 75. BERT generates an embedding for the whole sentence using its self-attention layers. A Dense layer with softmax activation is then added to classify the sentence into offensive or not. The whole pretrained architecture in addition to the added dense layer are then fine-tuned using the tagged dataset. The model is fine-tuned for three epochs using a learning rate of 10^{-5} and with L2 regularization.

- Fine-tuning AraBERT (a publicly released BERT model trained on Arabic text [2]). The text is tokenized using Farasa (Abdelali et al., 2016) which is a segmenter that is developed to segment an Arabic word into its affixes. Then, the tokens are fed to the BERT model. The default values provided by the model's authors were used in the fine-tuning process. The training dataset was divided into batches of size 32, where each sample was tokenized to have a length of 64. Six epochs were used to fine-tune the pre-trained AraBERT model on the training dataset of 7000 samples with a learning rate of 10^{-5}.

Moreover, We have built a list of profanity words and used simple augmentation rules to generate the different forms of each word. Mubarak et. al (2017) have demonstrated the effectiveness of using a list of words to detect abusive content in text documents. They used a seed list of bad words and collected user data from twitter to find other candidate words that: 1) are used by those who have any of the seed words in their tweets. 2) aren't used by those who don't have any of the seed words in their tweets. We build on the same idea of having a list of profanity words to automatically mark some tweets as offensive irrespective of their context but we have used a morphological approach for augmenting our seed list of bad words. First, we used a list of bad words that is available online[3]. The list of bad words was manually augmented to include other common forms of an Arabic word by substituting ة (Taa-marbuta) with ه (Haa) and substituting ز (Zain) with ذ (Zaal). Then, the list was further augmented by other bad words that could be found in the training data-set using manual inspection. Finally, a list of prefixes and suffixes were used to generate the different morphological forms of each word. For example, if the word was a verb then the list of prefixes to be added would be (ا، ي، ت، ن، ه، سا) and the list of suffixes would be (ني، ك، ها، هم، كم، هن، نا). e.g.: For the verb هزم, 113 different morphological forms are generated. The following words represent a sample of these forms:

هزم، اهزم، اهزمك، اهزمكم، اهزمنا، اهزمني، اهزمها، اهزمهم، اهزمهن، يهزم، يهزمك، يهزمكم، يهزمنا، يهزمني، يهزمها، يهزمهم، يهزمهن

A seed list of 87 bad words was augmented to reach 5497 different words. Some combinations of the prefixes and suffixes might result in a word that is not linguistically valid but our intuition is since the word isn't part of the language then nobody will use it and thus considering a word that is impossible to be used to be a bad word won't affect the model's precision.

Throughout our experiments, we have faced problems with reproducing the results for models that are trained using GPUs among multiple runs given that we had used a random seed of value 42 in all our experiments. This seems like a problem that isn't widely discussed. The reproducibility problem can be partially mitigated by training the model multiple times while saving the trained weights for each training run and then choosing the best performing version of the model.

3. Results

Table 1 reports the accuracy and the macro-averaged precision, recall and F1 scores for the training and development datasets respectively on subtask A. Our best model

---

[2]The initial version of AraBERT can be found through: `https://github.com/zaidalyafeai/ARBML/ issues/18#issuecomment-580924000`

[3]https://github.com/LDNOOBW/List-of-Dirty-Naughty-Obscene-and-Otherwise-Bad-Words

Table 1: Results of the developed models on the training and development datasets

Model name	Training dataset				Development dataset			
	Accuracy	*Precision*	*Recall*	*F*1	*Accuracy*	*Precision*	*Recall*	*F*1
tfidf + logistic regression	0.889	0.938	0.725	0.778	0.888	**0.921**	0.694	0.746
CNN + Aravec	0.982	0.985	0.959	0.971	0.928	0.906	0.838	0.867
BiLSTM	**0.999**	**0.998**	**0.998**	**0.998**	0.920	0.856	**0.884**	0.869
Multi-lingual BERT	0.978	0.975	0.956	0.965	0.905	0.855	0.805	0.826
AraBERT	0.998	0.998	0.994	0.996	**0.928**	0.881	0.871	**0.876**

Table 2: Effect of using the list of profane words on the fine-tuned AraBERT reported on the development dataset

Model name	*Accuracy*	*Precision*	*Recall*	*F*1
AraBERT	0.928	0.881	0.871	0.876
AraBERT + augmented list of profane words	**0.930**	**0.883**	**0.877**	**0.880**

for subtask A was the AraBERT based model which performed better than the cased multilingual BERT model that is trained using the dumps of the 104 most represented languages on wikipedia. Researchers focusing on langauges other than English have found that a BERT model trained specifically for a certain language such as: German, Greek and Dutch (de Vries et al., 2019) achieves better results than the multilingual BERT model that might under-represent some languages. Additionally, The results of the Offenseval 2019 (Zampieri et al., 2019) competition reported that 7 out of the top 10 teams have used BERT to build their models. Risch, et al. (2019) have also showed that using a BERT model that is trained using large German corpora performs better than all the other baseline models.

The AraBERT based model was also succeeded by a simple look-up search that marks a sentence as offensive if it contains any of the words in the augmented profanity words list irrespective of the prediction of the AraBERT model. Using this hybrid approach has improved the macro-averaged precision and recall and consequently improved the macro-averaged F1 score as shown in table 2. The official macro-averaged F1 score of this hybrid system on the test and development datasets is 0.896 which is much better than that of our second best system that is based on the Bidirectional LSTM which achieved an official score of 0.856.

For subtask B, We have fine-tuned AraBERT using the whole training dataset of 7000 tweets with the same configuration and hyperparameters that were used in subtask A. Our official macro-averaged F1 score is 0.807 which put our team in the third place on the scoreboard.

4. Error Analysis

One of the important steps to carry-out on training a machine learning model is to check the mis-classified samples and try to find reasonable explanations for such errors. This task might be hard for text data since one can't easily find relations between different samples unlike images for example. On checking a random sample of 50 mis-classified samples, we found that most of the errors were False Negatives (The sample is offensive yet it was classified as not offensive). Additionally, we found that all these samples contained the Arabic vocative article يا (Ya). This seemed

Table 3: Tweets containing bad words with mixed inconsistent labels

ID	Text	Label
2206	ده اللى كنت خايفة منه اصل تخيلى انزل صورى عادى و اجى الاقى الناس بتتبادل صورى و عليها رسم اسهم ودواير عشان نبين الفوتوشوب فين ا** ده انا هخاف و طبيعى همسحها مبقولش ان ده خداع و انه مش صح بس خوفى انى اجرحها يخلينى يا اسكت يا اما اعلق تعليق بسيط	NOT OFF
7177	لا ثانية واحدة كدة هى اسمها كان يا ما كان يا سادة يا كرام مش يا سعد يا إكرام ا***	OFF

like a really serious problem that needs to be fixed until we discovered that (6986 out of 7000) of the sentences in the training and (999 out of 1000) of the sentences in the development data-sets contain the article يا (Ya). The effect of such observation on the model needs more analysis but clearly this article was used by the data-set creators to query sentences (tweets) and it might limit the distribution of the corpus.

4.1. Issues with the Annotation scheme

Human annotation is a tiresome task especially in the field of natural language processing since text might sometimes be ambiguous in a way that the same sentence might carry different meanings. In this section, we will shed the lights on different issues that we have spotted on performing error analysis.

Presence of a bad word in a non-negative context: The way people perceive and use bad words might depend on different factors such as: the dialect that they use or their society's culture. Some words might be accepted in some regions but are completely inappropriate in other regions.

Table 4: Tweets with offensive semantic meaning and sarcastic pragmatic meaning

ID	Text	Label
261	RT @USER: وشوشنى وديتها فين يا محول يا أبو عين واحده ؟! أول هام أسمها أعور .. لما تحب تهزئنى هزئنى صح URL	OFF
7868	It seems like تاني يا زكي يا تافه .. رحتلهم تاني عشان يضربوك وياخدوا هدومك تاني	NOT OFF

Table 5: Tweets containing Offensive content with incorrect labels

ID	Text	Label
7106	إلى بحط جدول المحاضرات بالجامعة اقسم بالله ما بكون صاحي ! يا غبي ٣ مواد تخصص بنفس الساعة كييف؟؟ أكيد بكون يا نايم يا بحلم بذكرني بأركان وهو بكتب أحداث كارا دينيز	NOT OFF - NOT HS
7491	@USER @USER التهريج مش بكلام هشام التهريج بكلامك الاستزلامي و الانبطاحي و السوقية بتوجيهك الكلام الو. عادي الاستزلاميين هيدي لغتن مش انو شي جديد الزلمي بكلامو ما كان في اهانات و تجريح بعكس انتي يلي مفروض يا متعلمة يا بتوعت المدارس. عموما يعط	NOT OFF - NOT HS
7358	يا عيباه يا حسافاه اليمني يهان بكل مكان وهذا كله بسبب قيادته الملعونه المرتزقة والمشكله نحن كجنوبيين والله ثم والله اننا نحترم ونقدر الشعب في الشمال وكل خلافنا سببة قادتهم السرق واعمالهم في الجنوب متى يصحى الشعب اليمني ويشوف الاهانات من كل البلدان متى ويبني علاقة حب مع الجنوبيين	NOT OFF - NOT HS

Additionally, Annotators might neglect the presence of a bad word if the context isn't offensive while others consider the whole sentence to be offensive if it contains a bad word. Table 3 demonstrates the disagreement problem between human annotators where the same bad word (with different forms) was found in a non-offensive context. Annotators have considered the first to be not offensive but marked the second one as offensive.

Usage of sarcastic speech quoting popular movie scenes: Our Arabic culture relies heavily on quoting conversations from popular movies. The semantic meaning of these words might be offensive but the pragmatic meaning will depend on the context in which they are used. Ambiguity is an issue that rises in almost all the systems that operate on linguistic data. Table 4 shows two examples where quotes from movies were used. Although the fact that the model can only depend on the semantic meaning of the sentence, we believe that annotators should pick a side and mark them as either offensive or not. The two sentences have offensive speech yet one of them was annotated as offensive and the other was annotated as non offensive.

Wrong annotations: Having errors in annotations generated by humans is a problem that is almost unavoidable especially if the dataset was of a large size (10,000 tweets) and annotators are asked to provide two different labels for each tweet (Offensive or not offensive and Hate speech or not hate speech). In table 5, we believe that all these samples should have marked as offensive and as hate speech.

5. Conclusion

Our experiments reveals that the contextualized word embeddings generated using BERT yield better classifiers for offensive text detection. A BERT model that is pre-trained on large text corpora achieves state-of-the-art results. On the other hand, multilingual BERT seemed to lack the ability to represent Arabic text. This might be attributed to the fact that Arabic text needs to be tokenized in a different way than the other languages that are supported by multilingual BERT. Additionally, using a hybrid approach improved our system that is used for subtask A. Relying on a manually prepared list to mark a sentence that contains a profane word as offensive is a logical solution to support machine learning based models.

6. Bibliographical References

Abdelali, A., Darwish, K., Durrani, N., and Mubarak, H. (2016). Farasa: A fast and furious segmenter for arabic. 06.

de Vries, W., van Cranenburgh, A., Bisazza, A., Caselli, T., van Noord, G., and Nissim, M. (2019). Bertje: A dutch bert model. *ArXiv*, abs/1912.09582.

Devlin, J., Chang, M.-W., Lee, K., and Toutanova, K. (2019). BERT: Pre-training of deep bidirectional transformers for language understanding. In *Proceedings of the 2019 Conference of the North American Chapter of the Association for Computational Linguistics: Human Language Technologies, Volume 1 (Long and Short Papers)*, pages 4171–4186, Minneapolis, Minnesota, June. Association for Computational Linguistics.

Howard, J. and Ruder, S. (2018). Universal language model fine-tuning for text classification. In *Proceedings of the 56th Annual Meeting of the Association for Computational Linguistics (Volume 1: Long Papers)*, pages 328–339, Melbourne, Australia, July. Association for Computational Linguistics.

Kingma, D. P. and Ba, J. (2014). Adam: A

method for stochastic optimization. *arXiv preprint arXiv:1412.6980.*

Malmasi, S. and Zampieri, M. (2017). Challenges in discriminating profanity from hate speech. *Journal of Experimental & Theoretical Artificial Intelligence,* 30(2):187202, Dec.

Mohammad, A. B., Eissa, K., and El-Beltagy, S. (2017). Aravec: A set of arabic word embedding models for use in arabic nlp. *Procedia Computer Science,* 117:256–265, 11.

Mubarak, H., Darwish, K., and Magdy, W. (2017). Abusive language detection on Arabic social media. In *Proceedings of the First Workshop on Abusive Language Online,* pages 52–56, Vancouver, BC, Canada, August. Association for Computational Linguistics.

Risch, J., Stoll, A., Ziegele, M., and Krestel, R. (2019). hpidedis at germeval 2019: Offensive language identification using a german bert model. In *Preliminary proceedings of the 15th Conference on Natural Language Processing (KONVENS 2019). Erlangen, Germany: German Society for Computational Linguistics & Language Technology,* pages 403–408.

Wu, Y., Schuster, M., Chen, Z., Le, Q. V., Norouzi, M., Macherey, W., Krikun, M., Cao, Y., Gao, Q., Macherey, K., Klingner, J., Shah, A., Johnson, M., Liu, X., ukasz Kaiser, Gouws, S., Kato, Y., Kudo, T., Kazawa, H., Stevens, K., Kurian, G., Patil, N., Wang, W., Young, C., Smith, J., Riesa, J., Rudnick, A., Vinyals, O., Corrado, G., Hughes, M., and Dean, J. (2016). Google's neural machine translation system: Bridging the gap between human and machine translation.

Zampieri, M., Malmasi, S., Nakov, P., Rosenthal, S., Farra, N., and Kumar, R. (2019). SemEval-2019 task 6: Identifying and categorizing offensive language in social media (OffensEval). In *Proceedings of the 13th International Workshop on Semantic Evaluation,* pages 75–86, Minneapolis, Minnesota, USA, June. Association for Computational Linguistics.

Proceedings of the 4th Workshop on Open-Source Arabic Corpora and Processing Tools, pages 71–75
with a Shared Task on Offensive Language Detection.
Language Resources and Evaluation Conference (LREC 2020), Marseille, 11–16 May 2020
© European Language Resources Association (ELRA), licensed under CC-BY-NC

OCAST4 Shared Tasks: Ensembled Stacked Classification for Offensive and Hate Speech in Arabic Tweets

Hafiz Hassaan Saeed[1], Toon Calders[2], Faisal Kamiran[1]
[1] Information Technology University, Pakistan, {hassaan.saeed,faisal.kamiran}@itu.edu.pk
[2]University of Antwerp, Belgium, toon.calders@uantwerpen.be

Abstract

In this paper, we describe our submission for the OCAST4 2020 shared tasks on offensive language and hate speech detection in the Arabic language. Our solution builds upon combining a number of deep learning models using pre-trained word vectors. To improve the word representation and increase word coverage, we compare a number of existing pre-trained word embeddings and finally concatenate the two empirically best among them. To avoid under- as well as over-fitting, we train each deep model multiple times, and we include the optimization of the decision threshold into the training process. The predictions of the resulting models are then combined into a tuned ensemble by stacking a classifier on top of the predictions by these base models. We name our approach "ESOTP" (Ensembled Stacking classifier over Optimized Thresholded Predictions of multiple deep models). The resulting ESOTP-based system ranked 6th out of 35 on the shared task of Offensive Language detection (sub-task A) and 5th out of 30 on Hate Speech Detection (sub-task B).

Keywords: ESOTP, Arabic Hate Speech, Arabic Offensive Language, Stacked Deep Predictions

1. Introduction

Social media platforms have become a widely-used mode of communication among individuals or groups from diverse backgrounds. With the increasing freedom of expression in user-generated content on these platforms, the menace of offensive and hate speech is also on the rise (Santosh and Aravind, 2019), causing adverse effects on users and society at large (Lee and Kim, 2015). Because of this menace, the identification of offensive or hateful statements towards individuals or groups has become a priority nowadays and many social media companies have already invested millions for building automated systems to detect offensive language and hate speech (Gambäck and Sikdar, 2017).

In this paper, we address the task of offensive language and hate speech detection in the Arabic language by presenting our contributions to two shared tasks (A and B) in OCAST4 2020. The objective in shared subtask A is to identify offensive language whereas the objective in shared subtask B is to identify hate speech in the given tweets. We developed a common methodology for both tasks, and executed the classification pipeline twice, once for each of both subtasks.

As a first attempt, we applied classical text classification techniques including Naïve Bayes, Logistic Regression, Support Vector Machines, and Random Forests based on the traditional encoding of the tweets as TF.IDF vectors. Subsequently, more advanced deep learning techniques using pre-trained word embeddings were applied and compared to the classical techniques. Both approaches were compared empirically, showing superior performance for the deep models.

The superiority of the deep models motivated further exploration in the direction of deep learning. We compared a number of pre-trained word-level embeddings available for Arabic language processing, and in the end, concatenated the two empirically best performing pre-trained word-level embeddings.

Using this combined embedding, several network architectures and ways of pre-processing were tried out, and the resulting models were combined in a tuned ensemble as follows. The different deep networks were trained and optimized several times, saving their predictions for both tasks. Finally, a classifier was stacked on top of these predictions to combine them in one ensemble. The resulting classifier was further fine-tuned, therefore, we name our approach "ESOTP" which stands for *Ensembled Stacking classifier over Optimized Thresholded Predictions of multiple deep models*.

2. Related Work

Hate speech detection has been studied extensively in recent years, especially for highly-resourced languages like English. (Yin et al., 2009) were among the first ones to apply supervised machine learning approaches in hate speech detection. They applied Support Vector Machines to detect harassment in posts from famous social platforms like MySpace. Similarly, (Warner and Hirschberg, 2012) trained a Support Vector Machine classifier on word n-grams and used it to detect hate speech. In recent years, (Waseem and Hovy, 2016) showed that character n-grams are better than word n-grams as predictive features for hate speech detection. Their best performing model was a Gradient Boosted Decision Trees classifier trained on word embeddings learned using LSTMs.

There exists, however, very little literature on the problem of Hate Speech detection in Arabic. Some of the few works are discussed next. (Magdy et al., 2015) collected a large number of Arabic tweets and trained a Support Vector Machine classifier to predict if a user supports or opposes ISIS. (Mubarak et al., 2017) proposed a methodology for the detection of profane tweets by using an automatically created and expanded list of obscene and offensive words. (Haidar et al., 2017) proposed a multilingual system that detects cyberbullying attacks in both English and Arabic texts. They scrapped the data from Facebook and Twitter. The data collected from Facebook was kept for validating the system. Their proposed system was a multilingual cyberbullying detection system and two machine learning models Naive Bayes and Support Vector Machine were used in it. In another related work, (Albadi et al., 2018) prepared the first publicly available Arabic dataset that was especially annotated for religious hate speech detection. They also developed multiple classifiers using lexicon-based, n-gram-based, and deep learning approaches. They found a simple Recurrent Neural Network (RNN) architecture with Gated Recurrent Units (GRU) and pre-trained word embeddings to be the best performing model for the detection of religious hate speech in Arabic. (Mohaouchane et al., 2019) compared multiple deep models including CNN, BLSTM with Attention, BLSTM and Combined CNN-LSTM for detecting offensive language in Arabic. They showed that CNN-LSTM achieved best recall scores whereas CNN achieved highest f1 scores in 5-fold cross validation. Recently, (Chowdhury et al., 2019) proposed ARHNET to detect religious hate speech in Arabic by using word embeddings and social network graphs with deep learning models and improved the classification scores than (Albadi et al., 2018). The overview of OSACT4 Arabic Offensive Language Detection Shared Task is discussed by (Mubarak et al., 2020).

3. Methodology

Starting from pre-processing, we now discuss the overall methodology (classification pipeline) followed for both subtasks in OCAST4 2020.

3.1. Pre-processing

One pre-processing step was already done over the original tweets by the competition's organizers, i.e., mentions of a specific user were replaced with @USER, URLs were replaced with URL, and empty lines with <LF>. We removed all these replaced tokens along with emoticons, emojis, punctuation marks (both Arabic and English), English characters, digits (both Arabic and English) and Arabic diacritics. We then normalized a few Arabic characters like *Hamza*, *Ya*, *Ha*, and *Qaf*, and finally removed a repeating character in the string if it is repeated more than 3 times consecutively. An additional pre-processing step is taken for out-of-word-embeddings-vocabulary (OOWEV) words with the models that use pre-trained word embeddings, which is to split an OOWEV word into 2 tokens (i.e., the first character and the rest of the word) if the first character is *Wa*, *Fa*, or *Sa*. The intuition behind this additional step is that *Wa*, *Fa*, or *Sa* appearing at the beginning of an Arabic word function like a grammatical particle as *Wa* gives added meaning of ("and" or "vow" or "oath"), *Fa* gives added meaning of (result to a previous statement) and *Sa* gives added meaning of (in very near future). This way a few more words are covered from the pre-trained word embeddings.

3.2. Pre-trained Word Vectors

A number of pre-trained word vectors are available for Arabic language processing like FastText (Grave et al., 2018), Word2Vec[1] (Continuous Skip gram trained over Arabic CoNLL17 corpus), AraVec (Soliman et al., 2017), N-Gram and Uni-Gram models, and recent BERT[2] multilingual vectors. We empirically evaluated these available word embeddings based on the given evaluation metric and concatenated the two best among them which were FastText (300 dimensional vectors) and Word2Vec (100 dimensional vectors) resulting in a 400 dimensional vector representation for words in the corpus.

The resulting concatenation of word embeddings yields 4 types of words: **type 1)** words which exist in both embeddings; **type 2)** words which exist in the first embedding but do not exist in the second; **type 3)** words which exist in the second embedding but do not exist in the first; **type 4)** words which neither exist in the first nor in the second embedding.

	FastText$_{300\,D}$	W2V$_{100\,D}$
W_{type_1}	E_1	E_2
W_{type_2}	E_1	$N\,(\mu_2, \sigma_2)$
W_{type_3}	$N\,(\mu_1, \sigma_1)$	E_2
W_{type_4}	$N\,(\mu_1, \sigma_1)$	$N\,(\mu_2, \sigma_2)$

Figure 1: Assigning vectors to the respective types of words yielded from the concatenation of FastText and Word2Vec word embeddings.

The strategy adopted for assigning vectors to all four types of words is shown in Figure 1 and is explained as:

Let E_1 be vector components from the FastText embedding, E_2 be vector components from the Word2Vec embedding, μ_1 be the mean of all vectors in FastText, μ_2 be the mean of vectors in Word2Vec, σ_1 be the standard deviation of the vectors in FastText, σ_2 be the standard deviation of the vectors in Word2Vec, then the vectors assigned to the types of words are: **type 1)** get E_1 and E_2; **type 2)** get E_1 and initialize last 100 components with Gaussian distribution using μ_2 & σ_2; **type 3)** get E_2 and initialize first 300 components with Gaussian distribution using μ_1 & σ_1; **type 4)** initialize first 300 components with Gaussian distribution using μ_1, σ_1 and last 100 components with Gaussian distribution using μ_2, σ_2.

3.3. Models Used

We used four different types of neural architectures for both tasks of offensive language and hate speech detection, namely: 1) Convolutional Neural Networks (CNN); 2) Nets based on Bidirectional Long Short-Term Memory (BLSTM); 3) Nets based on Bidirectional Gated Recurrent Units (BGRU); and 4) Nets based on Bidirectional LSTMs with CNN (BLSTM+CNN). We briefly explain these architectures.

---

[1] http://vectors.nlpl.eu/repository/20/31.zip

[2] https://github.com/google-research/bert/blob/master/multilingual.md

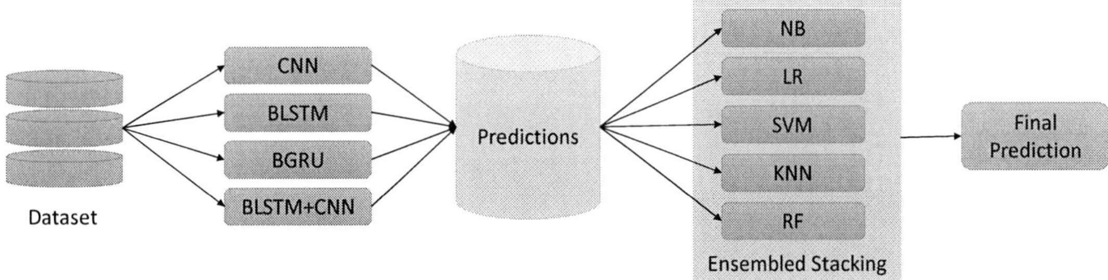

Figure 2: Classification pipeline followed to detect offensive language and hate speech in Arabic language

3.3.1. CNN

This architecture is based on the one presented by (Kim, 2014). The input layer in this architecture is an embedding layer, attached to a 1D spatial dropout layer that is then reshaped to a 2D matrix of $M \times V$, where M is maximum length of tweets in the corpus and V is the size of embedding vectors. After reshaping the input, 5 convolutional layers are attached in parallel having 128 kernels in each layer with kernel dimensions ranging from $1 \times V$, to $5 \times V$. All these parallel layers are then attached to a global max-pooling layer and concatenated to make a single feature vector, connected then to a dropout layer, followed by fully connected layers of 100, 50 and 1 units respectively. The activation function in the last layer is a sigmoid whereas for the rest of the network we use the exponential linear unit (ELU) function.

3.3.2. BLSTM

This architecture is taken from (Saeed et al., 2018). The input to this architecture is an embedding layer followed by a 1D spatial dropout layer, which is then attached to two parallel blocks of Bidirectional Long-Short Term Memory (BLSTM) where the first block has 128 units and the second block 64 units. Global max-pooling and global average-pooling layers are attached to both parallel blocks and are concatenated to make one feature vector, which is then attached to fully connected layers of 100, 50, and 1 units respectively. The activation function in the last layer is a sigmoid whereas the BLSTM layers use the tanh activation function and for the rest of the network we use the exponential linear unit (ELU) function.

3.3.3. BGRU

This architecture is also taken from (Saeed et al., 2018) and is similar to the BLSTM architecture. The only difference between this architecture and BLSTM is that we use GRU instead of LSTM. The rest of the architecture is same as that of BLSTM.

3.3.4. BLSTM+CNN

This architecture has an input embedding layer connected to a 1D spatial dropout layer. The output from the 1D spatial dropout layer is given as input to a bidirectional LSTM layer with 128 units and then a 1D convolutional layer is attached with 64 kernels of size 4, connected on its turn with a global max-pooling layer, followed by a dropout layer, and again 3 fully connected layers having 100, 50 and 1 units respectively.

3.4. Ensembled Stacking Classifier

The overall classification pipeline is shown in Figure 2. We train all four models: CNN, BLSTM, BGRU, and BLSTM+CNN, for 250, 200, 70 and 30 times respectively. The decision threshold is optimized for F1 as part of the training phase. We hence get 550 predictions for each sample in the validation set. Using these 550 predictions as a new training set, we built a stacking classifier that is an ensemble of a Naïve Bayes classifier, a Logistic Regression model, a Support Vector Machine, a Nearest Neighbours classifier and a Random Forest. We fine-tune this new Ensembled Stacking Classifier as well. We named our approach "ESOTP", which stands for *Ensembled Stacking classifier over Optimized Thresholded Predictions of multiple deep models*.

4. Experimentation & Results

We used Keras deep learning framework with Tensorflow backend to build our deep classification pipeline. The evaluation metric used to test the classification system is macro averaged f1 score. We report cross-validation scores as our results in this paper, as there was a limit of 10 submissions at maximum per team during the OCAST4 testing phase.

4.1. Hyper-parameter Tuning

We tune hyper-parameters of the deep models used in this study by mixing grid search with manual tuning. The hyper-parameters include batch size, optimizers, learning rate, the number of kernels in CNN, the number of units in recurrent layers, and the dropout rates. The hyper-parameters in ensembled stacking classifier include penalty, solver and regularization parameter for Logistic Regression; penalty, kernel function, regularization parameter and gamma for Support Vector Machine; values of K in Nearest Neighbours; and number of estimators, splitting criterion and max. depth of trees in Random Forest.

4.2. Pre-trained Word Vectors

We compared pre-trained word embeddings with CNN architecture over 20 runs only due to time limitations. The average of 20 runs for both subtasks is shown in Table 1, which shows that Word2Vec and FastText achieved the

Word Embeddings	OFF	HS
Bert Multilingual	83.10 ± 0.75	73.45 ± 1.09
AraVec-300-SG	77.94 ± 0.28	72.64 ± 1.57
AraVec-300-CBOW	77.62 ± 0.70	72.77 ± 1.39
AraVec-100-SG	77.51 ± 0.39	72.95 ± 1.52
AraVec-100-CBOW	77.97 ± 0.53	72.56 ± 1.33
Word2Vec	**87.03 ± 0.33**	**75.98 ± 1.21**
FastText	**87.13 ± 0.23**	**76.68 ± 1.04**

Table 1: Comparison of pre-trained word embeddings averaged over 20 runs for macro f1 score.

highest f1 scores on our cross-validation when used as pre-trained word vectors, and therefore we selected both these embeddings to concatenate them for the representation of words from both embeddings.

4.3. Main Results

The main results are shown in Table 2. Naïve Bayes (NB), Logistic Regression (LR), Random Forest (RF) and Support Vector Machines (SVM) give lower F1 scores as compared to deep models in our cross-validation. Besides the deep models described in section 3.3., we trained two additional deep models: 1) BLSTM with Attention; 2) BLSTM with some statistical features like number of punctuation marks, number of characters, number of words, number of rare words, number of out-of-vocabulary words, etc. The cross-validation scores showed deterioration instead of improvement, therefore, we ignored them from being into our ensembled stacking classification.

The scores in Table 2 shown for CNN are averaged over 250 runs, for BLSTM over 200 runs, for BGRU over 70 runs and for BLSTM+CNN over 30 runs. The scores of "ESTOP" are marked with asterisk (*) sign because we split the validation set further (into train and validation) to fine-tune the ensembled stacking classifier.

Models	OFF	HS
NB+TF.IDF	64.73	48.87
LR+TF.IDF	84.55 ± 0.22	71.12 ± 0.38
RF+TF.IDF	80.92 ± 0.46	72.41 ± 1.25
SVM+TF.IDF	84.86 ± 0.29	72.88 ± 0.11
CNN	88.67 ± 0.47	75.68 ± 1.04
BLSTM	89.02 ± 0.43	76.83 ± 1.40
BGRU	88.75 ± 0.38	76.63 ± 1.36
BLSTM+CNN	87.84 ± 0.42	75.82 ± 1.42
ESTOP	95.51*	77.79*

Table 2: Macro averaged F1 cross-validation scores for both subtasks

We submitted predictions from CNN, BLSTM, BGRU, BLSTM+CNN and ESTOP for the actual test set one-by-one. The test scores indicated that CNN, BLSTM and BGRU were over-fitting whereas BLSTM+CNN was under-fitting. Overall, ESTOP approximated better generalized predictions for the actual test set as it achieved 87.37% f1 for subtask A (ranked 6/35) and 79.85% for subtask B (ranked 5/30).

5. Conclusion

We present our submission to the shared tasks of offensive language and hate speech detection in OCAST4 2020. To develop a good classification pipeline for both tasks, we select the empirically best word representations using available pre-trained word embeddings with some language-specific pre-processing, and afterwards compare a number of deep learning approaches. Our final submission is based on fine-tuning a stacking classifier where we use an ensemble of multiple models as the stacking classifier, built over different deep models trained for several times. Our classification pipeline (ESTOP) results in better generalization as compared to individual deep models.

6. Acknowledgements

We thank Louis Bruyns Foundation, Belgium, for their support in this research study.

7. Bibliographical References

Albadi, N., Kurdi, M., and Mishra, S. (2018). Are they our brothers? analysis and detection of religious hate speech in the arabic twittersphere. In *2018 IEEE/ACM International Conference on Advances in Social Networks Analysis and Mining (ASONAM)*, pages 69–76. IEEE.

Chowdhury, A. G., Didolkar, A., Sawhney, R., and Shah, R. R. (2019). Arhnet - leveraging community interaction for detection of religious hate speech in arabic. In Fernando Alva-Manchego, et al., editors, *Proceedings of the 57th Conference of the Association for Computational Linguistics, ACL 2019, Florence, Italy, July 28 - August 2, 2019, Volume 2: Student Research Workshop*, pages 273–280. Association for Computational Linguistics.

Gambäck, B. and Sikdar, U. K. (2017). Using convolutional neural networks to classify hate-speech. In *Proceedings of the First Workshop on Abusive Language Online, ALW@ACL 2017, Vancouver, BC, Canada, August 4, 2017*, pages 85–90.

Grave, E., Bojanowski, P., Gupta, P., Joulin, A., and Mikolov, T. (2018). Learning word vectors for 157 languages. In *Proceedings of the Eleventh International Conference on Language Resources and Evaluation, LREC 2018, Miyazaki, Japan, May 7-12, 2018*.

Haidar, B., Chamoun, M., and Serrhrouchni, A. (2017). Multilingual cyberbullying detection system: Detecting cyberbullying in arabic content. In *2017 1st Cyber Security in Networking Conference (CSNet)*, pages 1–8. IEEE.

Kim, Y. (2014). Convolutional neural networks for sentence classification. In *Proceedings of the 2014 Conference on Empirical Methods in Natural Language Processing, EMNLP 2014, October 25-29, 2014, Doha, Qatar, A meeting of SIGDAT, a Special Interest Group of the ACL*, pages 1746–1751.

Lee, S. and Kim, H. (2015). Why people post benevolent and malicious comments online. *Commun. ACM*, 58(11):74–79.

Magdy, W., Darwish, K., and Weber, I. (2015). # failedrevolutions: Using twitter to study the antecedents of isis support. *arXiv preprint arXiv:1503.02401*.

Mohaouchane, H., Mourhir, A., and Nikolov, N. S. (2019). Detecting offensive language on arabic social media using deep learning. In Mohammad A. Alsmirat et al., editors, *Sixth International Conference on Social Networks Analysis, Management and Security, SNAMS 2019, Granada, Spain, October 22-25, 2019*, pages 466–471. IEEE.

Mubarak, H., Darwish, K., and Magdy, W. (2017). Abusive language detection on arabic social media. In *Proceedings of the First Workshop on Abusive Language Online*, pages 52–56.

Mubarak, H., Darwish, K., Magdy, W., Elsayed, T., and Al-Khalifa, H. (2020). Overview of osact4 arabic offensive language detection shared task. In *Proceedings of the 4th Workshop on Open-Source Arabic Corpora and Processing Tools (OSACT)*, volume 4.

Saeed, H. H., Shahzad, K., and Kamiran, F. (2018). Overlapping toxic sentiment classification using deep neural architectures. In *2018 IEEE International Conference on Data Mining Workshops, ICDM Workshops, Singapore, Singapore, November 17-20, 2018*, pages 1361–1366. IEEE.

Santosh, T. Y. S. S. and Aravind, K. V. S. (2019). Hate speech detection in hindi-english code-mixed social media text. In *Proceedings of the ACM India Joint International Conference on Data Science and Management of Data, COMAD/CODS 2019, Kolkata, India, January 3-5, 2019*, pages 310–313.

Soliman, A. B., Eissa, K., and El-Beltagy, S. R. (2017). Aravec: A set of arabic word embedding models for use in arabic NLP. In *Third International Conference On Arabic Computational Linguistics, ACLING 2017, November 5-6, 2017, Dubai, United Arab Emirates*, pages 256–265.

Warner, W. and Hirschberg, J. (2012). Detecting hate speech on the world wide web. In *Proceedings of the Second Workshop on Language in Social Media*, pages 19–26, Montréal, Canada, June. Association for Computational Linguistics.

Waseem, Z. and Hovy, D. (2016). Hateful symbols or hateful people? predictive features for hate speech detection on twitter. In *Proceedings of the NAACL student research workshop*, pages 88 93.

Yin, D., Xue, Z., Hong, L., Davison, B. D., Kontostathis, A., and Edwards, L. (2009). Detection of harassment on web 2.0. *Proceedings of the Content Analysis in the WEB*, 2:1–7.

Proceedings of the 4th Workshop on Open-Source Arabic Corpora and Processing Tools, pages 76–81
with a Shared Task on Offensive Language Detection.
Language Resources and Evaluation Conference (LREC 2020), Marseille, 11–16 May 2020
© European Language Resources Association (ELRA), licensed under CC-BY-NC

Arabic Offensive Language Detection with Attention-based Deep Neural Networks

Bushr Haddad*, Zoher Orabe*, Anas Al-Abood*, Nada Ghneim**
*Damascus University
Damascus, Syria
**AlSham Private University
Damascus, Syria
{bushr.haddad, zoherorabe999, anasabood3}@gmail.com
n.ghneim@aspu.edu.com

Abstract

The abusive content on Arabic social media such as hate speech, sexism, racism has become pervasive, and it has a lot of negative psychological effects on users. In this paper, we introduce our work aiming to detect Arabic offensive language and hate speech. We present our two deep neural networks Convolutional Neural Network (CNN) and Bidirectional Gated Recurrent Unit (Bi-GRU) used to tackle this problem. These models have been further augmented with attention layers. In addition, we have tested various pre-processing and oversampling techniques to increase the performance of our models. Several machine learning algorithms with different features have been also tested. Our bidirectional GRU model augmented with attention layer has achieved the highest results among our proposed models on a labeled dataset of Arabic tweets, where we achieved 0.859 F1 score for the task of offensive language detection, and 0.75 F1 score for the task of hate speech detection.

Keywords: Abusive Language, Text Mining, Arabic Language, Social Media Mining, Deep Learning, Convolutional Neural Network, Gated Recurrent Unit, Attention Mechanism, Machine Learning.

1. Introduction

The internet and social media provide people with a range of benefits and opportunities to empower themselves in a variety of ways. There are millions of people using social media platforms to maintain social connections and support networks that otherwise would not be possible. All of these benefits led to a huge growth of social media interactions in the last few years. Arabic language has a very high rate of growth in social networking usage. Based on the Arab social media report (Salem, 2017), the average rate of using Arabic language in social media reaches 55% in 2017.

With the massive increase of the social connections, there has also been an increase of abusive language that should be detected and eliminated from these networks, due to its negative impacts on users. This paper has been prepared for the competition of OSACT4 shared task on offensive language detection (Mubarak et al., 2020). The competition was divided into two sub-tasks; sub-task A (offensive language detection) and sub-task B (hate speech detection). Offensive language is defined as any implicit or explicit insult or attack against other people, or any inappropriate language, while hate speech[1] is defined as any abusive speech targeting individuals (a politician, a celebrity, etc.) or particular groups (a gender, a religion, a country, etc.).

Hate speech is known to be complex and ambiguous because it was not just a words identification. (Zhang and Luo, 2019) showed that detecting a hateful content is a challenging task compared to non-hateful content due to their lack of unique, discriminative linguistic features. On the other hand, Arabic language is known to be difficult and ambiguous, the Arabic content on social media is noisy with different dialects, and most Arabic users do not care about using correct grammar, or spelling. All of these factors made these tasks nearly impossible in the past to detect and identify using conventional features widely adopted in many language-based tasks.

Based on (Al-Hassan and Al-Dossari, 2019), offensive language detection task depends mainly on text mining approaches such as NLP and machine learning algorithms.

In the rest of this paper, a brief of related works are summarized in section 2. In section 3, we represent our data preparation process, then our proposed models are presented in section 4. In section 5, a brief discussion on the results is addressed. At the end, a short summary and insights for the future are presented.

2. Related Works

Different researches have addressed both offensive language detection, and hate detection subjects. (Cambray and Podsadowski, 2019) evaluated their model on OffensEval 2019 English dataset and presented their best model as a bidirectional LSTM; followed by a two-branch bidirectional LSTM and GRU architecture (macro F1 of 73% for offensive language detection task and 61% for targeted hate speech detection).

(Mubarak, Darwish, and Magdy, 2017) have created a list of 288 of Arabic obscene words and other list of 127 of hashtags. They used this list in addition to patterns to collect Arabic abusive tweets from Twitter API during 2014. They classified tweet users into two groups, namely: those who authored tweets that did not include a single obscene word from list words (clean group) and those who used at least one of the words in list at least once (obscene

---

[1] https://www.dictionary.com/browse/hate-speech

group). They computed unigram and bigram counts in both of them and computed the Log Odds Ratio (LOR) for each word unigram and bigram that appeared at least 10 times. (Alakrot, Murray, and Nikolov, 2018) have collected a dataset of 15,050 comments from YouTube and labelled them manually by three annotators. This dataset was collected in July 2017. They applied some preprocessing operations on the dataset, and then applied SVM classifier on tf-idf features with different methods for text normalizing (macro F1 of 82%). (Mohaouchane, Mourhir, and Nikolov, 2019) have used the same YouTube dataset. They used Word2Vec embeddings and trained different neural networks models namely: convolutional neural network (CNN), bidirectional long short-term memory (Bi-LSTM), Bi-LSTM with attention mechanism, and combined CNN and LSTM. The CNN model achieved the highest accuracy (87.84%), precision (86.10%), and F1 score (84.05%) among other models.

Several works have investigated the problem of hate speech detection in English language. (Zhang and Luo, 2019) Firstly: they demonstrated that hateful content exhibits a 'long tail' pattern compared to non-hate, and secondly: they proposed two deep neural networks, CNN and GRU, to identify specific types of hate speech. They outperformed the previous state of the art methods by 5 percentage points in macro-average F1. (Gambäck and Sikdar, 2017) evaluated CNN model on various word embeddings, and achieved their best score (F1 score of 78%) with CNN model trained on Word2Vec word embeddings. (Badjatya et al, 2017) evaluated several neural architectures on a 16 K annotated tweets benchmark dataset. Their best setup involved a two-step approach using a short-term word-level memory (LSTM) model, tuning GLoVe or randomly initializing word embedding, and then training a gradient boosted decision tree (GBDT) classifier on the average of the tuned embedding in each tweet. They achieved the best results using randomly initialized embeddings (macro F1 of 93%).

In Arabic language there was a limited number of works in this area. (Mulki et al., 2019) constructed a Levantine hate speech and abusive dataset from Twitter. (Haddad, Mulki, and Oueslati, 2019) constructed a Tunisian hate and abusive speech dataset. (Albadi, Kurdi, and Mishra, 2018) built a lexicon of Arabic terms related to religion abuse along with hate score, the labeled dataset is then used to train several classification models using lexicon-based, n-grams-based, and deep-learning based approaches. Their best model achieved 0.84 area under receiver operating characteristic curve (AUROC).

3. Data Preparation

The main dataset used in this work, is the one that was firstly presented at OffensEval 2020. This dataset contains 10000 tweets, only 5% of tweets are labeled as hate speech while 19 % of the tweets are labeled as offensive and the other 81% as inoffensive tweets. The data has been given by the following format: a tweet followed by a label indicating its class {OFF/HS, NOT_OFF/NOT_HS}, all hate speech tweets considered to be offensive language, but not vice versa. The dataset was divided into 70% *train* data, 10% *validation* data, and the rest 20% *test* data.

3.1 Data Preprocessing

This dataset run through a series of pre-processing steps in order to get the most normalized language form. Twitter data is known for its unstructured and unformed language. So, making a good preprocessing steps will results in a much better text representation. As a first step, we removed non-Arabic words, diacritization, punctuations, emoticons and some other stopwords, while we replaced some words with their simplified Arabic equivalent, (example: "URL" will be substituted with "يورل"). We intend to study the effect of the emoticons in a future work. Normalization step was also applied (example, replacing "ة" with "ه", "ى" with "ي", "[إأآ]" with "ا"). In addition, elongated and some consecutive repetitive characters that people usually write on their dialect speech are converted back to their original form (example: "هههههه" was be converted to "هه", and "غوووول" to "غول"). This step is very important as some Arabic speakers tend to repeat and elongate some characters on their dialect speech.

3.2 Data Balancing

After preprocessing, and as the provided dataset is imbalanced, we applied different methods to balance out the classes for better model performance. Researches shows that classifiers trained on imbalanced dataset may tend to have a high number of false negatives (offensive tweets which are misclassified as inoffensive tweets) and thus a lower recall (Mohaouchane, Mourhir, and Nikolov, 2019). Such detection systems are preferable to identify offensive language even if it sometimes mistakes inoffensive language as offensive. Because the number of inoffensive language exceeds the number of offensive language, so it is preferable to have a higher recall comparing to a higher precession. A lot of ways have been used previously trying to balance out the data like loss function weighting (Cui et al., 2019), down sampling and oversampling. For our case and for subtask A we used an external augmenting technique by adding some offensive and inoffensive comments from an already constructed Arabic dataset collected from YouTube comments (Alakrot, Murray, and Nikolov, 2018) (as YouTube have a similar type of language to Twitter). Thus, augmenting our data from this YouTube comments data guarantee the compatibility of the language added with our given data. We have achieved a balanced dataset that contains approximately the same number of offensive and inoffensive samples.

For subtask B, we did not use the same technique used for sub-task A. Different reasons were behind this decision: insufficient hate speech examples in these datasets (only 468 tweets) (Mulki et al., 2019), some datasets are specific for one kind of hate speech, like religious hate speech (Albadi, Kurdi, and Mishra, 2018), and some datasets are specific for one or more Arabic dialectical form (example: Tunisian (Haddad, Mulki, and Oueslati, 2019) or Levantine (Mulki et al., 2019)). However, for future works, we intend to test augmenting our given data with the combination of all the existing hate speech datasets. Instead, we used the random oversampling technique by shuffling the words into hate speech tweets to create new samples. This method repeated many times over the undersampling class (hate speech) until each class in the dataset is represented apporoximately equally. Table 1 presents the number of tweets in each category before and after balancing.

	Before	After
Offensive	1330	7184
Inoffensive	5670	8705
Subtask A total	7000	15889
Hate Speech	361	7486
Not Hate Speech	6639	6639
Subtask B total	7000	14125

Table 1: Number of samples before and after balancing

3.3 Data Representation

The main idea of data representation is to represent words as feature vectors. Each entry in a word vector stands for one hidden feature inside the word meaning. Word embedding is one of the best data representation neural network depends on. Word embedding can reveal semantic or syntactic dependencies. We used the publically available Word2Vec Arabic model (AraVec) (Mohammad et al., 2017) that supports two types of words embeddings skipGram and CBOW, each of which has been trained on one of three datasets: tweets, Wikipedia articles, or web pages. AraVec also provides multiple dimensions for its word vectors. The choice of words embeddings used in this work is the vectors that was trained on the twitter dataset with the skipGram architecture. The choice of twitter model is to be compatible with the language used in the given dataset and also to ensure a huge cover of the dialectical words found on the tweets. We have further checked the overlap between our balanced dataset and the AraVec Twitter model. Table 2 shows the number of tokens that has been found on the final balanced datasets, number of dataset tokens found on the AraVec Twitter model and the percentage of overlapping between them.

N. of tokens	Balanced Dataset	AraVec Twitter	Overlapping
Sub-task A	40562	33777	83%
Sub-task B	24504	21592	88%

Table 2: Number of tokens found on the balanced datasets, dataset tokens found on the AraVec Twitter model, and the percentage of overlapping.

4. Proposed Approaches

Before introducing our attention based models. We will introduce two deep neural models; convolutional neural network and Gated Recurrent unit, and then augment these models with an attention layer, and finally compare the attention models with the original versions.

4.1 Convolutional Neural Network (CNN)

Although the main purpose of creating CNN was to convolve over image data, CNN have recently been used a lot in document classification, and experiment on textual data has shown improvements in multiple tasks (Kim, 2014). In this work, we use relatively the same model presented in (Kim, 2014), (Mohaouchane, Mourhir, and Nikolov, 2019), and (Gong et al., 2016), with some parameters' changes (number of filters and filter sizes). The

first layer of this model is an embedding layer (represents a lookup table for words already in the table, and others are initialized with random weights, and tuned jointly while learning). The second layer contains a number of filters with different filter sizes to capture different contextual features. Then, a Max-pooling layer was used to capture the most important features. After that, all feature vectors is concatenated together in order to be passed for a fully connected layer of one neuron. The output layer is responsible of classifying the tweet into a positive class (offensive/ hate speech) or a negative class (inoffensive/ not hate speech). We refer to this model as CNN. This model is shown at figure 1.

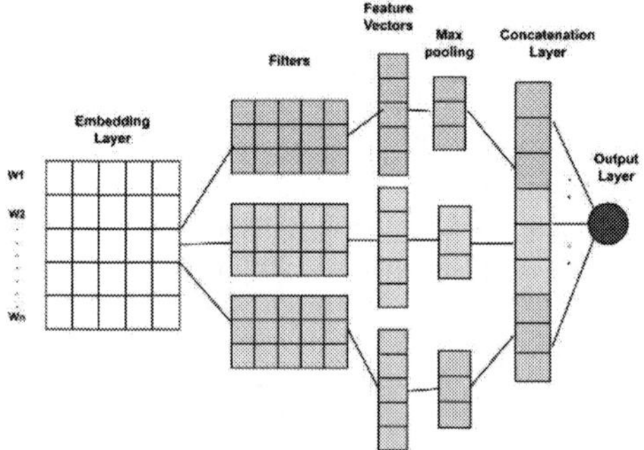

Figure 1: CNN Model

4.2 Bidirectional Gated Recurrent Unit (Bi-GRU)

Bidirectional GRUs are a type of bidirectional recurrent neural networks with only the input and forget gates. It allows for the use of information from both previous time steps and later time steps to make predictions about the current state. We stack two layers of bidirectional GRU on top of each other, followed by a fully connected layer of one neuron to predict the output. We refer to this model as Bi-GRU, figure 2 shows the model.

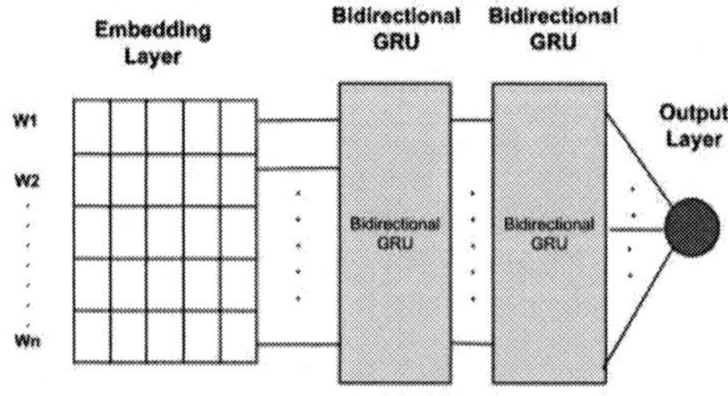

Figure 2: Bi-GRU Model

4.3 Convolution Neural Network with Attention (CNN_ATT)

Certainly, some words on the sentence plays more important role than others and some words are more important than others to the class of the tweet. (Bahdanau, Cho, and Bengio, 2014) was the first to present this type of attention in seq2seq model to improve machine translation model. After that, attention-based neural networks have been used in various tasks and achieved promising performance, such as (Gong et al., 2016) retweet prediction, (Xu et al., 2015) image captioning, (He and Golub, 2016) question answering, and so on.

In this section, we present a CNN neural network model augmented with an attention layer. Using an attention layer after the max pooling layer can learn which max pooled feature vectors are most important and thus learn which n-grams are most important for classification. So, after max pooling the feature vectors, they are stacked above each other and fed into an attention layer to learn the most important feature vectors. We refer to this model as CNN_ATT, Figure 3 shows the model.

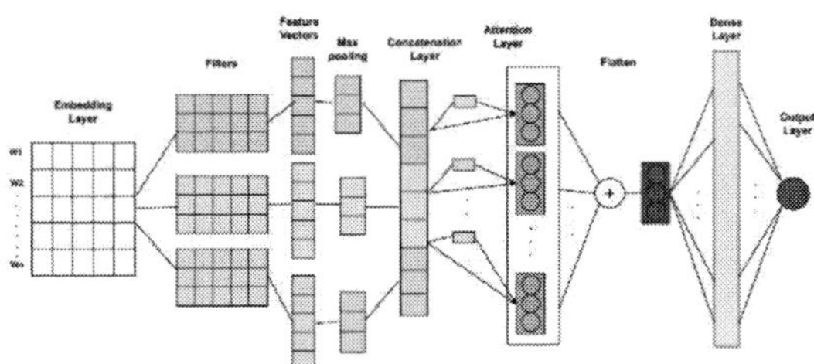

Figure 3: CNN_ATT Model

4.4 Bidirectional Gated Recurrent Unit with Attention (Bi-GRU_ATT)

Although Bidirectional Recurrent model has achieved a very good results in many tasks, they still treat all steps as equal. In this model, we stack the vectors of all computed steps, and then we calculate the score function of each step and then implement a folding layer to generate a context vector indicating the importance of each step vector. This is followed by one dense layer of 64 neurons with Relu activation function (to increase the nonlinear property of this model). After that, we add a fully connected layer with one neuron of a sigmoid activation function as the output layer. This model is referred as Bi-GRU_ATT and shown in figure 4.

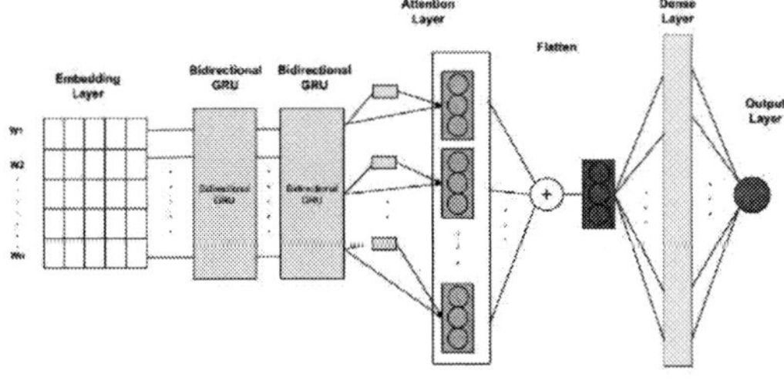

Figure 4: Bi-GRU_ATT Model

4.5 Basic machine Learning Models

We compared our proposed model with three basic machine learning classifiers (Ridge, SVM, and Logistic Regression). The Ridge classifier used RMSE and l2 penalty on both bag of word features (Bow_Ridge) or Tf-idf features (Tf-idf_Ridge). The SVM classifier was trained on bag of word (Bow_SVM) or tf-idf features (Tf-idf_SVM). In this method, we conducted a grid search to obtain the best parameters of SVM kernel. The Logistic Regression classifier was trained on bag of word features (Bow_LR) or tf-idf features (Tf-idf_LR).

5. Experimental Results

For Subtask A and B, we used the Adam optimizer, to adapt the learning rate and optimize the training of the neural networks. For both subtasks, we used the binary cross-entropy loss function. We also used an early stopping strategy based on a long-term moving-average of the F1 score evaluated at the end of every epoch.

Number of filters, recurrent units and neurons in dense layers have been optimized using a grid search. We used filter sizes of 1, 2, 3, and 4 to capture unigram, bigram, trigram, and quad-gram features. These filters are not organized in a sequential order, but rather in parallel to each other as shown in Fig. 1 and Fig. 3.

We used an early stopping strategy to determine the number of epochs that should be used. For other hyper-parameter optimization, we performed a manual twerking over successive runs on the validation set.

As a result, we found that the following parameters yielded the best validation performance based on our experiment.

- Maximum Tweet length= 100
- Filter sizes = [1,2,3,4]
- Number of Filters = 64
- Recurrent unit in Bidirectional GRUs' = 128, 64
- Neurons number in dense layers = 64
- Dropout rate = 0.2 and 0.3
- Batch size = 512
- Number of epochs = 5

To initialize the word vectors, the publicly available AraVec word vectors were used (Mohammad et al., 2017) (skipGram model from Twitter, with 1,476,715 tokens). The dimension of the vectors used is 100. Table 2 shows a good overlapping with our data, and for words that are not found in the vocabulary of pre-trained words, we initialized them with random vectors and tuned them while training.

Hereafter, we present our *validation* results. Table 3 and 4 lists the results of using various baseline machine learning classifiers (Bow_LR, Tf-idf_LR, Bow_Ridge, Bow_SVM, Tf-idf_Ridge, and Tf-idf_SVM).

Subtask A	Avg. Acc	Avg. P	Avg. R	Avg. F1
Bow_LR	0.86	0.77	0.79	0.78
Tf-idf_LR	0.85	0.75	0.79	0.77
Bow_Ridge	0.880	0.8	0.78	0.79
Tf-idf_Ridge	0.905	**0.85**	0.8	**0.83**
Bow_SVM	0.872	0.78	0.77	0.78
Tf-idf_SVM	**0.906**	**0.85**	**0.81**	**0.83**

Table 3: Performance of baseline models on subtask A

Subtask B	Avg. Acc	Avg. P	Avg. R	Avg. F1
Bow_LR	0.491	0.49	0.45	0.36
Tf-idf_LR	**0.492**	**0.51**	0.55	**0.37**
Bow_Ridge	0.463	0.5	0.49	0.35

Tf-idf_Ridge	0.462	**0.51**	**0.57**	0.36
Bow_SVM	0.391	0.49	0.46	0.31
Tf-idf_SVM	0.386	0.5	0.52	0.31

Table 4: Performance of baseline models on subtask B

Comparing the models of Tf-idf and Bow features, we can see that tf-idf features is relatively better than Bow features, which may be due to the tf-idf's ability to determine how relevant a given word is in a particular document. We can also observe that Tf-idf_SVM achieved a high performance on subtask A, this may be because SVM generalized better with nonlinear kernel that has been found by a grid search over its parameters.

Table 5 and 6 shows the comparison of the proposed models (CNN, Bi-GRU, CNN_ATT, and Bi-GRU_ATT) when evaluated on subtask task A and B respectively.

Subtask A	Avg. Acc	Avg. P	Avg. R	Avg. F1
CNN	0.92	0.63	0.84	0.85
CNN_ATT	0.92	0.86	0.85	**0.86**
Bi-GRU	0.91	0.85	**0.86**	0.85
Bi-GRU_ATT	**0.93**	**0.91**	0.83	**0.86**

Table 5: Performance of proposed models on subtask A

Subtask B	Avg. Acc	Avg. P	Avg. R	Avg. F1
CNN	0.91	0.63	0.78	0.67
CNN_ATT	0.9	0.63	**0.84**	0.67
Bi-GRU	0.92	0.65	0.78	0.69
Bi-GRU_ATT	**0.93**	**0.66**	0.79	**0.7**

Table 6: Performance of proposed models on subtask B

We can observe that baseline models was less efficient compared to our proposed models in both subtasks. The proposed models have increased the F1 measure of the baseline models on subtask B (from 37% to 70%). We also can observe that models augmented with attention layer can achieve a better performance than the models without the attention layer. The improvement is in the order of 1 to 2% in Recall and F1 score. However, attention layer has achieved a significant improvement in Precision, which means that attention layer helps in detecting the right offensive and hate speech words and thus raising precision. Bi-GRU_ATT achieved the highest accuracy, Precision and F1 score for both subtasks A and B, and outperformed the CNN models. This may be due to the fact that GRU models have more information of text sequence dependencies and order that CNN models does not have. These features seems to be very important for such tasks as shown in (Zhang and Luo, 2019).

Table 7 shows the results of our best model (Bi-GRU_ATT) evaluated on the *test* data.

Bi-GRU_ATT	Avg. Acc	Avg. P	Avg. R	Avg. F1
Subtask A	0.91	0.88	0.83	0.85
Subtask B	0.95	0.75	0.74	0.75

Table 7: *Test* performance of Bi-GRU_ATT on subtasks A and B

We observe that Bi-GRU_ATT performance on *test* data - for both subtasks is close to performance on the *validation* data, which is a good indication of a good generalization of the model. We can also notice that general performance on sub-task B is less efficient than performance on sub-task A, due to the hard separation of hate speech from other instances of offensive language.

6. Conclusion

In this paper, we tackle the problem of offensive language and hate speech detection. We proposed our methods for data preprocessing and balancing, and then we presented our Convolutional Neural Network (CNN) and bidirectional Gated Recurrent Unit (GRU) models used. After that, we augmented these models with attention layer. The best results achieved was using the Bidirectional Gated Recurrent Unit augmented with attention layer (Bi-GRU_ATT). Comparing the Precision results of models without attention layers and models with attention layer reveals that attention layer enabled our model to effectively select the relevant input series to the output class, and thus raising Precision score. Future work will consider the same problem working with both character-level and word-level features. Another improvement of models could be using LSTM instead of GRU to capture long range dependencies in tweets, which plays a big role in offensive language and hate speech detection tasks.

7. Bibliographical References

Alakrot, A., Murray, L., & Nikolov, N. S. (2018). Dataset construction for the detection of anti-social behaviour in online communication in Arabic. Procedia Computer Science, 142, 174-181.

Alakrot, A., Murray, L., & Nikolov, N. S. (2018). Towards accurate detection of offensive language in online communication in arabic. Procedia computer science, 142, 315-320.

Albadi, N., Kurdi, M., & Mishra, S. (2018, August). Are they our brothers? Analysis and detection of religious hate speech in the Arabic Twittersphere. In 2018 IEEE/ACM International Conference on Advances in Social Networks Analysis and Mining (ASONAM) (pp. 69-76). IEEE.

Al-Hassan, A., & Al-Dossari, H. (2019). Detection of hate speech in social networks: a survey on multilingual corpus. In 6th International Conference on Computer Science and Information Technology.

Badjatiya, P., Gupta, S., Gupta, M., & Varma, V. (2017, April). Deep learning for hate speech detection in tweets. In Proceedings of the 26th International Conference on World Wide Web Companion (pp. 759-760).

Bahdanau, D., Cho, K., & Bengio, Y. (2014). Neural machine translation by jointly learning to align and translate. arXiv preprint arXiv:1409.0473.

Cambray, A., & Podsadowski, N. (2019). Bidirectional Recurrent Models for Offensive Tweet Classification. arXiv preprint arXiv:1903.08808.

Cui, Y., Jia, M., Lin, T. Y., Song, Y., & Belongie, S. (2019). Class-balanced loss based on effective number of samples. In Proceedings of the IEEE Conference on Computer Vision and Pattern Recognition (pp. 9268-9277).

Gambäck, B., & Sikdar, U. K. (2017, August). Using convolutional neural networks to classify hate-speech. In

Proceedings of the first workshop on abusive language online (pp. 85-90).

Golub, D., & He, X. (2016). Character-level question answering with attention. arXiv preprint arXiv:1604.00727.

Haddad, H., Mulki, H., & Oueslati, A. (2019, October). T-HSAB: A Tunisian Hate Speech and Abusive Dataset. In International Conference on Arabic Language Processing (pp. 251-263). Springer, Cham.

Kim, Y. (2014). Convolutional neural networks for sentence classification. arXiv preprint arXiv:1408.5882.

Mohaouchane, H., Mourhir, A., & Nikolov, N. S. (2019, October). Detecting Offensive Language on Arabic Social Media Using Deep Learning. In 2019 Sixth International Conference on Social Networks Analysis, Management and Security (SNAMS) (pp. 466-471). IEEE.

Mubarak, H., Darwish, K., & Magdy, W. (2017, August). Abusive language detection on Arabic social media. In Proceedings of the First Workshop on Abusive Language Online (pp. 52-56).

Mubarak, H., Darwish, K., Magdy, W., Elsayed, T., & Al-Khalifa, H. (2020). Overview of OSACT4 Arabic Offensive Language Detection Shared Task. Proceedings of the 4th Workshop on Open-Source Arabic Corpora and Processing Tools (OSACT), 4.

Mulki, H., Haddad, H., Ali, C. B., & Alshabani, H. (2019, August). L-HSAB: A Levantine Twitter Dataset for Hate Speech and Abusive Language. In Proceedings of the Third Workshop on Abusive Language Online (pp. 111-118).

Salem, F. (2017). Social media and the internet of things towards data-driven policymaking in the Arab world: potential, limits and concerns. The Arab Social Media Report, Dubai: MBR School of Government, 7.

Soliman, A. B., Eissa, K., & El-Beltagy, S. R. (2017). Aravec: A set of arabic word embedding models for use in arabic nlp. Procedia Computer Science, 117, 256-265.

Xu, K., Ba, J., Kiros, R., Cho, K., Courville, A., Salakhudinov, R., ... & Bengio, Y. (2015, June). Show, attend and tell: Neural image caption generation with visual attention. In International conference on machine learning (pp. 2048-2057).

Zhang, Q., Gong, Y., Wu, J., Huang, H., & Huang, X. (2016, October). Retweet prediction with attention-based deep neural network. In Proceedings of the 25th ACM international on conference on information and knowledge management (pp. 75-84).

Zhang, Z., & Luo, L. (2019). Hate speech detection: A solved problem? The challenging case of long tail on twitter. Semantic Web, 10(5), 925-945.

Proceedings of the 4th Workshop on Open-Source Arabic Corpora and Processing Tools, pages 82–85
with a Shared Task on Offensive Language Detection.
Language Resources and Evaluation Conference (LREC 2020), Marseille, 11–16 May 2020
© European Language Resources Association (ELRA), licensed under CC-BY-NC

Offensive Language Detection in Arabic using ULMFiT

Mohamed Abdellatif, Ahmed Elgammal

Rutgers University - Computer Science
Piscataway, NJ, USA
{mma215, elgammal}@cs.rutgers.edu

Abstract

In this paper, we approach the shared task OffenseEval 2020 by Mubarak et al. (2020) using ULMFiT Howard and Ruder (2018) pre-trained on Arabic Wikipedia Khooli (2019) which we use as a starting point and use the target data-set to fine-tune it. The data set of the task is highly imbalanced. We train forward and backward models and ensemble the results. We report confusion matrix, accuracy, precision, recall and F_1 of the development set and report summarized results of the test set. Transfer learning method using ULMFiT shows potential for Arabic text classification.

Keywords: language models, text classification, transfer learning, opinion mining

1. Introduction

Imbalanced data set is a data set that has at least one (minority) class with *significantly* smaller population than others (majority). If the minority class is a label of interest (to study and predict), imbalanced data represents a challenge since during the training there is relatively no sufficient representation of the minority class(es) to stand out in the trained model. Examples of applications include: finance (e.g. fraud transaction detection), security (e.g. intrusion detection), networking (e.g. anomaly traffic detection), systems (e.g. irregular resource usage detection), medical (e.g. disease [e.g. cancer] detection), nature (e.g. volcano eruption, earthquake, tsunami predictions) and text processing (e.g. opinion mining and spotting hate speech).

Opinion mining and spotting hate speech in the context of social networking using deep learning attracted researchers' attention recently. For example, Park & Fung combined results from CNN (convolutional neural network) and LR (logistic regression) in Park and Fung (2017). They applied their method on the data set by Waseem and Hovy (2016). The same data-set was subject for experimenting a combination of both convolutional and recurrent units by Zhang et al. in Zhang et al. (2018).

State of the art text classification has been recently pushed forward by the advancements of the Transfer Learning (e.g. Devlin et al. (2018), Howard and Ruder (2018) and Radford et al. (2018))

From the work by Mahendran and Vedaldi (2016), inspecting neural network of more than one layer that was trained on a certain data-set of images (say a cats vs dogs binary classification task), the earlier layers tend to capture high level features (e.g. edges, contours .. etc) while the later layers tend to capture low level features (e.g. dogs faces, cats faces .. etc). Even though both types of features are extracted from the same data-set, the high level one is more general so it can be made use of in training the same network for a different task (since almost any kind of image classification will benefit from capturing edges and contours [and similarly general image features] in the weights of the model as concluded by Sharif Razavian et al. (2014)). Observing that, Howard & Ruder (Howard and Ruder (2018)) applied gradual unfreezing associated with dis-

criminative fine-tuning and slanted triangular learning rates (as concluded by Smith (2017)) and successfully apply it on text classification.

Our goal is to investigate applying ULMFiT on the imbalanced Arabic data-sets OffenseEval 2020. Khooli pre-trained ULMFiT on Arabic Wikipedia in Khooli (2019). We use their model as a starting point and use the Arabic data-set of interest to fine tune it.

The rest of the paper is organized as follows: we illustrate the data-sets properties in section 2.. In section 4. we describe the model, training parameters and experiments. We show results in section 5. and finally conclude the work in section 6..

2. Data sets

For this work, we use data provided by the organizers of OSACT4. The target of the shared task is to achieve as high macro F_1 score as possible. 10k Arabic tweets were collected. They are splitted to train (7k), development (1k) and test (2k) subsets. The train and development are released along with labels while the test set is released without them. The task has two sub tasks, sub task A is classifying the tweet as 'offensive' vs 'not offensive' while sub task B is about classifying the tweet as 'hateful' vs 'not hateful'. So each tweet is labeled twice. The labeled data sets in both cases are imbalanced with sub task B more so than A.

2.1. Sub task A

A tweet is considered *offensive* if it has any level of profanity. Table 1 shows instances count of different classes of sub task A. As the table shows the distribution of both training and development data sets show imbalance between the two existing classes.

2.2. Sub task B

A tweet is considered *hateful* if it has an attack against one or more person based on their nationality, ethnicity, gender, political affiliation, sport affiliation or religious belief. Table 2 shows instances count of different classes of sub task B. As the table shows the distribution of both training and development data sets show imbalance between the two ex-

Figure 1: Part of vocabulary words

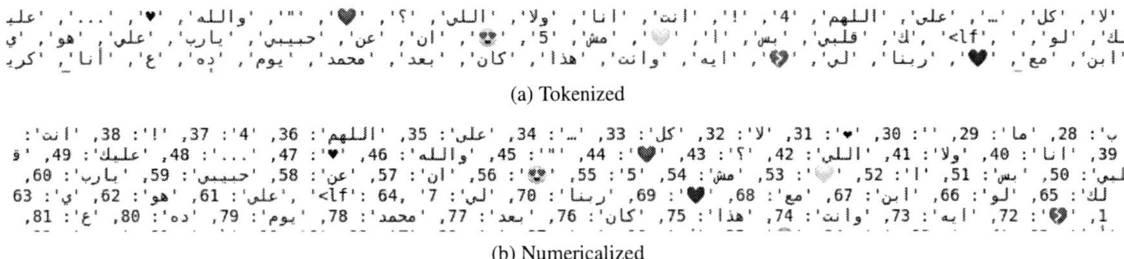

Class	Train	Development	Test
Not offensive (regular)	5.6k	821	-
Offensive	1.4k	179	-
Total	7k	1k	2k

Table 1: Classes distribution of sub task A

isting classes that is more significant than in case of sub task A.

3. Approach

3.1. Pre-processing

We do simple tokenization based on white-spaces and keep words that appeared more frequently than a certain threshold (replaced by 'xxunk'). Since pre-processing is not specific to Arabic, we kept all the non-Arabic words as long as they exist above the threshold (e.g. mentions). Among the special tokens: 'xxpad' is a padding token, 'xxeos' is an end of scentence token, 'xxup' is used to indicate the next word is capitalized (for English parts), 'xxrep' and 'xxwrep' are used to indicate repetition. After segmentation/tokenization, we convert the set of tokens to unique ids. Figure 1 shows part of the resulting vocabulary.

3.2. Method

Language modeling is a problem that deals with learning the joint probability function of sequences of words in this language. Such that given a sequence of a certain number of words, it can assigns a probability for it (as defined in Bengio et al. (2003)).

Inductive transfer learning is to make use of the knowledge learned by training a model (model A) on a source problem to be used towards building another model (model B) that handles a target (different) problem (as defined in Ruder et al. (2019)). In the case of ULMFiT, the source problem is unlabeled (language modeling) and the target problem is (text classification).

ULMFiT transfer learning method (by Howard and Ruder (2018)) can be summarized as three steps applied on two neural networks. The first neural network is a Language Model (LM) the second one is a text classifier. The three steps are 1- pre-training the LM on a general corpus (we used the model by Khooli (2019) for this step), 2- ~~training~~ fine-tuning the LM on the target data-set and then saving a part off the LM (the encoder) and 3- Loading the saved part of the LM (result of step 2) and attaching it to the classifier then ~~train~~ fine-tuning the classifier with the target data-set. Following Howard and Ruder (2018) For both the language model and classifier networks, we used LSTM AWD (by Merity et al. (2017)) which uses a 3 layers LSTM.

4. Experimental Setup

4.1. Experiments

Following the original work by Howard and Ruder (2018), we fine-tune two separate (forward and backward) models, classify twice and average results for each sub-task. That was shown to be always better on all the six of the English data-sets experimented on by Howard and Ruder (2018). We report three different sets of results for each sub task as well to study whether the same conclusion can be made on Arabic imbalanced data-set in question.

Since the source task of the transfer learning (language modeling) needs unlabeled data, we use all the available unlabeled Arabic text (both train and validation) to fine-tune and save (forward and backward) language models and use their encoders for two separate classifiers (two [forward and backward] for each sub task).

4.2. Settings and training

We use fastai library [1] and adjust the hyper-parameters based on the observed performance of training on the development set. The forward language model was trained for 2 epochs while the backward one was trained for 3. After applying a 3-steps of gradual unfreezing, both the forward and the backward classifiers of sub task A were unfrozen and fine-tuned for 3 epochs. Similar steps were followed for sub task B, except we ended up with 30 epochs for fine tuning the forward classifier and only 3 to fine tune the backward one. We use an Nvidia Titan X with 12 GB of memory that allowed us to use a batch size of 64.

---

[1] https://github.com/fastai/fastai

Class	Train	Development	Test
Not hateful (regular)	6.6k	956	-
Hateful	0.4k	44	-
Total	7k	1k	2k

Table 2: Classes distribution of sub task B

Model	Accuracy	Weighted			Macro		
		precision	recall	F_1	precision	recall	F_1
Forward	86	85	86	85	77	71	74
Backward	87	87	87	87	78	78	78
Averaged	89	88	89	89	82	78	80

Table 3: Validation results (%) of sub-task A

5. Results

We report accuracy, weighted and macro F_1 as evaluation metrics for the validation set while we report accuracy and only the macro F_1 for the test set. F_1 is the harmonic mean of Precision (the ratio between the true positives and all the positive) and Recall (the ratio between the true positives and all the true). The macro version adds the metrics values of separate classes with equaly weights while the weighted version weights them by the ratio of class population. Recall that Both the language model and the classifier networks use AWD LSTM (Merity et al. (2017)).

5.1. Validation results

Table 3 presents validation results of sub task A while table 4 present task B. Since we have access to validation labels, we show the results of the forward, backward and averaged models. Since weighted measures favor majority classes (they aggregate using a weighted average), they are not very descriptive of the performance in case of imbalanced datasets where the minority class is important (like in our case). This can be seen from the tables. In terms of validation results, training two models instead of one and averaging results boosts the results in terms of macro F_1 in both sub tasks. The confusion matrix of the validation set is illustrated in figure 2.

5.2. Test results

Table 5 shows the test results of both sub tasks. Inspecting this table, the imbalance of the data-sets under question renders accuracy metric not descriptive of the performance. The very low population minor classes (offensive and hateful tweets in tasks A and B respectively) receive little attention from the trained classifier (relative to the majority class) since they are not as well represented in the training either. This is reflected in the low recall which drags F_1 down.

6. Conclusion and future work

We applied ULMFiT pre-trained on Arabic Wikipedia to approach the problem of classifying imbalanced Arabic data sets. Experiments on imbalanced data-sets of OffenseEval 2020 show that using two models (forward and

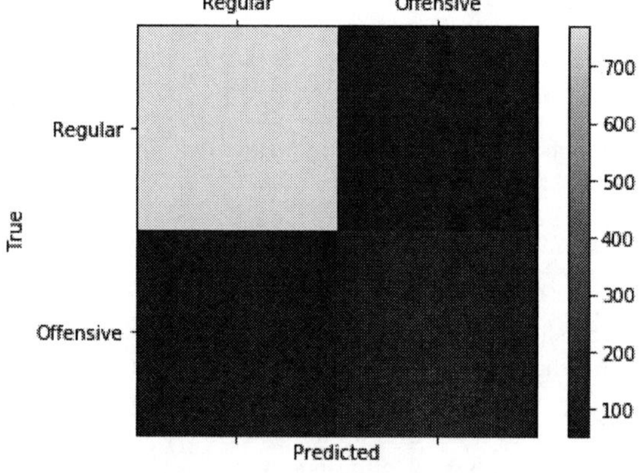

(a) Sub task A

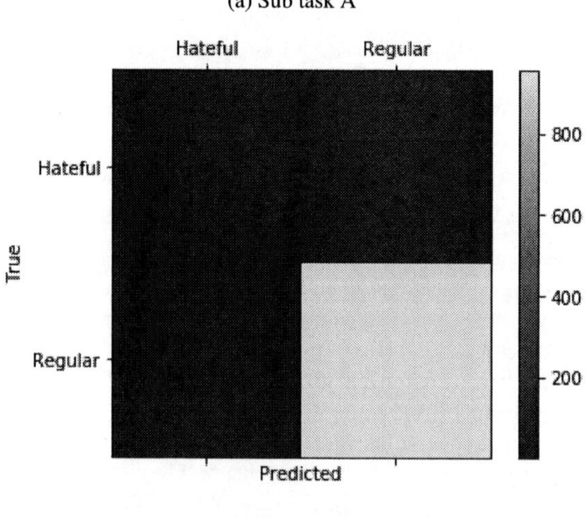

(b) Sub task B

Figure 2: Confusion matrix

backward) helps the final result in terms of macro F_1. Arabic-specific tokenization (e.g. based on Arabic morphological rules) may help building a better representation of Arabic text and hence improve performance, we leave this for future work. Another avenue for future work would be

Model	Accuracy	Weighted			Macro		
		Precision	Recall	F_1	Precision	Recall	F_1
Forward	96	94	96	94	75	57	60
Backward	96	95	96	95	77	58	61
Averaged	96	95	96	95	86	57	61

Table 4: Validation results (%) of sub-task B

Sub task	Accuracy	Macro		
		precision	recall	F_1
A	86	79	76	77
B	95	75	56	58

Table 5: Test results (%)

using generative models (e.g. language modelling) as a way of over-sampling the minor classes in imbalanced data sets. It can be experimented with by its own or associated with other (existing) techniques (e.g. random Ghazikhani et al. (2012) and SMOTE Chawla et al. (2002)).

7. Bibliographical References

References

Y. Bengio, R. Ducharme, P. Vincent, and C. Jauvin. A neural probabilistic language model. *Journal of machine learning research*, 3(Feb):1137–1155, 2003.

N. V. Chawla, K. W. Bowyer, L. O. Hall, and W. P. Kegelmeyer. Smote: synthetic minority over-sampling technique. *Journal of artificial intelligence research*, 16: 321–357, 2002.

J. Devlin, M.-W. Chang, K. Lee, and K. Toutanova. Bert: Pre-training of deep bidirectional transformers for language understanding. *arXiv preprint arXiv:1810.04805*, 2018.

A. Ghazikhani, H. S. Yazdi, and R. Monsefi. Class imbalance handling using wrapper-based random oversampling. In *20th Iranian Conference on Electrical Engineering (ICEE2012)*, pages 611–616. IEEE, 2012.

J. Howard and S. Ruder. Universal language model fine-tuning for text classification. *arXiv preprint arXiv:1801.06146*, 2018.

A. Khooli. Applied data science. `https://github.com/abedkhooli/ds2`, 2019.

A. Mahendran and A. Vedaldi. Visualizing deep convolutional neural networks using natural pre-images. *International Journal of Computer Vision*, 120(3):233–255, 2016.

S. Merity, N. S. Keskar, and R. Socher. Regularizing and optimizing lstm language models. *arXiv preprint arXiv:1708.02182*, 2017.

H. Mubarak, K. Darwish, W. Magdy, T. Elsayed, and H. Al-Khalifa. Overview of osact4 arabic offensive language detection shared task. 4, 2020.

J. H. Park and P. Fung. One-step and two-step classification for abusive language detection on twitter. *arXiv preprint arXiv:1706.01206*, 2017.

A. Radford, K. Narasimhan, T. Salimans, and I. Sutskever. Improving language understanding by generative pre-training. *URL https://s3-us-west-2. amazonaws. com/openai-assets/researchcovers/languageunsupervised/language understanding paper. pdf*, 2018.

S. Ruder, M. E. Peters, S. Swayamdipta, and T. Wolf. Transfer learning in natural language processing. In *Proceedings of the 2019 Conference of the North American Chapter of the Association for Computational Linguistics: Tutorials*, pages 15–18, 2019.

A. Sharif Razavian, H. Azizpour, J. Sullivan, and S. Carlsson. Cnn features off-the-shelf: an astounding baseline for recognition. In *Proceedings of the IEEE conference on computer vision and pattern recognition workshops*, pages 806–813, 2014.

L. N. Smith. Cyclical learning rates for training neural networks. In *2017 IEEE Winter Conference on Applications of Computer Vision (WACV)*, pages 464–472. IEEE, 2017.

Z. Waseem and D. Hovy. Hateful symbols or hateful people? predictive features for hate speech detection on twitter. In *Proceedings of the NAACL student research workshop*, pages 88–93, 2016.

Z. Zhang, D. Robinson, and J. Tepper. Detecting hate speech on twitter using a convolution-gru based deep neural network. In *European semantic web conference*, pages 745–760. Springer, 2018.

Proceedings of the 4th Workshop on Open-Source Arabic Corpora and Processing Tools, pages 86–90
with a Shared Task on Offensive Language Detection.
Language Resources and Evaluation Conference (LREC 2020), Marseille, 11–16 May 2020
© European Language Resources Association (ELRA), licensed under CC-BY-NC

Multitask Learning for Arabic Offensive Language and Hate-Speech Detection

Ibrahim Abu-Farha[1] and Walid Magdy[1,2]
[1] School of Informatics, The University of Edinburgh
Edinburgh, United Kingdom
[2] The Alan Turing Institute
London, United Kingdom
i.abufarha@ed.ac.uk, wmagdy@inf.ed.ac.uk

Abstract

Offensive language and hate-speech are phenomena that spread with the rising popularity of social media. Detecting such content is crucial for understanding and predicting conflicts, understanding polarisation among communities and providing means and tools to filter or block inappropriate content. This paper describes the SMASH team submission to OSACT4's shared task on hate-speech and offensive language detection, where we explore different approaches to perform these tasks. The experiments cover a variety of approaches that include deep learning, transfer learning and multitask learning. We also explore the utilisation of sentiment information to perform the previous task. Our best model is a multitask learning architecture, based on CNN-BiLSTM, that was trained to detect hate-speech and offensive language and predict sentiment.

Keywords: Arabic, hate-speech, offensive language

1   Introduction

Social media platforms provide a versatile medium for people to communicate with each other, share ideas and express opinions. These user-driven platforms have a challenge when it comes to controlling the content being fed into them. People have different intentions, while some might use these platforms for their intended purposes, others might be sharing inappropriate content such as pornographic images or racist speech towards others. Detecting such content is very important for these platforms. For example, it is necessary to add filtration features to hide adult-only content in order to protect children (Mubarak et al., 2017). Also, such detection systems are important to provide real time monitoring of the content being fed to these platforms, which could be promoting hate crimes or racism against various groups of people. An early detection of this phenomena could help in preventing the escalation from speech to actions (Waseem and Hovy, 2016). Platforms such as Twitter, Facebook and YouTube are putting effort into fighting the spread of hate-speech, racism and xenophobia on their platforms. Thus, having robust detection systems is extremely important (Waseem and Hovy, 2016). According to Cambridge Dictionary[1] hate-speech is defined as "public speech that expresses hate or encourages violence towards a person or group based on something such as race, religion, sex or sexual orientation". There has been a large amount of studies on how to automatically detect hate-speech, offensive language and obscene content. The approaches vary from using word-lists, syntactic and semantic features to deep learning models.

This paper is a description of our submission (SMASH team) to the shared task of offensive language and hate-speech detection (Mubarak et al., 2020). This task is a part of the Open-Source Arabic Corpora and Corpora Processing Tools (OSACT4) workshop. In this paper, we explore various approaches to detect hate-speech and offensive language, which include deep learning, transfer learning and multitask learning. Our best model is a multitask learning architecture that was trained to detect both hate-speech and offensive language.

2   Related Work

There has been some work on tasks related to hate-speech and offensive language detection, especially in English. Most of the work view the problem as a classification task where the goal is to assign a specific label to a given input. Early work on such task includes (Yin et al., 2009), where the authors used multiple features such as n-grams and sentiment to train a classifier for harassment detection. In their work, they used a manually labelled dataset of discussion threads. Razavi et al. (2010) proposed a multilevel classifier to detect offensive messages, in which they utilised a set of manually collected words and phrases. Nobata et al. (2016) proposed a machine learning based approach for abusive language detection. They utilised multiple features such as n-grams, linguistic features, syntactic features and word embeddings. They also created a new dataset using comments from Yahoo Finance and News. Davidson et al. (2017) built a corpus of tweets that contain hate-speech. In their work, they utilised a lexicon of hate-speech keywords in order to collect relevant tweets. The collected data was labelled into three classes: hate-speech, offensive language and neither. They built a classifier to detect hate-speech, their analysis showed that raciest and homophobic are likely to be classified as hate-speech. In (Malmasi and Zampieri, 2017), the authors trained an SVM classifier for hate-speech detection, the classifier relies on n-gram based features. In 2019, OffensEval (Zampieri et al., 2019) was introduced to be part of SemEval. This competition has multiple sub-tasks such as offensive language detection, offence categorisation and offence target identification. Regarding Arabic, there were few attempts to approach the problems of offensive language and hate-speech detection. These include the work of Mubarak et al. (2017), where the

---

[1]https://dictionary.cambridge.org/dictionary/english/

authors proposed a method to automatically expand word lists for obscene and offensive content. In their work, they created an initial list of seed words, which was used to collect a set of tweets. From the collected tweets, they extracted the patterns that are used to express offensiveness. They followed that with manual assessment and used other resources to create the final word-list. In another work (Mubarak and Darwish, 2019), the authors used the word-list as a seed to create a training set, which they used to experiment with and create an offensive language detector. Alakrot et al. (2018) proposed a method to detect abusive language, they used SVM with n-gram features for the classification where they achieved an F1-score of 0.82. They collected their own dataset from YouTube comments. Albadi et al. (2018) created a dataset of religious hate-speech discussions on Twitter, they used this data to train an RNN based classifier for automatic detection of hate-speech, they achieved 0.84 Area under the ROC curve. The authors also used their dataset to create multiple hate-speech lexicons. Haidar et al. (2017) experimented with cyberbullying detection, where they utilised a dataset that they collected from Facebook and Twitter. They used n-gram features and experimented with multiple classifiers such as Naive Bayes and SVM.

3 Dataset Description

The dataset is the same one provided in SemEval 2020 Arabic offensive language task. It consists of 10,000 tweets labelled for offensive language and hate-speech. The annotation assumes that a tweet is offensive if it contains an insult, attack or inappropriate language. While a tweet is assumed to contain hate-speech if it was directed towards a group or an entity. Table 1 shows the statistics of the training and development sets. The test set, which contains 2000 tweets, was not released for evaluation purposes.

Label	Training Set	Development Set
Hate-Speech	361	44
Non hate-speech	6,639	956
Offensive	1,410	179
Non-offensive	5,590	821

Table 1: Dataset statistics.

4 Proposed Models

In this section, we provide details of the different steps and models we used in the experiments.

4.1 Data Preprocessing

This step is important in order to clean data from unnecessary content and transform it into a coherent form, which can be processed and analysed easily. Since we are using Mazajak's word embeddings (Abu Farha and Magdy, 2019), we used the same steps used by the authors as follows:

- Letter normalisation: unifying the letters that appear in different forms. We replace { أ ، إ ، آ } with {ا}, {ة} with {ه} and {ى} with {ي} (Darwish et al., 2014).

- Elongation removal: removing the repeated letters which might appear specially in social media data (Darwish et al., 2012).

- Cleaning: removing unknown characters, diacritics, punctuation, URLs, etc.

4.2 Text Representation

In this step, we transform textual data into a representation that can be used for the task we are aiming to accomplish. There are different ways to represent textual information, in our implementation we use word embeddings. Word embeddings are a dense vector representation of the words, we utilised the word embeddings provided by (Abu Farha and Magdy, 2019). These are skip-gram word2vec embeddings, which were built using a corpus of 250M tweets.

4.3 Models

This section provides details of the different approaches and models tested for the different tasks.

BiLSTM

Long short-term memory (LSTM)(Hochreiter and Schmidhuber, 1997) networks are quite powerful at capturing relations over sequences. However, they capture the dependencies in one direction, and sometimes they might lose important information, here where bidirectional LSTMs (BiLSTM) are useful. BiLSTMs are two LSTMs where each one goes over the input in a different direction. This configuration allows the network to have a representation of the whole sequence at any point. The output of the LSTM is passed to a dense layer with softmax activation which emits the final output.

CNN-BiLSTM

This architecture consists of a convolutional neural network (CNN) followed by a BiLSTM network. Such architecture is commonly used in the literature for text classification tasks. The benefits of such architecture is that the CNN has the capability to capture patterns and correlations within the input. The CNN would work as a feature extractor and these features are fed into a BiLSTM network which captures dependencies within these features.

This architecture consists of a 1D convolutional layer followed by a max-pooling layer, then the BiLSTM part. Finally, we have a dense layers followed by the output layer.

Transfer Learning

Transfer learning has been a turning point in the field of computer vision which led to huge improvements and breakthroughs. In the last couple of years, the research in natural language processing (NLP) has caught up with the introduction of pre-trained language models such as Elmo(Peters et al., 2018) and ULMFit(Howard and Ruder, 2018). The introduction of Bidirectional Encoder Representation from Transformers (BERT) (Devlin et al., 2019) led to a revolution in the NLP world. BERT-based models achieved state-of-the-art results in many tasks. In the proposed architecture, we utilise a pre-trained language model and fine tune it for a specific task, i.e. transfer learning. In our experiments we use the multilingual BERT which was trained on 104 languages. It utilises a vocabulary of 110K WordPeice tokens. BERT's architecture consists of 12 layers with 768 hidden units in each of them, and 12 attention heads.

In the experiments we fine tune BERT to be used for classification. This is done by adding a fully connected layer and a softmax layer after the the pre-trained model. Then the model is trained for a small number of epochs to adjust the weights for the specific task.

Multitask Learning

In multitask learning (MTL), the objective is to utilise the process of learning multiple tasks in order to improve the performance on each of them (Caruana, 1997). These tasks are usually related and have some common aspects between them. Thus, having the model to learn these tasks would give it the ability to utilise some cues from one task to improve the other. MTL has been used to improve many NLP tasks such as syntactic chunking and POS-tagging (Søgaard and Goldberg, 2016), even BERT (Devlin et al., 2019) was built using multitask learning settings.

In this architecture, we utilise that the data is labelled for both tasks, hate-speech and offensive language. Based on the given definitions of the tasks and the annotated data, we can assume that if a sentence contains hate-speech, it is offensive. Thus, we try to utilise this correlation and train the model for both tasks at once (the model is called MTL).

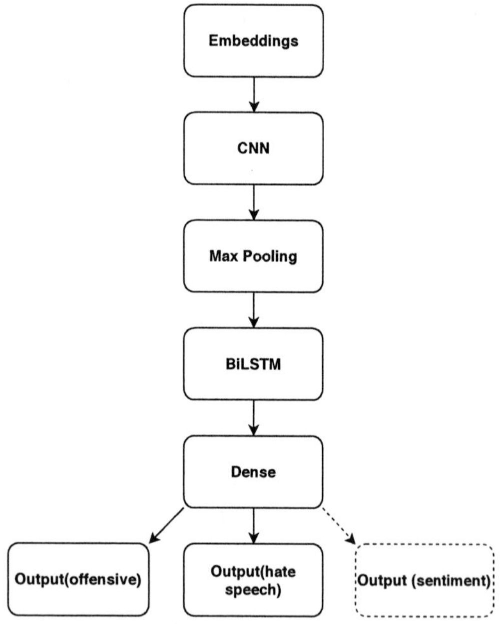

Figure 1: CNN-BiLSTM architecture in multitask learning configuration.

To extend this idea, we decided to incorporate more information through adding sentiment information. The reason for this is that offensive language or hate-speech are usually sentimental and express a negative emotion towards the target. In order get the sentiment labels, we used Mazajak sentiment analyser (Abu Farha and Magdy, 2019). With the sentiment labels added as an objective, the new model (MTL-S) learns to predict three labels, sentiment, hate-speech, and offensive language.

An issue that might occur is that when we use the sentiment from another system, we might be propagating some of error and uncertainty to the new model. In order to reduce such uncertainty in the sentiment labels, we had two variants of the experiment. In the first one, we used the labels returned from Mazajak as they are. In the second, we masked the sentiment to be negative if the sentence was originally labelled as hate-speech or offensive language. The notion behind this experiment is that a hate-speech or offensive content are always bearing negative sentiment, but those might be expressed in an indirect way which could result in an incorrect sentiment label, this model is called (MTL-S-N). In this architecture, we utilised the CNN-BiLSTM architecture, the only difference is that we have a forking before the output layer to accommodate for the different outputs as shown in Figure 1.

5   Performance and Evaluation

5.1   Experimental Setup

In the implementation, we used Python as the programming language for all the experiments. For the deep learning experiments, *Keras* (Chollet and others, 2015) was used on top of *Tensorflow* (Abadi et al., 2015) back-end. For all the experiments, *ReLU* activation and *Adam* optimiser with learning rate of 0.0001 were used. Table 2 shows the hyper-parameters for each Architecture. Regarding the experiments with BERT, we utilised HuggingFace's Transformers library (Wolf et al., 2019). We used the provided *BertForSequenceClassification* implementation along with BertAdam optimiser. We trained the models for 4 epochs with learning rate of $1e-5$. The maximum sequence length was set to the maximum length seen in the training set.

Hyper-parameter	BiLSTM	CNN-BiLSTM
#LSTM cells	128	128
recurrent dropout	0.2	0.2
dropout	0.2	0.2
#filters	-	300
filter size	-	3
pooling size	-	2
#hidden units	-	128

Table 2: Hyper-parameters used for each architecture.

5.2   Results and evaluation

We experimented with the different models mentioned previously. To have an initial measure of the performance, we used two different baselines. One where we always assign the majority label (baseline-1), this was done for both tasks. The second baseline (baseline-2) was Multinomial Naive Bayes (MNB) trained on unigram and bigram TF-IDF representation of the input. The evaluation metric for both tasks is macro-average F1-score. Table 3 shows the results on the development set. From the table, it is noticeable that the multitask learning models (MTL and MTL-S-N) achieved the best results on the development set. This shows that the extra information learned through learning multiple objectives was effective to improve the performance. It is noticeable that the BERT based model achieved relatively lower results compared to the other models. This is due to the fact that BERT has a limited vocabulary and was trained on the Arabic Wikipedia, which is in modern standard Arabic (MSA). Thus, BERT was not able to effectively handle the dialectal content within the dataset. In general, the models are better in detecting offensive language than hate-speech. This is due to the small number of training examples of hate-speech data.

Model	OFF	HS
baseline-1	0.450	0.490
baseline-2	0.490	0.390
BiLSTM	0.896	0.671
BERT	0.857	0.719
CNN-BiLSTM	0.901	0.702
MTL	0.899	**0.737**
MTL-S	0.899	0.712
MTL-S-N	**0.904**	0.730

Table 3: Macro F1 scores achieved on the development set for hate-speech (HS) and offensive language (OFF) detection tasks.

5.3 Submission Results

These tasks are part of a shared competition organised in OSACT4 (Mubarak et al., 2020), where we participated as SMASH team. For each task, we submitted the best performing model as our primary submission, the results are shown in Table 4. For the hate-speech task we submitted the MTL model which achieved a macro F1-score of 0.76 on the test set (ranked 6th out of 13). For the offensive language task, we submitted the MTL-S-N model which achieved and F1-score of 0.877 on test set (ranked 5th out of 14).

Model	OFF	HS
MTL	-	0.76
MTL-S-N	0.877	-

Table 4: Macro F1 scores achieved by the best models on the test set for hate-speech (HS) and offensive language (OFF) detection tasks.

6 Conclusion and Future Work

In this work, we presented our system to perform hate-speech and offensive language detection. The experiments show that using a multitask learning setting was extremely useful due to the high correlation between the two tasks. We also explored the effect of adding sentiment information, which proved to be useful. This is explained by the fact that hate-speech and offensive content always bear negative sentiment. Thus, sentiment information is correlated with hate-speech and offensive language. In the future, we hope to improve the results through the utilisation of other resources such as lexicons and experimenting with more multitask learning settings.

Acknowledgements

This work was supported by the D&S Programme of The Alan Turing Institute under the EPSRC grant EP/N510129/1.

7 References

Abadi, M., Agarwal, A., Barham, P., Brevdo, E., Chen, Z., Citro, C., Corrado, G. S., Davis, A., Dean, J., Devin, M., Ghemawat, S., Goodfellow, I., Harp, A., Irving, G., Isard, M., Jia, Y., Jozefowicz, R., Kaiser, L., Kudlur, M., Levenberg, J., Mané, D., Monga, R., Moore, S., Murray, D., Olah, C., Schuster, M., Shlens, J., Steiner, B., Sutskever, I., Talwar, K., Tucker, P., Vanhoucke, V., Vasudevan, V., Viégas, F., Vinyals, O., Warden, P., Wattenberg, M., Wicke, M., Yu, Y., and Zheng, X. (2015). TensorFlow: Large-scale machine learning on heterogeneous systems. Software available from tensorflow.org.

Abu Farha, I. and Magdy, W. (2019). Mazajak: An online Arabic sentiment analyser. In *Proceedings of the Fourth Arabic Natural Language Processing Workshop*, pages 192–198, Florence, Italy, August. Association for Computational Linguistics.

Alakrot, A., Murray, L., and Nikolov, N. S. (2018). Towards accurate detection of offensive language in online communication in arabic. *Procedia computer science*, 142:315–320.

Albadi, N., Kurdi, M., and Mishra, S. (2018). Are they our brothers? analysis and detection of religious hate speech in the arabic twittersphere. In *2018 IEEE/ACM International Conference on Advances in Social Networks Analysis and Mining (ASONAM)*, pages 69–76. IEEE.

Caruana, R. (1997). Multitask learning. *Machine learning*, 28(1):41–75.

Chollet, F. et al. (2015). Keras. https://keras.io.

Darwish, K., Magdy, W., and Mourad, A. (2012). Language processing for arabic microblog retrieval. In *Proceedings of the 21st ACM international conference on Information and knowledge management*, pages 2427–2430. ACM.

Darwish, K., Magdy, W., et al. (2014). Arabic information retrieval. *Foundations and Trends® in Information Retrieval*, 7(4):239–342.

Davidson, T., Warmsley, D., Macy, M., and Weber, I. (2017). Automated hate speech detection and the problem of offensive language. In *Eleventh international aaai conference on web and social media*.

Devlin, J., Chang, M.-W., Lee, K., and Toutanova, K. (2019). BERT: Pre-training of deep bidirectional transformers for language understanding. In *Proceedings of the 2019 Conference of the North American Chapter of the Association for Computational Linguistics: Human Language Technologies, Volume 1 (Long and Short Papers)*, pages 4171–4186, Minneapolis, Minnesota, June. Association for Computational Linguistics.

Haidar, B., Chamoun, M., and Serhrouchni, A. (2017). A multilingual system for cyberbullying detection: Arabic content detection using machine learning. *Advances in Science, Technology and Engineering Systems Journal*, 2(6):275–284.

Hochreiter, S. and Schmidhuber, J. (1997). Long short-term memory. *Neural Computation*, 9(8):1735–1780.

Howard, J. and Ruder, S. (2018). Universal language model fine-tuning for text classification. In *Proceedings of the 56th Annual Meeting of the Association for Computational Linguistics (Volume 1: Long Papers)*, pages 328–339, Melbourne, Australia, July. Association for Computational Linguistics.

Malmasi, S. and Zampieri, M. (2017). Detecting hate speech in social media. In *Proceedings of the International Conference Recent Advances in Natural Language Processing, RANLP 2017*, pages 467–472, Varna, Bulgaria, September. INCOMA Ltd.

Mubarak, H. and Darwish, K. (2019). Arabic offensive language classification on twitter. In *International Conference on Social Informatics*, pages 269–276. Springer.

Mubarak, H., Darwish, K., and Magdy, W. (2017). Abusive language detection on Arabic social media. In *Proceedings of the First Workshop on Abusive Language Online*, pages 52–56, Vancouver, BC, Canada, August. Association for Computational Linguistics.

Mubarak, H., Darwish, K., Magdy, W., Elsayed, T., and Al-Khalifa, H. (2020). Overview of osact4 arabic offensive language detection shared task. 4.

Nobata, C., Tetreault, J., Thomas, A., Mehdad, Y., and Chang, Y. (2016). Abusive language detection in online user content. In *Proceedings of the 25th International Conference on World Wide Web*, WWW '16, page 145–153, Republic and Canton of Geneva, CHE. International World Wide Web Conferences Steering Committee.

Peters, M., Neumann, M., Iyyer, M., Gardner, M., Clark, C., Lee, K., and Zettlemoyer, L. (2018). Deep contextualized word representations. In *Proceedings of the 2018 Conference of the North American Chapter of the Association for Computational Linguistics: Human Language Technologies, Volume 1 (Long Papers)*, pages 2227–2237, New Orleans, Louisiana, June. Association for Computational Linguistics.

Razavi, A. H., Inkpen, D., Uritsky, S., and Matwin, S. (2010). Offensive language detection using multi-level classification. In *Canadian Conference on Artificial Intelligence*, pages 16–27. Springer.

Søgaard, A. and Goldberg, Y. (2016). Deep multi-task learning with low level tasks supervised at lower layers. In *Proceedings of the 54th Annual Meeting of the Association for Computational Linguistics (Volume 2: Short Papers)*, pages 231–235, Berlin, Germany, August. Association for Computational Linguistics.

Waseem, Z. and Hovy, D. (2016). Hateful symbols or hateful people? predictive features for hate speech detection on twitter. In *Proceedings of the NAACL Student Research Workshop*, pages 88–93, San Diego, California, June. Association for Computational Linguistics.

Wolf, T., Debut, L., Sanh, V., Chaumond, J., Delangue, C., Moi, A., Cistac, P., Rault, T., Louf, R., Funtow-icz, M., and Brew, J. (2019). Huggingface's transformers: State-of-the-art natural language processing. *ArXiv*, abs/1910.03771.

Yin, D., Xue, Z., Hong, L., Davison, B. D., Kontostathis, A., and Edwards, L. (2009). Detection of harassment on web 2.0. *Proceedings of the Content Analysis in the WEB*, 2:1–7.

Zampieri, M., Malmasi, S., Nakov, P., Rosenthal, S., Farra, N., and Kumar, R. (2019). SemEval-2019 task 6: Identifying and categorizing offensive language in social media (OffensEval). In *Proceedings of the 13th International Workshop on Semantic Evaluation*, pages 75–86, Minneapolis, Minnesota, USA, June. Association for Computational Linguistics.

Proceedings of the 4th Workshop on Open-Source Arabic Corpora and Processing Tools, pages 91–96
with a Shared Task on Offensive Language Detection.
Language Resources and Evaluation Conference (LREC 2020), Marseille, 11–16 May 2020
© European Language Resources Association (ELRA), licensed under CC-BY-NC

Combining Character and Word Embeddings for the Detection of Offensive Language in Arabic

Abdullah I. Alharbi[1,2], Mark Lee[1]
[1]School of Computer Science, University of Birmingham, Birmingham, UK
[2]Faculty of Computing and Information Technology, King Abdulaziz University, Rabigh, KSA
{aia784, m.g.lee}@cs.bham.ac.uk
aamalharbe@kau.edu.sa

Abstract

Twitter and other social media platforms offer users the chance to share their ideas via short posts. While the easy exchange of ideas has value, these microblogs can be leveraged by people who want to share hatred. and such individuals can share negative views about an individual, race, or group with millions of people at the click of a button. There is thus an urgent need to establish a method that can automatically identify hate speech and offensive language. To contribute to this development, during the OSACT4 workshop, a shared task was undertaken to detect offensive language in Arabic. A key challenge was the uniqueness of the language used on social media, prompting the out-of-vocabulary (OOV) problem. In addition, the use of different dialects in Arabic exacerbates this problem. To deal with the issues associated with OOV, we generated a character-level embeddings model, which was trained on a massive data collected carefully. This level of embeddings can work effectively in resolving the problem of OOV words through its ability to learn the vectors of character n-grams or parts of words. The proposed systems were ranked 7th and 8th for Subtasks A and B, respectively.

Keywords: character-level embeddings, word-level embeddings, Arabic offensive language detection

1. Introduction

Microblogging platforms, such as Twitter, offer users a channel through which they can share ideas and opinions via short messages. In the case of Twitter, these are known as tweets. While social media channels can be used for constructive purposes, they can also be exploited by people who wish to share their hatred. These people can share their negative views about an individual, a race or a group with millions of people at the click of a button. To counteract this, there is a significant need to develop an effective method that will automatically identify messages containing offensive language or hate speech. Much research has been undertaken on detecting offensive language in English, but as yet, little research has focused on the detection of offensive language in Arabic (Mubarak and Darwish, 2019).

To contribute to the development of this area, a shared task on 'Arabic offensive language detection' was conducted at the OSACT4 workshop (Mubarak et al., 2020). This shared task included two subtasks: Subtask A was to detect offensive language, and Subtask B was to detect hate speech. These subtasks shared a dataset of 10,000 tweets that comprised an Arabic offensive language dataset. The challenges of this shared task included the following:

(i) The distribution of the targeted classes was imbalanced in both subtasks. However, Subtask B is more challenging than Subtask A as only 5% of the tweets were labelled as hate speech and fell under Subtask B, 19% of the tweets are labelled as offensive and included in Subtask A.

(ii) The language used on social media has unique characteristics, such as sentences that are grammatically incorrect, and the use of symbols and emojis resulting in an out-of-vocabulary (OOV) problem.

(iii) This problem becomes even more challenging when considering that Arabic social media users employ various dialects and sub-dialects in their communication. In contrast to Modern Standard Arabic (MSA), the forms of dialectical Arabic vary widely, and there is a general lack of rules and standards (Salameh et al., 2018).

To deal with the issues associated with OOV, we generated a character-level (char-level) embeddings model, which was trained on a massive carefully collected dataset. This level of embeddings can work effectively in resolving the problem of OOV words through its ability to identify the vectors of character n-grams or parts of words. Our proposed systems were ranked 7th and 8th for Subtasks A and B, respectively.

The rest of this paper is organized in the following manner. Section two provides a brief overview of current literature on hate-speech and offensive speech detection. Section three includes an overview of the methodology, including the experimental setup for our proposed systems. Section four provides an evaluation and analysis of results and some discussion. Finally, section five concludes the paper with suggestions for future work.

2. Related Work

The use of offensive language and hate speech in the English language has been investigated widely, and various categories of hate speech have been identified, including sexism, religious hate speech and racial hate speech (Davidson et al., 2017; Malmasi and Zampieri, 2017; Kumar et al., 2018; Waseem et al., 2017; Zampieri et al., 2019). In contrast, limited studies have been done in this area in the Arabic language (Al-Hassan and Al-Dossari, 2019).

One of the earliest works on the detection of offensive language in Arabic was by Mubarak et al. (2017). They argued that some users have a higher likelihood of using offensive language than others. They used this insight to construct a list of Arabic words that are offensive. They subsequently developed an extensive corpus of Arabic tweets that were annotated manually into three categories: clean, obscene and offensive. Another contribution was made by Alakrot et al. (2018) who developed a corpus of offensive Arabic comments that had been shared on YouTube. This created a dataset that includes 16K Egyptian, Libyan and Iraqi comments, categorised into one of three classes: offensive, inoffensive and neutral. They trained a Support Vector Machine (SVM) classifier to detect the offensive comments. Based on their experiments, they concluded that using the N-gram feature improved the classifier's accuracy, while a combination of N-gram and stemming reduced the performance of the system. Albadi et al. (2018) focused on the detection of religious hate speech in Arabic but did not consider any other forms of hate speech. They constructed and scored a lexicon of the most frequently used religious hate terms and tested a variety of classifiers for their study.

More recently, Mubarak and Darwish (2019) extended the list of offensive words and used it to build a massive training corpus for automatic offensive tweet detection. They employed a character-level deep learning algorithm to classify each tweet as to whether or not it was offensive. In our work, we combined different levels of word embedding (character and word levels) and incorporated these into a supervised learning framework for the task of detecting offensive and hate speech tweets.

3. Data and Methodology

3.1. Data Description

The data released by the organisers included two sub-tasks: Subtask A (detecting offensive language) and Subtask B (detecting hate speech). The subtasks shared a common dataset of 10,000 tweets containing offensive language in Arabic. For Subtask A, the tweets were manually annotated using the term 'OFF' for offensive tweets and 'NOT_OFF' for tweets that were not offensive. In Subtask B, tweets were identified by 'HS' for hate speech and 'NOT_HS' for all other cases. An overview of the dataset is provided in Tables 1 and 2.

Dataset/Class	OFF	NOT_OFF	Total
Training	1410	5590	7000
Dev	179	821	1000
Test	402	1598	2000

Table 1: Distribution of classes in Subtask A

3.2. Preprocessing

We followed the procedure described by a number of researchers (Abu Farha and Magdy, 2019; Duwairi and El-Orfali, 2014), which involves the following steps:

- **Cleaning:** All unknown symbols and other characters are eliminated. For example, other language letters,

Dataset/Class	HS	NOT_HS	Total
Training	361	6639	7000
Dev	44	956	1000
Test	101	1899	2000

Table 2: Distribution of classes in Subtask B

diacritics, punctuation, etc. However, emojis are not removed and each emoji is represented by a vector as same as words.

- **Normalisation of letters:**Letters which appeared in different forms in the original tweets were rendered into a single form. For example, the "hamza" on characters {أ,إ} was replaced with {ا}, and the 't marbouta' {ة} was replaced with {ه}.

- **Segmenting {يا} phrases:** One of the most common phrases used in Arabic offensive language is the phrase that begins with (ya), followed by an offensive word. A large number of writers on social media do not use a space between these two words, so they will be recognized as one word. This issue cannot be handled even by state-of-the-art tools such as MADAMIRA (Pasha et al., 2014) and Farasa (Abdelali et al., 2016). We therefore treated this situation by using RegEx to segment any strings starting with (ya) into two words. However, this approach needs to improved in our future works to treat words such as Yasser or Yassin.

3.3. Embedding Models

Word embedding is one of the most important methods that have been applied recently to many natural language processing tasks (Devlin et al., 2014; Zhang et al., 2014; Lin et al., 2015; Bordes et al., 2014). Word embeddings are learned representations of text, with words of similar meanings represented in similar ways. An essential element of this methodology is the concept of employing densely distributed representations for every word. Every word is encoded to a real-valued vector with a few hundred dimensions. We employed different levels of word embedding models, which are detailed in the following subsections. Table 3 presents a summary of important information about each of these models including their sizes and pre-trained corpus.

Model	Corpus	Size
Ara2Vec	General - Twitter	77M tweets
Mazajak	Sentiment - Twitter	250M tweets
Our Model	Emotion - Twitter	10M tweets

Table 3: Different pre-trained Arabic word embeddings used for our systems

3.3.1. Word-level Embeddings

We used two Arabic pre-trained word embeddings: Ara2Vec (Soliman et al., 2017) as well as Mazajak

(Abu Farha and Magdy, 2019). One of the largest open-source word embeddings is Ara2Vec, consisting of six different word embedding models for the Arabic language. The researchers derived the training data from three separate sources: the Wikipedia, Twitter and Common Crawl web-pages crawl data. They employed two word-level models to learn word representations for general NLP tasks. In addition, we used Mazajak, which is considered the largest word-level embeddings. They used 250M Arabic tweets to generate a language model. Although these models are trained on a large number of words, they cannot capture all words that can be encountered in the real world. Due to OOV, the inability to identify words is one of the main limitations of this word-level model.

3.3.2. Char-level Embeddings

As mentioned in the introduction, the form of dialectical Arabic words used varies widely, which leads to the OOV problem. Therefore, effective resources and tools are needed to better understand and treat these various linguistic forms when targeting offensive language in Arabic tweets. Our main intuition is that while word-Level embeddings seems to give more importance to the semantic similarity, char-level embeddings are more likely to encode all variants of a word's morphology closer in the embedded space. Table 4 shows an example of offensive Arabic word, where the similarity of these words is mostly based on morphology for the char-level and semantics for the word-level. Therefore, combining these two different levels of embeddings into a supervised learning framework for the task of detecting offensive tweets can improve the results.

To learn the morphological features found within each word, we utilised FastText, a character n-grams model (Bojanowski et al., 2017). FastText can learn the vectors of character n-grams or word parts. Therefore, this feature enables the model to capture words that have similar meanings but have different morphological word formations. To train this model, we used an in-house unlabelled Arabic dataset (consisting of 10 million tweets) [1]. This large dataset contains varied sentiment and emotional words expressed in different Arabic dialects. We used these data not only because of their variety of Arabic dialects but also because we believe a correlation exists between negative emotions and offensive language words. We used the Gensim library [2] to implement the FastText method. Gensim is an open source Python library for natural language processing, which supports an implementation of different word embeddings, including FastText. The input for this char-level model was a composed of n-grams for each word in a given tweet. For example: the word (mnHTyn) will be treated as composed of 3-grams: '<mn','mnh',...,'yn>'. The '<' and '>' are special symbols which are appended to indicate the token start and end. We used the following parameters: 300 for size, five for the windows context and three to ignore words that had a total frequency of less than three. In addition, to control the length of character n-grams, we used three and six. We released our generated char-level model to be used as a pre-trained language model for applications

---

[1]https://github.com/aialharbi/ACWE

[2]https://radimrehurek.com/gensim/models/fasttext.html

and research relying on Arabic NLP.

Example of an offensive query term: منحط (mnHT)	
Mazajak	Our char-level model
ومنحط (wmnHT)	ومنحط (wmnHT)
قذر (q*r)	منحطه (mnHTh)
وقذر (wq*r)	ومنحطه (wmnHTh)
متخلف (mtxlf)	المنحط (AlmnHT)
ووق (wwqH)	منحطين (mnHTyn)

Table 4: The top five most similar words to a given query term using char and word level embeddings.

3.4. Classification Models

3.4.1. Logistic Regression

We selected logistic regression (LR) as our baseline model in order to investigate the lower bound performance that we should compare. We performed a number of experiments to compare the impact of the preprocessing techniques mentioned in section 3.2. We also used LR to compare the impact of using different features such as emojis, URL and user tags, and the combination of these features. We then reported the results with the highest scores to consider using them with other training models.

3.4.2. XGBoost Classifier

The XGBoost learning model (Chen and Guestrin, 2016) is frequently employed in different situations because it performs extremely well despite substantial challenges. This is an algorithm of decision trees in which new trees correct errors of those trees which are already part of the model. Trees are added to the model until no further changes can be made. We inputted tweet vector representations obtained from an average of real-value word vectors for every word with matching vector representations derived from the pre-trained embeddings.

3.4.3. Deep Learning Model

For the deep learning model, we utilized the Long Short-Term Memory (LSTM) (Hochreiter and Schmidhuber, 1997) which is an enhanced form of the recurrent neural network. It is able to tackle various problems and provide robust solutions, for example, to the vanishing gradient problem. The internal structure of the LSTM consists of four layers that interact with each other. These four layers can be described as Forget Gate, Input Gate, Modulation Gate and Output Gate. In order to achieve superior performance, we combined all word embedding models (see section 3.3), and these were then used to initialize the weights of the embedding layer. The weights of the embedding layer were then updated during training to be fine-tuned to each subtask. This was then connected to the rest of the layers in the networks. This embedding layer was followed by two layers each of 1-D convolutions with kernel size 3 and 128 filters. This was followed by two layers of the LSTM network, with 256 and 128 filters, respectively. In the LSTM layers, 0.2 dropouts were induced, and 0.2 recurrent dropouts were employed. Finally, a dense layer with one output was introduced by exploiting sigmoid as an activation function. For all other layers of the network, the ReLU activation function was utilized. We used the Adam optimizer as an optimization function for the network.

4. Experiment Results

The evaluation metrics for this shared task is evaluated by using Macro-F1. From our experiments on the Dev dataset of Subtask A, we selected the deep learning model as the first system and XGBoost algorithm as the second system. However, in Subtask B, the deep learning model performed poorly compared to XGBoost algorithm, therefore we swapped the proposed systems for this Subtask.One possible reason for this low performance is due to the significant imbalanced classes in Subtask B.

The results of subtask A are presented in Table 5. It can be seen that our model 1 provided an F1-score of 0.89 for the Dev dataset and 0.87 for the Test dataset with high precision and recall rates of 0.90 and 0.87, and 0.90 and 0.85, respectively. Similarly, model 2 produced an F1-score of 0.87 with 0.89 precision and 0.85 recall for the Dev dataset, and an F1 score of 0.85, with a precision of 0.88, and a recall of 0.84 for the Test dataset.

System	F1	Accuracy	Precision	Recall
Dev dataset				
1	0.885	0.935	0.901	0.871
2	0.870	0.928	0.895	0.849
Test dataset				
1	0.868	0.920	0.896	0.847
2	0.857	0.913	0.877	0.841

Table 5: Results for both systems with Dev and Test dataset for the Subtask A

The results of Subtask B are presented in Table 5. It can be seen that our model 1 provided an F1 score of 0.71 for the Dev dataset and a 0.74 F1 score for Test dataset with high precision and recall rates of 0.81 and 0.65, and 0.86 and 0.68, respectively. Similarly, model 2 produced an F1-score of 0.49 which is a little less, with 0.48 for precision and 0.50 for recall for the Dev dataset, while with the Test dataset, the F1 score was 0.49, with 0.47 precision, and 0.5 for recall. The confusion matrix of three sub-tasks are shown in fig 1 and 2, which is another way to explain the results discussed above.

Moreover, we evaluated the use of three pre-trained word embeddings: two open-source word-level models and our generated char-level model. We compared the performance of these models individually and by combining all of them. Our char-level model and Mazajak obtained an F1-score of 0.87, outperforming Ara2Vec (0.86). Although our generated model trained only on 10 million tweets, it achieved the same result as Mazajak, which trained on 250 million tweets. However, combining all these different levels of models improved the results by about 2%. We believe that with this combination, we take advantage of these large

System	F1	Accuracy	Precision	Recall
Dev dataset				
1	0.706	0.963	0.818	0.655
2	0.489	0.956	0.478	0.5
Test dataset				
1	0.742	0.963	0.864	0.685
2	0.487	0.950	0.475	0.5

Table 6: Results for both systems with Dev and Test dataset for the Subtask B

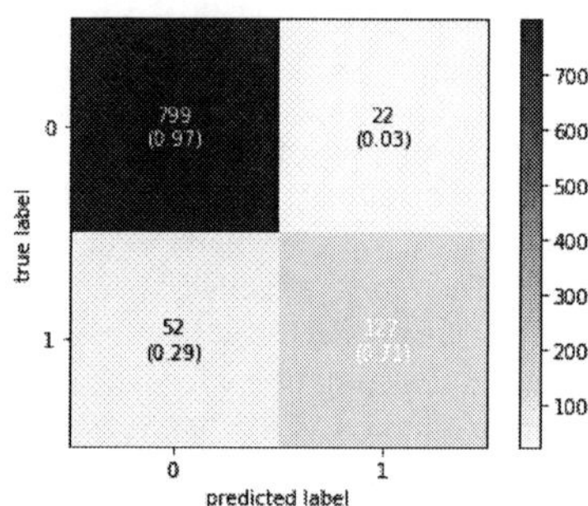

Figure 1: Confusion Matrix for system 1 for Sub-task A.

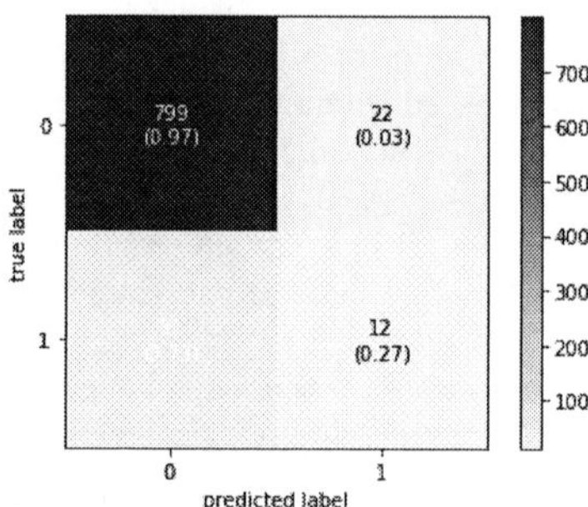

Figure 2: Confusion Matrix for system 1 for Sub-task B.

pre-trained word embeddings (Mazajak and Ara2Vec), and we also overcome their limitation by incorporating our char model to deal with the OOV problem. An example of OOV taken from the dataset of this shared task, an offensive word (الكلبوبه - Alklbwbh), meaning the small female dog, could not be realised by both aforementioned pre-trained word embeddings. However, our char-level model was able to capture its meaning by encoding this word close to other related words that either have the same semantic meaning or mostly a different form of this word.

5. Conclusion

In this work, we generated a character-level embeddings model, which was trained on a massive carefully collected dataset. We incorporated this model with other pretrained word embeddings into a supervised learning framework for the task of detecting offensive and hate speech tweets.

While the macro averaged F1 score for the majority base-line was 0.444 (given by the organisers), we achieved almost double this score. In future works, we hope to improve our results by applying more preprocessing techniques and exploiting a list of offensive language words. Additionally, we will investigate different methods to augment data into our training datasets to make them more robust.

6. Bibliographical References

Abdelali, A., Darwish, K., Durrani, N., and Mubarak, H. (2016). Farasa: A fast and furious segmenter for Arabic. In *Proceedings of the 2016 Conference of the North American Chapter of the Association for Computational Linguistics: Demonstrations*, pages 11–16, San Diego, California, June. Association for Computational Linguistics.

Abu Farha, I. and Magdy, W. (2019). Mazajak: An online Arabic sentiment analyser. In *Proceedings of the Fourth Arabic Natural Language Processing Workshop*, pages 192–198, Florence, Italy, August. Association for Computational Linguistics.

Al-Hassan, A. and Al-Dossari, H. (2019). Detection of hate speech in social networks: a survey on multilingual corpus. In *6th International Conference on Computer Science and Information Technology*.

Alakrot, A., Murray, L., and Nikolov, N. S. (2018). Towards accurate detection of offensive language in online communication in arabic. *Procedia Computer Science*, 142:315 – 320. Arabic Computational Linguistics.

Albadi, N., Kurdi, M., and Mishra, S. (2018). Are they our brothers? analysis and detection of religious hate speech in the arabic twittersphere. In *2018 IEEE/ACM International Conference on Advances in Social Networks Analysis and Mining (ASONAM)*, pages 69–76, Aug.

Bojanowski, P., Grave, E., Joulin, A., and Mikolov, T. (2017). Enriching word vectors with subword information. *Transactions of the Association for Computational Linguistics*, 5:135–146.

Bordes, A., Chopra, S., and Weston, J. (2014). Question Answering with Subgraph Embeddings. In *Proceedings of the 2014 Conference on Empirical Methods in Natural Language Processing (EMNLP)*, pages 615–620.

Chen, T. and Guestrin, C. (2016). Xgboost: A scalable tree boosting system. In *Proceedings of the 22nd acm sigkdd international conference on knowledge discovery and data mining*, pages 785–794.

Davidson, T., Warmsley, D., Macy, M., and Weber, I. (2017). Automated hate speech detection and the problem of offensive language. In *Eleventh international aaai conference on web and social media*.

Devlin, J., Zbib, R., Huang, Z., Lamar, T., Schwartz, R., and Makhoul, J. (2014). Fast and robust neural network joint models for statistical machine translation. In *Proceedings of the 52nd Annual Meeting of the Association for Computational Linguistics (Volume 1: Long Papers)*, volume 1, pages 1370–1380.

Duwairi, R. and El-Orfali, M. (2014). A study of the effects of preprocessing strategies on sentiment analysis for arabic text. *Journal of Information Science*, 40(4):501–513.

Hochreiter, S. and Schmidhuber, J. (1997). Long short-term memory. *Neural Comput.*, 9(8):1735–1780, November.

Kumar, R., Ojha, A. K., Malmasi, S., and Zampieri, M. (2018). Benchmarking aggression identification in social media. In *Proceedings of the First Workshop on Trolling, Aggression and Cyberbullying (TRAC-2018)*, pages 1–11, Santa Fe, New Mexico, USA, August. Association for Computational Linguistics.

Lin, C.-C., Ammar, W., Dyer, C., and Levin, L. (2015). Unsupervised POS Induction with Word Embeddings. In *Proceedings of the 2015 Conference of the North American Chapter of the Association for Computational Linguistics: Human Language Technologies*, pages 1311–1316.

Malmasi, S. and Zampieri, M. (2017). Detecting hate speech in social media. In *Proceedings of the International Conference Recent Advances in Natural Language Processing, RANLP 2017*, pages 467–472, Varna, Bulgaria, September. INCOMA Ltd.

Mubarak, H. and Darwish, K. (2019). Arabic offensive language classification on twitter. In *International Conference on Social Informatics*, pages 269–276. Springer.

Mubarak, H., Darwish, K., and Magdy, W. (2017). Abusive language detection on arabic social media. In *Proceedings of the First Workshop on Abusive Language Online*, pages 52–56.

Mubarak, H., Darwish, K., Magdy, W., Elsayed, T., and Al-Khalifa, H. (2020). Overview of osact4 arabic offensive language detection shared task. In *Proceedings of the 4th Workshop on Open-Source Arabic Corpora and Processing Tools (OSACT)*, volume 4.

Pasha, A., Al-Badrashiny, M., Diab, M., El Kholy, A., Eskander, R., Habash, N., Pooleery, M., Rambow, O., and Roth, R. (2014). MADAMIRA: A fast, comprehensive tool for morphological analysis and disambiguation of Arabic. In *Proceedings of the Ninth International Conference on Language Resources and Evaluation (LREC'14)*, pages 1094–1101, Reykjavik, Iceland, May. European Language Resources Association (ELRA).

Salameh, M., Bouamor, H., and Habash, N. (2018). Fine-grained Arabic dialect identification. In *Proceedings of the 27th International Conference on Computational Linguistics*, pages 1332–1344, Santa Fe, New Mexico, USA, August. Association for Computational Linguistics.

Soliman, A. B., Eissa, K., and El-Beltagy, S. R. (2017). Aravec: A set of arabic word embedding models for use in arabic nlp. *Procedia Computer Science*, 117:256–265.

Waseem, Z., Davidson, T., Warmsley, D., and Weber, I. (2017). Understanding abuse: A typology of abusive language detection subtasks. In *Proceedings of the First Workshop on Abusive Language Online*, pages 78–84, Vancouver, BC, Canada, August. Association for Computational Linguistics.

Zampieri, M., Malmasi, S., Nakov, P., Rosenthal, S., Farra,

N., and Kumar, R. (2019). SemEval-2019 task 6: Identifying and categorizing offensive language in social media (OffensEval). In *Proceedings of the 13th International Workshop on Semantic Evaluation*, pages 75–86, Minneapolis, Minnesota, USA, June. Association for Computational Linguistics.

Zhang, J., Liu, S., Li, M., Zhou, M., and Zong, C. (2014). Bilingually-constrained phrase embeddings for machine translation. In *Proceedings of the 52nd Annual Meeting of the Association for Computational Linguistics (Volume 1: Long Papers)*, volume 1, pages 111–121.

Proceedings of the 4th Workshop on Open-Source Arabic Corpora and Processing Tools, pages 97–101
with a Shared Task on Offensive Language Detection.
Language Resources and Evaluation Conference (LREC 2020), Marseille, 11–16 May 2020
© European Language Resources Association (ELRA), licensed under CC-BY-NC

Multi-Task Learning using AraBert for Offensive Language Detection

Marc Djandji, Fady Baly, Wissam Antoun, Hazem Hajj

American University of Beirut

{mgd10, fgb06, wfa07,hh63}@aub.edu.lb

Abstract

The use of social media platforms has become more prevalent, which has provided tremendous opportunities for people to connect but has also opened the door for misuse with the spread of hate speech and offensive language. This phenomenon has been driving more and more people to more extreme reactions and online aggression, sometimes causing physical harm to individuals or groups of people. There is a need to control and prevent such misuse of online social media through automatic detection of profane language. The shared task on Offensive Language Detection at the OSACT4 has aimed at achieving state of art profane language detection methods for Arabic social media. Our team "BERTologists" tackled this problem by leveraging state of the art pretrained Arabic language model, AraBERT, that we augment with the addition of Multi-task learning to enable our model to learn efficiently from little data. Our Multitask AraBERT approach achieved the second place in both subtasks A & B, which shows that the model performs consistently across different tasks.

Keywords: Offensive Language, Hate Speech, AraBERT, Multilabel, Multitask Learning

1. Introduction

Offensive language, including hate speech, is a violent behavior that is becoming more and more pervasive across public social media platforms (Fosler-Lussier et al., 2012). Hate speech was found to negatively impact the psychological well-being of individuals and to deteriorate inter-group relations on the societal level (Tynes et al., 2008). As such, detection and prevention mechanisms should be setup to deal with such content. Machine learning algorithms can be employed to automatically detect these behaviors by relying on recent techniques in natural language processing that have shown propitious performance.

A small number of works targeted the problem of simultaneously detecting both hate and offensive speech in Arabic. For example, Haddad et al. (2019) targeted the problem of hate and offensive speech detection for the Tunisian dialect using Support Vector Machine (SVM) and Naive Bayes classifiers trained on hand crafted features. Mulki et al. (2019) targeted the detection of profane language for the Levantine dialect using SVM and NB models trained on hand-crafted features. Although these works provided insights into the features that could be used for Arabic hate and offensive speech detection and introduced datasets for these specific dialects, they are limited to these specific dialects and do not target the problem of developing models that can learn efficiently with little data.

In the 4th Workshop on Open-Source Arabic Corpora and Processing Tools (OSACT4) (Mubarak et al., 2020) the shared task on offensive language aimed at offensive and hate speech detection in Arabic tweets. The task is split up into two Subtasks: Subtask A) which aimed at detecting whether a tweet is offensive or not and Subtask B) which aimed at detecting whether a tweet is hate-speech or not. The organizers labeled a tweet as offensive if it contained explicit or implicit insults directed towards other people or inappropriate language. While a tweet labeled as hate speech contains targeted insults towards a group based on their nationality, ethnicity, gender, political or sport affiliation. Each subtask is evaluated independently with a macro-F1 score. The dataset had the following issues that also needed to be addressed: (*i*) The labeled tweets were written in dialectal Arabic which had inconsistent writing style and vocabulary (*ii*) The class labels were highly imbalanced especially in the hate speech case where only 5% of the data was labeled as hate speech.

The models that we experimented with are all based on fine-tuning the Arabic Bidirectional Encoder Representation from Transformer (AraBERT) model (AUBMind-Lab, 2020) with different training classification schemes. To enable the model to learn from little data and not overfit to the dominant class, we train AraBERT in a multitask paradigm. Our contributions can be summarized as follows:

- Comprehensive evaluation including the impact of different sampling techniques and weighted loss functions that penalizes wrong predictions on the minority class in an attempt to balance the data.

- Propose a new model that combines AraBert and multi-task learning to achieve accurate predictions and address data imbalance.

- Propose a model that provides consistent performance on both hate and offensive speech detection with the presence of different Arabic dialects.

The rest of the paper is organized as follows: Section 2. reviews related work on offensive and hate-speech detection. In section 3., we provide details on our models. Section 4.3. provides and discusses the results of the conducted experiments. A conclusion of the work is presented in Section 5.

2. Related Work

2.1. Hate and Offensive Speech Detection in English

Hate Speech Detection Schmidt and Wiegand (2017) concluded that the most used models are Support Vector Machine (SVM) and Recurrent Neural Network (RNN) variant. The most used features are surface features such as bag of words, word and character n-gram, word generalization features such as word embeddings, and reported that lexicon features are usually used as a baseline. Waseem and Hovy (2016) investigated the usefulness of different features for hate speech detection, where they found that among character n-gram, gender, and location features, a combination of character n-gram and gender features yields the best macro-F1 score. Recently, different competitions has been organized to accelerate the development of accurate hate speech detection models. For example, HateEval competition (Basile et al., 2019) targeted the problem of detecting hate speech directed towards women and immigrants in English and Spanish tweets. The winning team in English achieved a 65.1% macro-F1 score using an SVM classifier with an RBF kernel trained on Universal Sentence Encoder embeddings (Cer et al., 2018). Mandl et al. (2019) organized a competition for hate speech detection in Hindi, English, and German, where the winning team for English hate speech detection has used a Long-short term memory (LSTM) with attention model.

Offensive Speech Detection Offensive speech detection was the topic of interest in the last offenseval competition (Zampieri et al., 2019), where it was shown that BERT (Devlin et al., 2018) trained with two epochs and 64 maximum sequence length achieved the first place outperforming Convolutional Neural Network (CNN), LSTM and SVM baselines and an ensemble of LSTM and Bidirectional-Gated Recurrent Unit (Bi-GRU) on word2vec embeddings.

Hate and Offensive Speech Detection Few works in the literature have targeted the problem of detecting hate and offensive tweets. Davidson et al. (2017) provided a dataset that contains both hate and offensive examples. They proposed the use of a combination of (bi, uni, tri)-gram features weighted by TF-IDF, lexicon sentiment score for each tweet, and Flesch-Kincaid grade level and Flesch Reading Ease scores. It was found that logistic regression with the L2 norm provided the best results among other shallow classifiers.

In summary, The most used features in the literature are character and word n-gram, TF-IDF feature weighing, Flesch-Kincaid grade, and ease of reading scores, word embeddings. The most popular classifiers in the literature are SVM, Logistic regression, LSTM, CNN, GRU, BERT. The best performing models are BERT and SVM with RBF kernel on sentence embeddings for offensive and hate-speech detection, respectively. The current work does not address the problem of providing a model that can learn efficiently from little data.

2.2. Hate and Offensive Speech Detection

Hate Speech Detection An extensive overview of the different works on hate speech detection was done by (Al-Hassan and Al-Dossari, 2019), but very few works in the literature target the problem of Arabic hate speech detection. Albadi et al. (2018) introduced the first dataset containing 6.6K Arabic hate-speech tweets targeting religious groups. The authors compared a lexicon-based classifier, SVM classifier trained with character n-gram features, and a Deep Learning approach consisting of a GRU trained on AraVec embeddings (Soliman et al., 2017). The GRU approach outperformed all other approaches with a 77% F1 score.

Offensive Speech Detection For offensive speech detection in Arabic, different approaches can be found in the literature. Alakrot et al. (2018), introduced a dataset for offensive speech in Arabic collected from 15K YouTube comments. For classifying the different comments, the data was preprocessed by removing stop words and diacritics, correcting misspelled words, then tokenization and stemming was performed in order to extract features that are used by a binary SVM classifier. Mohaouchane et al. (2019), explored the use of different Deep Learning architectures for offensive language detection. AraVec embeddings of each comment were used to train several models: CNN-LSTM, CNN-BiLSTM with attention, Bi-LSTM, and CNN model on the dataset proposed in (Alakrot et al., 2018) where the CNN model was found to provide the best F1 score. In Mubarak and Darwish (2019) 36 million tweets were collected and used it to train a FastText deep learning model and SVM classifier on character n-gram features where it was found that the Arabic FastText DL model provided the best results.

Hate and Offensive Speech Detection A very limited number of works targeted the problem of detecting both hate and offensive speech in Arabic. Haddad et al. (2019) created a dataset of 6K tweets containing hate and offensive speech in the Tunisian dialect. For binary (offensive, non-offensive) and multi-class (offensive, hate, or normal) classification of hate and offensive speech, the authors extracted several n-gram features from each tweet and applied Term Frequency (TF) weighing to select the most effective features. The extracted features were then used to develop an SVM and Naive Bayesian (NB) classifiers. The NB classifier provided superior performance with 92.3% and 83.6% F1 scores for binary and multi-class classification, respectively. Mulki et al. (2019) introduced a dataset of 6K tweets containing hate and offensive speech in the Levantine dialect. Similar to (Haddad et al., 2019), they extracted n-gram features with TF weighing and used the features to develop an SVM and NB classifiers. The NB classifier was found to be superior.

In summary, The most used features in the literature are character n-gram, stemming, and tokenization. The most popular classifiers in the literature are SVM, NB, LSTM, CNN, GRU. The best performing systems employed a CNN model and AraVec embeddings for offensive speech detection and a GRU model on AraVec embeddings for hate-speech detection. Very little work can be found in the literature for Arabic hate and offensive speech detection. The current work does not address the multiple dialects and little data challenges for these tasks.

3. Proposed Models

We based our approaches on the recently released AraBERT model. AraBERT is a Bidirectional representation of a text sequence, pretrained on a large Arabic corpus that achieved state of the art performance on multiple Arabic NLP tasks. Our best model is based on augmenting AraBERT with Multitask Learning, which solves the data imbalance problem by leveraging information from multiple tasks simultaneously. We also compare our best model with other approaches that are used to solve class imbalance issues such as balanced batch sampling and Multilabel classification.

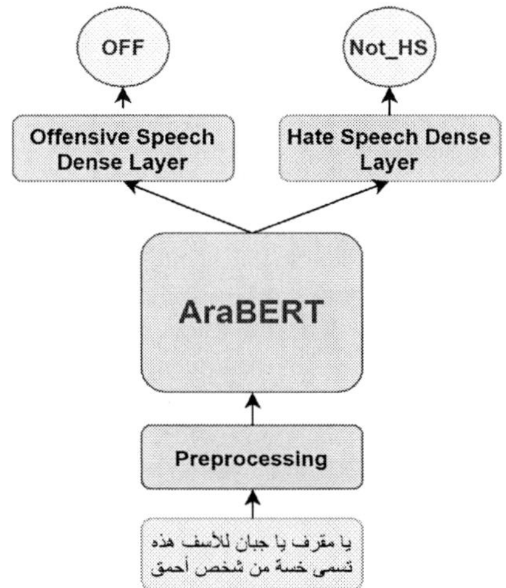

Figure 1: The trained Multitask Learning model given an input offensive tweet

3.1. Multitask Learning (MTL)

Multitask Learning is a learning paradigm that endows the developed models with the human-like abilities of transferring the important learned information between related tasks in what is called inductive transfer of knowledge under the assumption that commonalities exist between the learned tasks. Furthermore, the main advantages of MTL are that it reduces the requirements for large amounts of labeled data, improves the performance of a task with fewer data by leveraging the shared information from the related tasks with more data, and enables the model to be robust to missing observations for some tasks (Caruana, 1997; Qiu et al., 2017). Given that little data is available for both hate and offensive classes, we use an MTL approach to augment the initial AraBERT model such that it can learn both tasks simultaneously, which reduces the overfitting effect induced by the dominant not offensive and not hate examples. Our MTL-Arabert model consists of two components as can be seen in Figure 1: a part that gets trained by all the tasks' data in order to extract a general feature representation for all the tasks and a task-specific part that gets trained only by the task-specific examples to capture the task-specific characteristics.

1. Shared Part: Contains the pretrained AraBert model that gets tuned by the combined loss of both tasks in order to learn a shared set of information between both tasks

2. Task-specific layers: These consist of a task-specific dense layer that are dedicated to extracting the unique information per task.

3.2. Other Approaches

Multilabel Classification Multilabel classification is the task of classifying a single instance with multiple labels.

We considered using this approach for two main reasons. Firstly, the subtasks are very coherent as they both try to solve problems that behaviorally fall under the same general idea, detecting violent behaviors. Secondly, considering that subtask B has very little hate speech labeled data and that all hate speech data is also labeled as offensive, we assumed that a multilabel classifier would help leverage and provide a better understanding of the hate speech instances as they are being trained simultaneously with the offensive instances. We also explored oversampling the Task B instances and made sure that each training batch included samples of hate speech data.

Weighted Cross-Entropy loss Cross-entropy loss is useful in classification tasks, since the loss increases as the predicted probability diverges from the actual label. The Weighted version, penalizes each class differently, according to the given weight. The weighted cross-entropy loss of a class i with weight W_i is shown in 1, the weight vector is given in 2

$$\mathcal{L}(x_i) = -W_i \log \left(\frac{\exp(x_i)}{\sum_j \exp(x_j)} \right) \quad (1)$$

$$W_i = \frac{N^o Samples}{N^o Classes \times Count(i)} \quad (2)$$

Balanced batch sampling We re-sample the dataset in such a way that we under-sample the majority class and over-sample the minority class at the same time. Which reduces information loss due to under-sampling, and minimizes overfitting due to over-sampling, since the over/under-sampling is done to a lesser extent compared to independently implementing over/under-sampling.

4. Experiments

4.1. Data Description

The dataset for both tasks is the same containing 10K tweets that were annotated for offensiveness with labels (OFF or NOT_OFF) and hate speech with labels (HS or NOT_HS). The data was split by the competition organizers into 70% training set, 10% development set, and 20% test set. Table 1 shows the data distribution among the different labels and splits. By examining Table 1, it can be seen that the data is very imbalanced having only 5% of the examples labeled as hate speech and 20% of the examples labeled as offensive in the training dataset, which makes the tasks much harder and calls for methods that can learn efficiently from little data.

Table 1: The data distribution for both tasks. The first two rows show the class distribution of task A. The second two rows show the class distribution of task B

Class	Training	Developement
NOT_OFF	5468	821
OFF	1371	179
NOT_HS	6489	956
HS	350	44

4.2. Preprocessing

For preprocessing the data, we tokenized Arabic words with the Farasa Arabic segmenter (Abdelali et al., 2016) so that the input would be compatible with the AraBERT input. For example, "المدرسة - *Almadrasa*" becomes "ال + مدرس + ة - *Al+ madras +T*". We also removed all mentions of the user tokens "USER", retweet mentions "RT USER:", URL tokens, the "<LF>" tokens, diacritics, and emojis. As for hashtags, we replaced the underscore within a hashtag "_" with a white space to regain separate understandable tokens, and we pad the hashtag with a whitespace as well. For instance, "#أبو_ظبي" turns into "أبو ظبي". We should also mention that these preprocessing steps are precisely applied to all the experiments conducted for both subtasks.

4.3. Results

Both tasks were evaluated using the unweighted-average F1 of all classes, which is the macro-F1 score. Given the high imbalance in the dataset and that the macro-F1 score is penalized by the minority class, achieving a high macro-F1 score is challenging. Table 2 and 3 provide the results of our models on the development and test set, respectively. All three models were trained on the whole training set for five epochs with a batch size of 32 and a sequence length of 256 in a GPU-accelerated environment. The epoch-model that achieved the highest macro-F1 score on the dev-set is reported in Table 2.

Table 2: The performance of the different approaches on the development set for both tasks using the Macro-F1 score metric. It can be seen that the Multitask approach outperforms all other approaches

Model	Macro-F1	
	Offensive Language	**Hate Speech**
AraBERT	89.56	80.60
AraBERT-S*	87.24	79.42
AraBERT-W**	88.17	79.85
AraBERT-SW***	90.02	78.13
Multilable AraBERT	89.41	79.83
Multilable AraBERT*	89.55	80.81
Multitask AraBERT	**90.15**	**83.41**

* AraBERT with balanced batch sampling
** AraBERT with weighted loss
*** AraBERT with both balanced batch sampling and weighted loss

Table 3: The performance of the Multitask Learning (MTL) model on the test set for both tasks using the Macro-F1 score metric.

Model	Task A: Macro-F1	Task B: Macro-F1
Multitask AraBERT	90	82.28

We only show the results of our best MTL model on the test data in Table 3 as provided by the competition organizers. Our Multitask approach shows consistent performance on both the dev and test sets across both tasks. The results show that training both tasks jointly in a Multitask setting improves the model generalizability with the presence of little data for each task. The results for the hate speech task

are not as good as the offensive language task due to the minimal number of hate speech training examples, which constitute 5% of the training data. Although when combined, balanced batch sampling and weighted loss achieved the second best results on task A. When used separately, both approaches performed worse than the baseline model. This might be due to the overfitting effect of oversampling the minority class.

While examining the false predictions of our MTL model on the dev set, we noticed that the model was classifying tweets with a negative sentiment as offensive tweets. While it is intuitive for offensive tweets to have a negative sentiment by nature, our model did not capture the fact that not all tweets with negative sentiment are offensive. On another note, the use of words that are offensive in a non-offensive context was found to confuse the model. For example, the words "كلب" and "لئيم" in the following tweets (720, 828), respectively, were not used with an offensive intent and made the model classify both tweets as offensive.

We also found that the model has learned that a tweet cannot be hate-speech unless it is offensive, which would be ideal in case the offensive prediction was perfect. However, in our case, this also made the model falsely predict three tweets as hate-speech after they were falsely predicted as offensive. Furthermore, tweets 785, 881 in the dev set were found to be mislabeled as hate speech, and the model was able to detect this error showing a good understanding of what characterizes hate speech in a tweet. Finally, we found our model to falsely predict tweets that mostly contain mockery, sarcasm, or quoting other offensive/hateful statements.

Future work should explore the use of data augmentation techniques such as adversarial examples and learning from little data approaches such as meta-learning in order to enable state-of-the-art Natural Language Understanding (NLU) models such as AraBERT to be trained efficiently with little data.

5. Conclusion

The presence of hate speech and offensive language on Arabic social platforms is a major issue affecting the social lives of many individuals in the Arab world. The lack of annotated data and the presence of different dialects constitutes major challenges for automated Arabic offensive and hate speech detection systems. In this paper, we proposed the use of pre-trained Arabic BERT for accurate classification of the different tweets. We further augment the AraBERT model using Multitask Learning to enable the model to jointly learn both tasks efficiently with the presence of little labeled data per-task. Our results show the superiority of our proposed Multitask AraBERT model over single-task and Multilabel AraBERT. We explore different methods in order to cope with the presence of imbalanced training classes such as the use a weighted loss function and data re-sampling techniques, but found these methods to not introduce any improvements. Our method achieved the second place on both tasks in the OSACT4 competition.

6. References

Abdelali, A., Darwish, K., Durrani, N., and Mubarak, H. (2016). Farasa: A fast and furious segmenter for arabic. In *Proceedings of the 2016 Conference of the North American Chapter of the Association for Computational Linguistics: Demonstrations*, pages 11–16.

Al-Hassan, A. and Al-Dossari, H. (2019). Detection of hate speech in social networks: a survey on multilingual corpus. In *6th International Conference on Computer Science and Information Technology*.

Alakrot, A., Murray, L., and Nikolov, N. S. (2018). Towards accurate detection of offensive language in online communication in arabic. *Procedia computer science*, 142:315–320.

Albadi, N., Kurdi, M., and Mishra, S. (2018). Are they our brothers? analysis and detection of religious hate speech in the arabic twittersphere. In *2018 IEEE/ACM International Conference on Advances in Social Networks Analysis and Mining (ASONAM)*, pages 69–76. IEEE.

AUBMind-Lab. (2020). https://github.com/aubmind/arabert.

Basile, V., Bosco, C., Fersini, E., Nozza, D., Patti, V., Pardo, F. M. R., Rosso, P., and Sanguinetti, M. (2019). Semeval-2019 task 5: Multilingual detection of hate speech against immigrants and women in twitter. In *Proceedings of the 13th International Workshop on Semantic Evaluation*, pages 54–63.

Caruana, R. (1997). Multitask learning. *Machine learning*, 28(1):41–75.

Cer, D., Yang, Y., Kong, S.-y., Hua, N., Limtiaco, N., John, R. S., Constant, N., Guajardo-Cespedes, M., Yuan, S., Tar, C., et al. (2018). Universal sentence encoder. *arXiv preprint arXiv:1803.11175*.

Davidson, T., Warmsley, D., Macy, M., and Weber, I. (2017). Automated hate speech detection and the problem of offensive language. In *Eleventh international aaai conference on web and social media*.

Devlin, J., Chang, M.-W., Lee, K., and Toutanova, K. (2018). Bert: Pre-training of deep bidirectional transformers for language understanding. *arXiv preprint arXiv:1810.04805*.

Fosler-Lussier, E., Riloff, E., and Bangalore, S. (2012). Proceedings of the 2012 conference of the north american chapter of the association for computational linguistics: Human language technologies. In *Proceedings of the 2012 Conference of the North American Chapter of the Association for Computational Linguistics: Human Language Technologies*.

Haddad, H., Mulki, H., and Oueslati, A. (2019). T-hsab: A tunisian hate speech and abusive dataset. In *International Conference on Arabic Language Processing*, pages 251–263. Springer.

Mandl, T., Modha, S., Majumder, P., Patel, D., Dave, M., Mandlia, C., and Patel, A. (2019). Overview of the hasoc track at fire 2019: Hate speech and offensive content identification in indo-european languages. In *Proceedings of the 11th Forum for Information Retrieval Evaluation*, pages 14–17.

Mohaouchane, H., Mourhir, A., and Nikolov, N. S. (2019). Detecting offensive language on arabic social media using deep learning. In *2019 Sixth International Conference on Social Networks Analysis, Management and Security (SNAMS)*, pages 466–471. IEEE.

Mubarak, H. and Darwish, K. (2019). Arabic offensive language classification on twitter. In *International Conference on Social Informatics*, pages 269–276. Springer.

Mubarak, H., Darwish, K., Magdy, W., Elsayed, T., and Al-Khalifa, H. (2020). Overview of osact4 arabic offensive language detection shared task. 4.

Mulki, H., Haddad, H., Ali, C. B., and Alshabani, H. (2019). L-hsab: A levantine twitter dataset for hate speech and abusive language. In *Proceedings of the Third Workshop on Abusive Language Online*, pages 111–118.

Qiu, M., Zhao, P., Zhang, K., Huang, J., Shi, X., Wang, X., and Chu, W. (2017). A short-term rainfall prediction model using multi-task convolutional neural networks. In *2017 IEEE International Conference on Data Mining (ICDM)*, pages 395–404. IEEE.

Schmidt, A. and Wiegand, M. (2017). A survey on hate speech detection using natural language processing. In *Proceedings of the Fifth International Workshop on Natural Language Processing for Social Media*, pages 1–10.

Soliman, A. B., Eissa, K., and El-Beltagy, S. R. (2017). Aravec: A set of arabic word embedding models for use in arabic nlp. *Procedia Computer Science*, 117:256–265.

Tynes, B. M., Giang, M. T., Williams, D. R., and Thompson, G. N. (2008). Online racial discrimination and psychological adjustment among adolescents. *Journal of adolescent health*, 43(6):565–569.

Waseem, Z. and Hovy, D. (2016). Hateful symbols or hateful people? predictive features for hate speech detection on twitter. In *Proceedings of the NAACL student research workshop*, pages 88–93.

Zampieri, M., Malmasi, S., Nakov, P., Rosenthal, S., Farra, N., and Kumar, R. (2019). Semeval-2019 task 6: Identifying and categorizing offensive language in social media (offenseval). *arXiv preprint arXiv:1903.08983*.

Proceedings of the 4th Workshop on Open-Source Arabic Corpora and Processing Tools, pages 102–108
with a Shared Task on Offensive Language Detection.
Language Resources and Evaluation Conference (LREC 2020), Marseille, 11–16 May 2020
© European Language Resources Association (ELRA), licensed under CC-BY-NC

Leveraging Affective Bidirectional Transformers for Offensive Language Detection

AbdelRahim Elmadany, Chiyu Zhang, Muhammad Abdul-Mageed, Azadeh Hashemi

{a.elmadany,muhammad.mageeed,azadeh.hashemi}@ubc.ca, chiyuzh@mail.ubc.ca
Natural Language Processing Lab
University of British Columbia

Abstract

Social media are pervasive in our life, making it necessary to ensure safe online experiences by detecting and removing offensive and hate speech. In this work, we report our submission to the Offensive Language and hate-speech Detection shared task organized with the 4th Workshop on Open-Source Arabic Corpora and Processing Tools Arabic (OSACT4). We focus on developing purely deep learning systems, without a need for feature engineering. For that purpose, we develop an effective method for automatic data augmentation and show the utility of training both offensive and hate speech models off (i.e., by fine-tuning) previously trained affective models (i.e., sentiment and emotion). Our best models are significantly better than a vanilla BERT model, with 89.60% acc (82.31% macro F_1) for hate speech and 95.20% acc (70.51% macro F_1) on official TEST data.

1. Introduction

Social media are widely used at a global scale. Communication between users from different backgrounds, ideologies, preferences, political orientations, etc. on these platforms can result in tensions and use of offensive and hateful speech. This negative content can be very harmful, sometimes with real-world consequences. For these reasons, it is desirable to control this type of uncivil language behavior by detecting and removing this destructive content.

Although there have been a number of works on detecting offensive and hateful content in English (e.g. (Agrawal and Awekar, 2018; Badjatiya et al., 2017; Nobata et al., 2016)), works on many other languages are either lacking or rare. This is the case for Arabic, where there have been only very few works (e.g., (Alakrot et al., 2018; Albadi et al., 2018; Mubarak et al., 2017; Mubarak and Darwish, 2019)). For these motivations, we participated in the Offensive Language and hate-speech Detection shared task organized with the 4th Workshop on Open-Source Arabic Corpora and Processing Tools Arabic (OSACT4).

Offensive content and hate speech are less frequent online than civil, acceptable communication. For example, only 19% and $\sim$ 5% of the released shared task data are offensive and hate speech, respectively. This is the case in spite of the fact that the data seems to have been collected based on trigger seeds that are more likely to accompany this type of harmful content. As such, it is not easy to acquire data for training machine learning systems. For this reason, we direct part of our efforts to automatically augmenting training data released by the shared task organizers (Section 3.1.). Our experiments show the utility of our data enrichment method. In addition, we hypothesize trained affective models can have useful representations that might be effective for the purpose of detecting offensive and hateful content. To test this hypothesis, we fine-tune one sentiment analysis model and one emotion detection model on our training data. Our experiments support our hypothesis (Section 4.). All our models are based on the Bidirectional

Encoder from Transformers (BERT) model. Our best models are significantly better than competitive baseline based on vanilla BERT. Our contributions can be summarized as follows:

- We present an effective method for automatically augmenting training data. Our method is simple and yields sizable additional data when we run it on a large in-house collection.

- We demonstrate the utility of fine-tuning off-the-shelf affective models on the two downstream tasks of offensive and hate speech.

- We develop highly accurate deep learning models for the two tasks of offensive content and hate speech detection.

The rest of the paper is organized as follows: We introduce related works in Section 2., shared task data and our datasets in Section 3., our models in Section 4., and we conclude in Section 5..

2. Related Work

Thematic Focus: Research on undesirable content shows that social media users sometimes utilize *profane*, *obscene*, or *offensive* language (Jay and Janschewitz, 2008; Wiegand et al., 2018); *aggression* (Kumar et al., 2018; Modha et al., 2018); *toxic content* (Georgakopoulos et al., 2018; Fortuna et al., 2018; Zampieri et al., 2019), and *bullying* (Dadvar et al., 2013; Agrawal and Awekar, 2018; Fortuna et al., 2018).

Overarching Applications: Several works have taken as their target detecting these types of negative content with a goal to build applications for (1) content filtering or (2) quantifying the intensity of polarization (Barberá and Sood, 2015; Conover et al., 2011), (3) classifying trolls and propaganda accounts that often use offensive language (Darwish et al., 2017), (4) identifying hate speech that may correlate with hate crimes (Nobata et al., 2016), and (5) detecting signals of conflict, which are often

	Dataset	#tweets	# NOT_OFF	# OFF	OFF%	# NOT_HS	# HS	HS %
Shard-task data	TRAIN	6994	5585	1409	20%	6633	361	5%
	DEV	1000	821	179	18%	956	44	4%
	TEST	2000	-	-	-	-	-	-
Augmented data	AUG-TRAIN-HS	209780	-	-	-	199291	10489	5%
	AUG-TRAIN-OFF	480777	215365	265413	55%	-	-	-

Table 1: Offensive (OFF) and Hate Speech (HS) Labels distribution in datasets

preceded by verbal hostility (Chadefaux, 2014).

Methods: A manual way for detecting negative language can involve building a list of offensive words and then filtering text based on these words. As Mubarak and Darwish (2019) also point out, this approach is limited because (1) offensive words are ever evolving with new words continuously emerging, complicating the maintenance of such lists and (2) the offensiveness of certain words is highly context- and genre-dependent and hence a lexicon-based approach will not be very precise. Machine learning approaches, as such, are much more desirable since they are more nuanced to domain and also usually render more accurate, context-sensitive predictions. This is especially the case if there are enough data to train these systems.

Most work based on machine learning employs a supervised approach at either (1) character level (Malmasi and Zampieri, 2017), (2) word level (Kwok and Wang, 2013), or (3) simply employ some representation incorporating word embeddings (Malmasi and Zampieri, 2017). These studies use different learning methods, including Naive Bayes (Kwok and Wang, 2013), SVMs (Malmasi and Zampieri, 2017), and classical deep learning such as CNNs and RNNs (Nobata et al., 2016; Badjatiya et al., 2017; Alakrot et al., 2018; Agrawal and Awekar, 2018). Accuracy of the aforementioned systems range between 76% and 90%. It is also worth noting that some earlier works (Weber et al., 2013) use sentiment words as features to augment other contextual features. Our work has affinity to this last category since we also leverage affective models trained on sentiment or emotion tasks. Our approach, however, differs in that we build models free of hand-crafted features. In other words, we let the model learn its representation based on training data. This is a characteristic attribute of deep learning models in general. [1] In terms of the specific information encoded in classifiers, researchers use profile information in addition to text-based features. For example, Abozinadah (2017) apply SVMs on 31 features extracted from user profiles in addition to social graph centrality measures.

Methodologically, our work differs in three ways: (1) we train offensive and hate speech models off affective models (i.e., we fine-tune already trained sentiment and emotion models on both the offensive and hate speech tasks). (2)

We apply BERT language models on these two tasks. We also (3) automatically augment offensive and hate speech training data using a simple data enrichment method.

Arabic Offensive Content: Very few works have been applied to the Arabic language, focusing on detecting offensive language. For example, (Mubarak et al., 2017) develop a list of obscene words and hashtags using patterns common in offensive and rude communications to label a dataset of 1,100 tweets. Mubarak and Darwish (2019) applied character n-gram FasText model on a large dataset (3.3M tweets) of offensive content. Our work is similar to Mubarak and Darwish (2019) in that we also automatically augment training data based on an initial seed lexicon.

3. Data

In our experiments, we use two types of data: (1) data distributed by the Offensive Language Detection shared task and (2) an automatically collected dataset that we develop (Section 3.1.). The shared task dataset comprises 10,000 tweets manually annotated for two sub-tasks: *offensiveness* (Sub_task_A) [2] and *hate speech* (Sub_task_B) [3]. According to shared task organizers, [4], offensive tweets in the data contain explicit or implicit insults or attacks against other people, or inappropriate language. Organizers also maintain that hate speech tweets contains insults or threats targeting a specific group of people based on the nationality, ethnicity, gender, political or sport affiliation, religious belief, or other common characteristics of such a group. The dataset is split by shared task organizers into 70% TRAIN, 10% DEV, and 20% TEST. Both labeled TRAIN and DEV splits were shared with participating teams, while tweets of TEST data (without labels) was only released briefly before competition deadline.

It is noteworthy that the dataset is imbalanced. For *offensiveness* (Sub_task_A), only 20% of the TRAIN split are labeled as offensive and the rest is not offensive. For *hate speech* (Sub_task_B), only 5% of the tweets are annotated as hateful. Due to this imbalanced, the official evaluation metric is macro F_1 score. Table 1 shows the size and label distribution in the shared task data splits. [5]

---

[1] Of course hand-crafted features can also be added to a representation fed into a deep learning model. However, we do not do this here.

[2] https://competitions.codalab.org/competitions/22825.

[3] https://competitions.codalab.org/competitions/22826

[4] http://edinburghnlp.inf.ed.ac.uk/workshops/OSACT4/.

[5] Table 1 also shows size and class distribution for our auto-

The following are example tweets from the shared task TRAIN split.

Examples of *offensive* and *hateful* tweets:

(1) يا رب يا واحد يا أحد بحق يوم الاحد ان
تهلك بني سعود المجرمين. لاجل اطفال اليمن شاركوا.
Oh my Lord, O One and Only, destroy the family of Sau'd, for they are the criminals who put children of Yemen to suffer. [6]

(2) يا لبناني يا فضلات الاستعمار الفرنسي اللبنانيين
بالخليج يشغلون نسوانهم عاهرات
Hey, you Lebanese guy, you're the wastes of the French colonizers. The Lebanese in the Gulf put their women in prostitution work.

Examples for *offensive* but *not hate-speech* tweets:

(3) يا لطيف.. يا ساتر .أحمدوا ربكم إنها
مستقعدة كيف لو إنها واقفه
Oh my lord... Thank God she has disability. What would have happened if she were not disabled?

(4) يا ترى مخبيلنا ايه يا چون سنو انت
و الكلبوبة اللي جنبك دي
I wonder what you, and this little pitch by your side, are hiding for us, John Snow?

Examples for *not offensive* and *not hate-speech* tweets:

(5) يا بكون بحياتك الأهم يا إما ما بدي أكون
Either I become the most important in your life, or I become nothing at all.

(6) ايش الاكل الحلو ذا ياثُميه تسلم يدك ياعسل
ياقشطه ياحلوه ياشُكره يا طباخه يا فنانه يا كل شي
Wow! How wonderful this food is, Sumaia! You're such a honey, beauty, sweetie, and good cook! You're are artist! You're everything!

3.1. Data Augmentation

As explained earlier, the positive class in the offensive sub-task (i.e., the category 'offensive') is only 20% and in the hateful sub-task (i.e., the class 'hateful') it is only 5%. Since our goal is to develop exclusively deep learning

models, we needed to extend our training data such that we increase the positive samples. For this reason, we develop a simple method to automatically augment our training data. Our method first depends on extracting tweets that contain any of a seed lexicon (explained below) and satisfy a predicted sentiment label condition. We hypothesize that both offensive and hateful content would carry negative sentiment and so it would be intuitive to restrict any automatically extracted tweets to those that carry these negative sentiment labels. To further test this hypothesis, we analyzing the distribution of the sentiment classes in the TRAIN split using an off-the-shelf tool, *AraNet* (Abdul-Mageed et al., 2020). As shown in Figure 3, AraNet assigns sensible sentiment labels to the data. For the 'offensive' class, the tool assigns 65% negative sentiment tags and for the non-offensive class it assigns only 60% positive sentiment labels. [7] For the hate speech data, we find that AraNet assigns 72% negative labels to the 'hateful' class and 55% positive sentiment labels for the 'non-hateful' class. Based on this analysis, we decide to impose a sentiment-label condition on the automatically extended data as explained earlier. In other words, we only choose 'offensive' and 'hateful' class data from tweets predicted as negative sentiment. Similarly, we only choose 'non-offensive' and 'non-hateful' tweets assigned positive sentiment labels by AraNet. We now explain how we extend the dataset. We now explain our approach to extract tweets with an offensive and hateful seed lexicon.

To generate a seed lexicon, we extract all words that follow the *Ya* (*Oh, you*) in the shared task TRAIN split positive class in the two sub-tasks (i.e., 'offensive' and 'hateful'). The intuition here is that the word *Ya* acts as a trigger word that is likely to be followed by negative lexica. This gives us a set of 2,158. We find that this set can have words that are neither offensive nor hateful outside context and so we manually select a smaller set of 352 words that we believe are much more likely to be effective offensive seeds and only 38 words that we judge as more suitable carriers of hateful content. Table 2 shows samples of the offensive and hateful seeds. Table 3 shows examples of seeds in our initial larger set that we filtered out since these are less likely to carry negative meaning (whether offensive or hateful).

To extend the offensive and hateful tweets, we use 500K randomly sampled, unlabeled, tweets from (Abdul-Mageed et al., 2019) that each have at least one occurrence of the trigger word *Ya* and at least one occurrence of a word from either of our two seed lexica (i.e., the offensive and hateful seeds). [8] We then apply AraNet (Abdul-Mageed et al., 2020) on this 500K collection and keep only tweets assigned negative sentiment labels. Tweets that

---

matically extracted dataset, to which we refer to as augmented (AUG).

[6] Original tweets can be run-on sentences, lack proper grammatical structures or punctuation. In presented translation, for readability, while we maintain the meaning as much as possible, we render grammatical, well-structured sentence.

[7] AraNet (Abdul-Mageed et al., 2020) assigns only positive and negative sentiment labels. In other words, it does not assign neutral labels.

[8] The 500K collection is extracted via searching a larger sample of $\sim 21M$ tweets that all have the trigger word *Ya*. This corpus is also taken from (Abdul-Mageed et al., 2019). Note that a tweet can have both an offensive and a hateful seed.

Arabic Offensive	English	Arabic Hateful	English
يا خبيث	You, fat ass!	يا منجاوي	You're Manjawi
يا رعاع	You're mobby	يا دندرواي	You're Dandarawi
يا متشرد	You're a tramp	يا سعوديين	You Saudis
يا مجانين	You're crazy	يا دحباشي	You're Dahbashi
يا جعان	You, hungry man!	يا ادعائي	You, false claimer
يا فاجره	You, morally loose	يا حوثي	You, Houthi
يا ثمال	Oh, whore	يا شيعي	You, Shiite
يا زباله	You, junky	يا عميل	You, spay
يا بهايم	You, animals	يا اخوانجي	You, Ikhwangis
يا بغيض	You, hateful	يا اخوان	You, Ikhwan
يا وسخه	You, dirty woman	يا ابن الجرابيع	You, son of tramps
يا طاغيه	You, tyrant	يا ابن الحرام	You, bastard
يا فاجر	You, salacious	يا ابن الزنا	You, bastard
يا مغفل	You, idiot	يا ابن اليهوديه	You, son of Jewish woman
يا رخمه	You, silly woman	يا ابن الزانيه	You, son of adulterous woman
يا نحس	You, sinister	يا ابن الموهومه	You, son of deceived woman
يا غباء	You, stupid head	يا ابن العرص	You, son of pimp
يا كئيب	You, gloomy head	يا ابن المتاكه	You, son of adulterous
يا مرا	You, unworthy woman	يا امارات	You, Emirate
يا حمقي	You, fools	يا اتحادي	You, Itihadi

Table 2: Examples of offensive and hateful seeds in our lexica

carry offensive seeds are labeled as 'offensive' and those carrying hateful seeds are tagged as 'hateful'. This gives us 265,413 offensive tweets and 10,489 hateful tweets. For reference, the majority (%=67) of the collection extracted with our seed lexicon are assigned negative sentiment labels by AraNet. This reflects the effectiveness of our lexicon as it matches our observations about the distribution of sentiment labels in the shared task TRAIN split.

To add positive class data (i.e., 'not-offensive' and 'not-hateful') to this augmented collection, we randomly sample another 500K tweets that carry *Ya* from (Abdul-Mageed et al., 2019) that do not carry any of the two offensive and hateful seed lexica. We apply AraNet on these tweets and keep only tweets assigned a positive sentiment label (%=70). We use 215,365 tweets as 'non-offensive' but only 199,291 as 'non-hateful'. [9] Table 1 shows the size and distribution of class labels in our extended dataset.

Figure 2 and Figure 1 are word clouds of unigrams in our extended training data (offensive and hateful speech, respectively) after we remove our seed lexica from the data. The clouds show that the data carries lexical cues likely to occur in each of the two classes (offensive and hateful). Examples of frequent words in the offensive class include *dog, animal, son of, mother, dirty woman, monster, mad,* and *on you*. Examples in the hateful data include *shut up, dogs, son of, animal, dog, haha,* and *for this reason*. We note that the

hateful words do not include direct names of groups since these were primarily our seeds that we removed before we prepare the word cloud. Overall, the clouds provide sensible cues of our phenomena of interest across the two tasks.

Figure 1: A word cloud of unigrams in our extended training offensive data (AUG-TRAIN-OFF).

4. Models

4.1. Data Pre-Processing

We perform light Twitter-specific data cleaning (e.g., replacing numbers, usernames, hashtags, and hyperlinks by unique tokens NUM, USER, HASH, and URL respectively). We also perform Arabic-specific normalization (e.g., removing diacritics and mapping various forms of Alef and Yeh each to a canonical form). For text tokenization, we use byte-pair encoding (PBE) as implemented in

---

[9] We decided to keep only 199,291 'non-hateful' tweets since our augmented 'hateful' class comprises only 10,489 tweets.

Arabic Non-OFF/Non-HS	English
يا ابطال	You, heros
يا فنان	You, artist
يا عبسميع	You, Absemee'
يا عاالم	Oh, people
يا منسي	Oh, forgotten man
يا ماعندك	You have a lot
يا ماما	Oh, mum
يا قمرر	You, beautiful lady
يا جامد	You, wonderful man
يا طفل	Oh, child
يا قطه	Oh, delicate lady
يا حيلتها	You, lulled
يا ايتها	Oh you…
يا راعي	You, caregiver
يا حبيبي	Oh, darling
يا رب	Oh, my Lord
يا واحد	Oh, the One
يا ناس	You, people
يا اخر	Oh, the Last
يا بابا	Oh, daddy

Table 3: Examples of non-offensive/non-hateful seeds filtered out from our lexica.

Figure 2: A word cloud of unigrams in our extended training hate speech data (AUG-TRAIN-HS).

Multilingual Cased BERT model.

4.2. BERT

Our experiments are based on BERT-Base Multilingual Cased model released by (Devlin et al., 2018) [10]. BERT stands for **B**idirectional **E**ncoder **R**epresentations from **T**ransformers. It is an approach for language modeling that involves two self-supervised learning tasks, (1) masked language models (MLM) and (2) next sentence predication (NSP). BERT is equipped with an Encoder architecture which naturally conditions on bi-directional context. It randomly masks a given percentage of input tokens and attempts to predict these masked tokens. (Devlin et al., 2018) mask 15% of the tokens (the authors use

---

[10] https://github.com/google-research/bert/blob/master/multilingual.md.

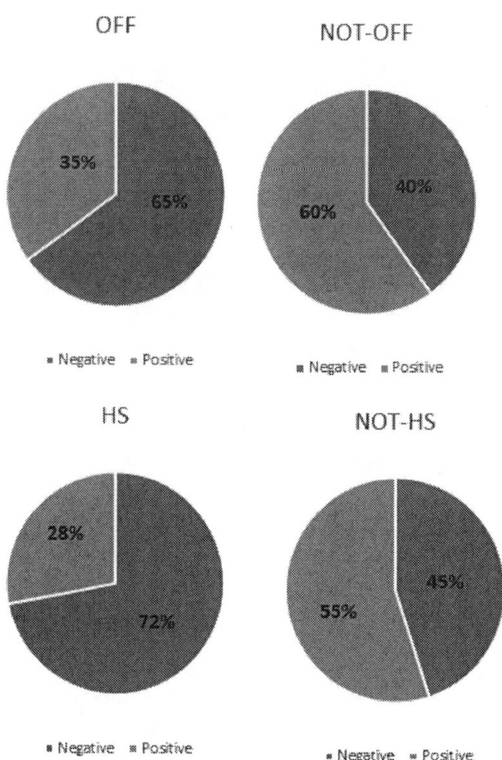

Figure 3: Distribution of Negative and Positive Tweets after applied AraNet on Shared-Task TRAIN Data

word pieces) and use the hidden states of these masked tokens from last layer for prediction. To understand the relationship between two sentences, the BERT also pre-trains with a binarized NSP task, which is also a type of self-supervises learning. For the sentence pairs (e.g., *A-B*) in pre-training examples, 50% of the time *B* is the actual next sentence that follows A in the corpus (positive class) and 50% of the time *B* is a random sentence from corpus (negative class). Google's pre-trained BERT-Base Multilingual Cased model is trained on 104 languages (including Arabic) with 12 layers, 768 hidden units each, 12 attention heads. The model has 119,547 shared word pieces vocabulary, and was pre-trained on the entire Wikipedia for each language.

In our experiments, we train our classification models on BERT-Base Multilingual Cased model. For all of our fine-tuning BERT models, we use a maximum sequence size of 50 tokens and a batch size of 32. We add a '[CLS]' token at the beginning of each input sequence and, then, feed the final hidden state of '[CLS]' to a Softmax linear layer to get predication probabilities across classes. We set the learning rate to $2e-6$ and train for 20 epochs. We save the checkpoint at the end of each epoch, report F1-score and accuracy of the best model, and use the best checkpoint to predict the labels of the TEST set. We fine-tune the BERT model under five settings. We describe each of these next.

	Dev				**Test**			
	OFF		**HS**		**OFF**		**HS**	
Model	**Acc**	**F1**	**Acc**	**F1**	**Acc**	**F1**	**Acc**	**F1**
BERT	87.10	78.38	**95.70**	**70.96**	87.30	77.70	**95.20**	**70.51**
BERT-SENTI	87.40	78.84	95.50	68.01	87.45	80.51	93.15	61.57
BERT-EMO	88.30	80.39	95.40	68.54	–	–	–	–
BERT-EMO-AUG	**89.60**	**82.31**	93.90	62.52	**89.35**	**82.85**	–	–

Table 4: Offensive (OFF) and Hate Speech (HS) results on DEV and TEST datasets

Vanilla BERT: We fine-tune BERT-Base Multilingual Cased model on TRAIN set of offensive task and hate speech task respectively. We refer these two models to BERT. The offensive model obtains the best result with 8 epochs. As Table 4 shows, for *offensive language* classification, this model obtains 87.10% accuracy and 78.38 F_1 score on DEV set. We submit the TEST prediction of this model to the shared task and obtain 87.30% accuracy and 77.70 F_1 on the TEST set. The *hate speech* model obtains best result (accuracy = 95.7-%, F1 = 70.96) with 6 epochs.

BERT-SENTI We use a BERT model fine-tuned with on binary Arabic sentiment dataset as released by (Abdul-Mageed et al., 2020). We use this off-the-shelf (already trained) model to further fine-tune on offensive and hate speech tasks, respectively. We replace the Softmax linear layer for sentiment classification with a randomly initialized Softmax linear layer for each task. We refer to these two models as BERT-SENTI. We train the BERT-SENTI models on the TRAIN sets for offensive and hate speech tasks respectively. On F_1 score, BERT-SENTI is 0.3 better than vanilla BERT on the offensive task, but 2.95 lower (than vanilla BERT) on the hate speech task. We submit the TEST predictions of both tasks. The offensive model obtain 87.45% accuracy and 80.51 F_1 on TEST. The hate speech model acquire 93.15% accuracy and 61.57 F_1 on TEST.

BERT-EMO Similar to BERT-SENTI, we use a BERT model trained on 8-class Arabic emotion identification from (Abdul-Mageed et al., 2020) to fine-tune on the offensive and hate speech tasks, respectively. We refer to this setting as BERT-EMO. We train the models on the TRAIN sets for both offensive and hate speech tasks for 20 epochs. The *offensive* model obtains its best result (accuracy = 88.30%, F_1 = 80.39) with 11 epochs. The *hate speech* model acquires its best result (accuracy = 95.40%, F_1 = 68.54) also with 11 epochs. We do not submit an BERT-EMO on the hate speech task TEST set.

BERT-EMO-AUG Similar to BERT-EMO, we also fine-tune the emotion BERT model (BERT-EMO) with the augmented offensive dataset (AUG-TRAIN-OFF) and augmented hate speech dataset (AUG-TRAIN-HS). On the DEV set, the *offensive model* acquires its best result (accuracy = 89.60%, F_1 = 82.31) with 13 epochs. The best results for the *hate speech model* (accuracy = 93.90%, F_1 = 62.52) is obtained with 9 epochs. Our best offensive predi-

cation on TEST is BERT-EMO-AUG. It which achieves an accuracy of 89.35% and F_1 of 82.85. We do not submit an BERT-EMO-AUG on the hate speech task TEST set.

5. Conclusion

We described our submission to the offensive language detection in Arabic shared task. We offered a simple method to extend training data and demonstrated the utility of such augmented data empirically. We also deploy affective language models on the two sub-tasks of offensive language detection and hate speech identification. We show that fine-tuning such affective models is useful, especially in the case of offensive language detection. In the future, we will investigate other methods for improving our automatic offensive and hateful language acquisition methods. We also explore other machine learning methods on the tasks. For example, we plan to investigate the utility of semi-supervised methods as a vehicle of improving our models.

6. Bibliographic References

Abdul-Mageed, M., Zhang, C., Elmadany, A., Rajendran, A., and Ungar, L. (2019). Dianet: Bert and hierarchical attention multi-task learning of fine-grained dialect. *arXiv preprint arXiv:1910.14243*.

Abdul-Mageed, Muhammad, Z. C., Nagoudi, E. M. B., and Hashemi, A. (2020). Aranet: A deep learning toolkit for arabic social media. In *The 4th Workshop on Open-Source Arabic Corpora and Processing Tools (OSACT4), LREC*.

Abozinadah, E. (2017). *Detecting abusive arabic language twitter accounts using a multidimensional analysis model.* Ph.D. thesis.

Agrawal, S. and Awekar, A. (2018). Deep learning for detecting cyberbullying across multiple social media platforms. In *European Conference on Information Retrieval*, pages 141–153. Springer.

Alakrot, A., Murray, L., and Nikolov, N. S. (2018). Towards accurate detection of offensive language in online communication in arabic. *Procedia computer science*, 142:315–320.

Albadi, N., Kurdi, M., and Mishra, S. (2018). Are they our brothers? analysis and detection of religious hate speech in the arabic twittersphere. In *2018 IEEE/ACM International Conference on Advances in Social Networks Analysis and Mining (ASONAM)*, pages 69–76. IEEE.

Badjatiya, P., Gupta, S., Gupta, M., and Varma, V. (2017). Deep learning for hate speech detection in tweets. In *Proceedings of the 26th International Conference on World Wide Web Companion*, pages 759–760.

Barberá, P. and Sood, G. (2015). Follow your ideology: Measuring media ideology on social networks. In *Annual Meeting of the European Political Science Association, Vienna, Austria. Retrieved from http://www. gsood. com/research/papers/mediabias. pdf.*

Chadefaux, T. (2014). Early warning signals for war in the news. *Journal of Peace Research*, 51(1):5–18.

Conover, M. D., Ratkiewicz, J., Francisco, M., Gonçalves, B., Menczer, F., and Flammini, A. (2011). Political polarization on twitter. In *Fifth international AAAI conference on weblogs and social media.*

Dadvar, M., Trieschnigg, D., Ordelman, R., and de Jong, F. (2013). Improving cyberbullying detection with user context. In *European Conference on Information Retrieval*, pages 693–696. Springer.

Darwish, K., Alexandrov, D., Nakov, P., and Mejova, Y. (2017). Seminar users in the arabic twitter sphere. In *International Conference on Social Informatics*, pages 91–108. Springer.

Devlin, J., Chang, M.-W., Lee, K., and Toutanova, K. (2018). Bert: Pre-training of deep bidirectional transformers for language understanding. *arXiv preprint arXiv:1810.04805.*

Fortuna, P., Ferreira, J., Pires, L., Routar, G., and Nunes, S. (2018). Merging datasets for aggressive text identification. In *Proceedings of the First Workshop on Trolling, Aggression and Cyberbullying (TRAC-2018)*, pages 128–139.

Georgakopoulos, S. V., Tasoulis, S. K., Vrahatis, A. G., and Plagianakos, V. P. (2018). Convolutional neural networks for toxic comment classification. In *Proceedings of the 10th Hellenic Conference on Artificial Intelligence*, pages 1–6.

Jay, T. and Janschewitz, K. (2008). The pragmatics of swearing. *Journal of Politeness Research. Language, Behaviour, Culture*, 4(2):267–288.

Kumar, R., Ojha, A. K., Malmasi, S., and Zampieri, M. (2018). Benchmarking aggression identification in social media. In *Proceedings of the First Workshop on Trolling, Aggression and Cyberbullying (TRAC-2018)*, pages 1–11.

Kwok, I. and Wang, Y. (2013). Locate the hate: Detecting tweets against blacks. In *Twenty-seventh AAAI conference on artificial intelligence.*

Malmasi, S. and Zampieri, M. (2017). Detecting hate speech in social media. *arXiv preprint arXiv:1712.06427.*

Modha, S., Majumder, P., and Mandl, T. (2018). Filtering aggression from the multilingual social media feed. In *Proceedings of the First Workshop on Trolling, Aggression and Cyberbullying (TRAC-2018)*, pages 199–207.

Mubarak, H. and Darwish, K. (2019). Arabic offensive language classification on twitter. In *International Conference on Social Informatics*, pages 269–276. Springer.

Mubarak, H., Darwish, K., and Magdy, W. (2017). Abusive language detection on arabic social media. In *Proceedings of the First Workshop on Abusive Language Online*, pages 52–56.

Nobata, C., Tetreault, J., Thomas, A., Mehdad, Y., and

Chang, Y. (2016). Abusive language detection in online user content. In *Proceedings of the 25th international conference on world wide web*, pages 145–153.

Weber, I., Garimella, V. R. K., and Batayneh, A. (2013). Secular vs. islamist polarization in egypt on twitter. In *Proceedings of the 2013 IEEE/ACM international conference on advances in social networks analysis and mining*, pages 290–297.

Wiegand, M., Siegel, M., and Ruppenhofer, J. (2018). Overview of the germeval 2018 shared task on the identification of offensive language.

Zampieri, M., Malmasi, S., Nakov, P., Rosenthal, S., Farra, N., and Kumar, R. (2019). Semeval-2019 task 6: Identifying and categorizing offensive language in social media (offenseval). *arXiv preprint arXiv:1903.08983.*

Quick and Simple Approach for Detecting Hate Speech in Arabic Tweets

Abeer Abuzayed
Islamic University of Gaza
Gaza, Palestine
aabuzayed1@students.iugaza.edu.ps

Tamer Elsayed
Qatar University
Doha, Qatar
telsayed@qu.edu.qa

Abstract

As the use of social media platforms increases extensively to freely communicate and share opinions, hate speech becomes an outstanding problem that requires urgent attention. This paper focuses on the problem of detecting hate speech in Arabic tweets. To tackle the problem efficiently, we adopt a "quick and simple" approach by which we investigate the effectiveness of 15 classical (e.g., SVM) and neural (e.g., CNN) learning models, while exploring two different term representations. Our experiments on 8k labelled dataset show that the best neural learning models outperform the classical ones, while distributed term representation is more effective than statistical bag-of-words representation. Overall, our best classifier (that combines both CNN and RNN in a joint architecture) achieved 0.73 macro-F1 score on the dev set, which significantly outperforms the majority-class baseline that achieves 0.49, proving the effectiveness of our "quick and simple" approach.

Keywords: Offensive language, Twitter, Text classification, Learning models, Neural models, Distributed term representation.

1. Introduction

Twitter is a place where 330 million users (in 2019)[1] from every background, race, religion, and nationality interact and communicate, and freely share their ideas, opinions, and beliefs. This makes Twitter easy to exploit in sharing content that targets and threatens individuals or groups based on their common characteristics or identities by spreading hate speech. According to Twitter hateful conduct policy[2], hate speech is to "attack or threaten other people on the basis of race, ethnicity, national origin, caste, sexual orientation, gender, gender identity, religious affiliation, age, disability, or serious disease", such as the tweet: "يا خوارج يا ارهابيين يا منبع اليهود" (O Kharijites, terrorists, the source of the Jews). Twitter encourages users to report any kind of hate speech that violates the hateful conduct policy, so that an action can be made such as suspending the user or deleting the tweet. Despite the considerable effort that social media sites are making in trying to curb hate speech, it is still threatening the online communities and users are still seeing it on many platforms. As hate speech might result in serious physical or mental abuse, there is an imperative need to detect and prevent such content on social media platforms.

Several researchers studied hate speech in the social media domain and proposed various approaches to detect it with more focus on English language, e.g., Malmasi and Zampieri (2018), Watanabe et al. (2018), Zhang and Luo (2018), and Zhang et al. (2018). However, detecting hate speech in Arabic content is still nascent. The richness and complexity of the nature and structure of the Arabic language, the variety of dialects, and the problems at orthographic, morphological, and syntactic levels make detecting hate speech in Arabic very challenging.

In this work, we conduct a preliminary study on the detection of hate speech in Arabic tweets as part of our participation in the Hate Speech Detection subtask in OSACT4 workshop[3] (Mubarak et al., 2020). Given the tight time we had for participation[4], we aim to tackle the classification problem in a simple, quick, yet effective approach. We elect to use "simple" features that are not problem-specific but easy to compute or use, while leveraging the richness, maturity, and strong support for "quick" development that current popular machine learning frameworks (e.g., Keras) provide. Adopting this *quick* and *simple* approach for developing our classification system for hate speech detection, we investigate the performance of several learning models and aim to answer two research questions in the context of this problem:

RQ1. Is distributed (latent) word representation (e.g., Word2Vec embeddings) more effective than standard statistical bag-of-words representation (e.g., tf-idf)?

RQ2. Are neural models more effective than classical machine learning models?

To answer both questions, we conducted experiments over seven classical and eight neural learning models using the labelled dataset of 8,000 tweets, provided by the shared task organizers, and submitted two runs on the test set. Our results show that, surprisingly, the bag-of-words tf-idf representation is more effective than distributed word embeddings representation; however the best neural models outperform classical models. Overall, our best classifier achieved a reasonable 0.73 macro-F1 score on the dev set, which significantly outperforms the majority-class baseline that achieves 0.49, proving the effectiveness of our quick and simple approach.

Our contribution in this work is two-fold:

1. We conducted a preliminary study investigating the performance of 15 different classical and neural learning models for detecting hate speech in Arabic tweets.
2. We demonstrated a simple and quick approach of developing a system that is implemented in less than 3 days to tackle the problem, yet achieved reasonable performance. We make all of our code open-source for the research community[5].

The paper is organized as follows. Section 2 describes related work. Section 3 outlines our approach in tackling the problem. Section 4 presents our experimental

---

1 https://www.statista.com/statistics/282087/number-of-monthly-active-twitter-users/

2 https://help.twitter.com/en/rules-and-policies/hateful-conduct-policy

3 http://edinburghnlp.inf.ed.ac.uk/workshops/OSACT4/

4 We only had 3 days before the submission deadline.

5 https://github.com/AbeerAbuZayed/QUIUG_Hate-Speech-Detection_OSACT4-Workshop

evaluation results. Section 5 concludes our work with potential future work.

2. Related Work

As mentioned earlier, there are several research studies conducted to study hate speech in online communities over English content. Mondal et al. (2017) conducted a study in online social media to understand how social media platforms are rich with hate speech and to investigate the most popular hate expressions and the main targets of online hate speech. Malmasi and Zampieri (2018) aimed to distinguish hate speech from general profanity using a dataset annotated as "hate, offensive, and ok", with advanced ensemble classifiers and stacked generalization along with various features such as n-grams, skip-grams, and clustering-based word representations. Additionally, Watanabe et al. (2018) classify tweets based on three labels (clean, offensive and hateful) using sentiment-based features, semantic features, unigram features, and pattern features. Zhang and Luo (2018) and Zhang et al. (2018) also conducted studies on Twitter hate speech for the English language.

Other researchers focused on detecting *offensive language* over *Arabic* content, where a number of studies were conducted to detect offensive and abusive language for Arabic Tweets and for YouTube comments (Mubarak and Darwish, 2019; Alakrot et al., 2018; Mohaouchane et al., 2018; Mubarak et al., 2017). However, *hate speech* is different from offensive and abusive language (Malmasi and Zampieri, 2018). Also, Zhang and Luo (2018) argue the same point and pointed out that the term "hate speech" might be overlapping with other terms such as "offensive", "profane" and "abusive". In order to distinguish them, they defined hate speech as "targeting individuals or groups on the basis of their characteristics and demonstrating a clear intention to incite harm, or to promote hatred and this speech may or may not use offensive or profane words".

Consequently, hate speech should be distinguished from other offensive and profane languages. Thus, other studies focus only on hate speech detection. Albadi et al. (2018) developed a system to detect religious hate speech in Arabic tweets. They used three various approaches to tackle this problem. Firstly, they constructed an Arabic lexicon of religious hate speech and used it to classify tweets to "hate" if the tweet terms exist in the lexicon, otherwise it is labelled as "not hate". Secondly, they trained Logistic Regression and SVM classifiers using n-gram models. Finally, a GRU model with the pre-trained embedding model AraVec (Twitter-CBOW 300D architecture) showing 0.77 F1 score was adopted.

Moreover, Chowdhury et al. (2019) studied religious hate speech in Arabic tweets too, where they argued that considering the community interactions can raise the ability to detect hate speech content on social media. To investigate this, Arabic word embedding (AraVec, Twitter-CBOW 300D architecture), social network graphs, and neural networks (e.g., RNN+CNN) were used. They pointed out that considering community interactions significantly improves the result and outperforms Albadi et al. (2018) performance, where the combination of social network graphs and joint LSTM and CNN model achieved 0.78 F1 score.

Furthermore, there are studies on hate speech detection in multilingual tweets including Arabic. Ousidhoum et al. (2019) used the bag of words (BOW) as features with Logistic Regression (LR) and deep learning models to detect hate speech in multilingual tweets. Smedt et al. (2018) conducted an experiment to detect online Jihadist hate speech in multilingual tweets, where SVM was used to classify tweets.

In this study, we focus on detecting hate speech in Arabic tweets using several classical and neural learning models with tf-idf and word embeddings features. We adopt a quick and simple approach of developing our classifiers and conducting our experiments, focusing on unigram representations that are problem-independent, while leveraging the power and ease-of-use of existing learning frameworks.

3. Approach

We approach hate speech detection as a supervised learning problem. In our study, we experimented with several classical and neural learning models trained for detecting Arabic hate speech on Twitter. We adopted basic text preprocessing and two main feature extraction techniques for comparison.

3.1 Preprocessing

To prepare our dataset for the feature extraction process, basic text preprocessing is done as follows:

- Punctuations, foreign characters and numbers (including user mentions and URLs), and diacritics (tashdid, fatha, tanwin fath, damma, tanwin damm, kasra, tanwin kasr, sukun, and tatwil/kashida) are all removed. We also removed repeated characters.
- The remaining Arabic text is normalized. Letters are normalized as follows:
    - {"آإأ" to "ا"}
    - {"ي" to "ى"}
    - {"ؤ" to "ء"}
    - {"ئ" to "ء"}
    - {"ة" to "ه"}
    - {"ﺟ" to "ك"}

While some normalization has been done through building the pre-trained word embedding model (AraVec2.0) used in our experiment, we augmented it with additional steps.

3.2 Feature Extraction

We adopted two main simple and problem-independent feature extraction techniques: tf-idf and word embeddings.

Firstly, tf-idf term weight (term frequency-inverse document frequency) indicates how relevant a term is to a document in a collection of documents. In our experiments, tf-idf weights are only used with the classical machine learning algorithms in order to compare against using word embeddings as features.

Secondly, word embeddings are the most popular distributed representation of words (or terms). Each word in the vocabulary is represented as a vector of a few hundred dimensions, where words that have the same meaning are closer to each other, while the words with different meanings are far apart. This is done by learning the vector representation of the words through the contexts in which they appear. One of the popular techniques for efficiently learning a standalone word embedding from a text corpus is Word2Vec (Mikolov et al., 2013). There are two different learning models to learn the embeddings, Skip Gram and Continuous Bag of Words (CBOW). The CBOW model learns the embeddings by predicting the current word using the context as an input, while the continuous skip-gram takes the current word as input and learns the embeddings by predicting the surrounding words (Mikolov et al., 2013).

In our experiments, we used the pre-trained Arabic word embedding model AraVec2.0 (Soliman et al., 2017), which provides various pre-trained Arabic word embedding model architectures; each is trained on one of three different datasets: tweets, Web pages, and Wikipedia Arabic articles. Moreover, for each dataset, two models are built: one using Skip Gram and another using CBOW. For the purpose of this study, we used the pre-trained SkipGram 300D-embeddings trained on more than 77M tweets, since we work on tweets. We used the pre-trained model in both classical and neural learning approaches. To use it with classical learning algorithms, the average vector of all the embeddings of the tweet words is computed and used as the feature vector of the tweet. However, for the neural learning models, the embedding vectors are used to initialize the weights of the embedding layer, which is then connected to the rest of the layers in the network.

3.3   Models

This section describes the classical and neural learning models used in our experiments.

3.3.1   Classical Learning Models

We experimented with various classical machine learning models, namely SVM, Random Forest, XGBoost, Extra Trees, Decision Trees, Gradient Boosting, and Logistic Regression. These models are trained along with both types of features we described earlier, tf-idf and pre-trained word embeddings.

3.3.2   Neural Learning Models

We experimented with two types of neural models, Recurrent Neural Networks (RNN), and Convolutional Neural Networks (CNN). We tried different RNN architectures, namely Long Short-Term Memory (LSTM), Bidirectional LSTM (BLSTM), and Gated Recurrent Unit (GRU).

We also tried a combination of both CNN and RNN. Previous studies showed that the joint CNN and RNN architecture outperforms CNN or RNN alone in natural language processing tasks such as sentiment analysis and text classification tasks (Wang et al., 2016 and Zhou et al. 2015). This combined architecture allows the network to learn local features from the CNN, and long-term dependencies, positional relation of features, and global features from the RNN (Wang et al., 2016). The combined architecture used in this work consists of one CNN layer with max-pooling and time distributed layer, followed by one RNN layer and dropout layer, as shown in the example joint CNN and LSTM architecture in Figure 1.

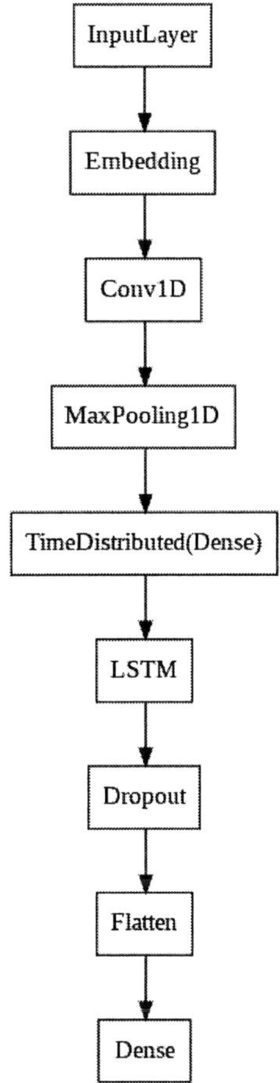

Figure 1: Joint CNN and LSTM model architecture.

4.   Experimental Evaluation

In this section, we present and analyze the performance of our trained models. We start with the experimental setup, followed by the analysis of the two experiments we conducted to answer the two research questions. Finally, we discuss the results of our two submitted runs to the shared task.

4.1   Experimental Setup

For the purpose of this study, we use SemEval 2020 Arabic offensive language dataset (OffensEval 2020, Subtask B for detecting hate speech) (Mubarak et al., 2020). The dataset was split into train, dev, and test sets (70%, 10%, and 20% respectively). There are 7,000 training tweets, only 361 of them (about 5.2%) are labelled as hate speech. There are 1,000 dev tweets, only 44 of them (4.4%) are labelled as hate speech. This shows how the two classes in the dataset are clearly unbalanced.

As expected, we used the training set to learn each model's parameters and the dev set to tune its hyperparameters. The hyperparameters and their tuned values are listed in Table 1.

Hyperparameter	Value
Number of filters (CNN)	25
Kernel size (CNN)	5
Number of hidden units (RNN)	16
Dropout rate (Regularizer)	0.5
Learning rate (Adam optimizer)	0.001

Table 1: Tuned values of the hyperparameters.

To answer the two research questions we listed in Section 1, we conducted two main experiments. The first compares the use of tf-idf vs word embeddings features, conducted on classical machine learning models. The second compares classical vs. neural models.

We evaluated the performance of our models using two measures: macro-averaged F1 (the official shared task measure) and F1 score on the hate speech (HS) class (since the target HS class is scarce). All reported results in this section are on the dev set unless otherwise mentioned. Notice that the majority-class baseline on the dev set yields a 0.49 macro-F1 score.

It is worth noting that all of our development and experiments were performed through Google Colaboratory using Python and Keras libraries.

4.2 RQ1: tf-idf vs. Word Embeddings

To answer RQ1, we conducted an experiment over the seven classical models listed in Section 3.3.1 using both tf-idf and pre-trained word embeddings (AraVec 2.0).

Figures 2 depicts the performance of the models in each of the two cases measured in macro-averaged F1. There are several interesting observations. First, we notice that the performance using tf-idf varies from 0.49 to 0.68, while using word embeddings it varies from 0.51 to 0.57. Second, some models (e.g., SVM) exhibited slightly better performance using word embeddings, however more models (e.g., Random Forest) exhibited much better performance using tf-idf. Overall, the best three models (namely Extra Trees, Random Forest, and Gradient Boosting, respectively) are all indeed using tf-idf. This is a surprising result, since tf-idf features neither capture meaning nor are contextualized; both attributes are (or at least should be) captured by word embeddings. This observation definitely needs more investigation.

Figure 3 illustrates the performance of the models in each of the two cases, but this time measured in F1 over

the positive class. It indicates very similar, but even stronger, observations. Moreover, it clearly shows that the task of detecting the HS tweets is, not surprisingly, much harder than non-HS, achieving an F1 score of 0.39 at best.

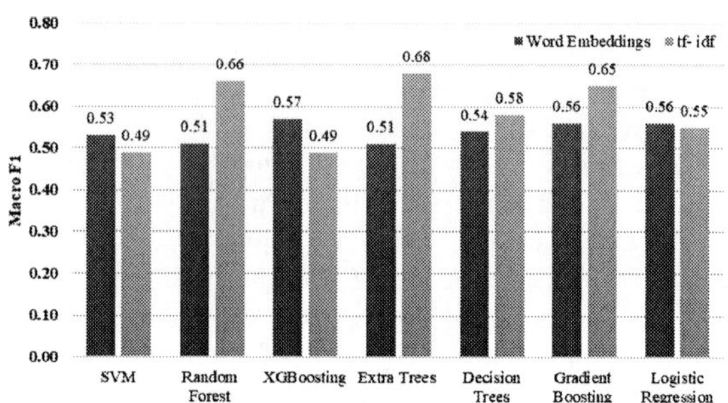

Figure 2: Macro F1 of classical learning models.

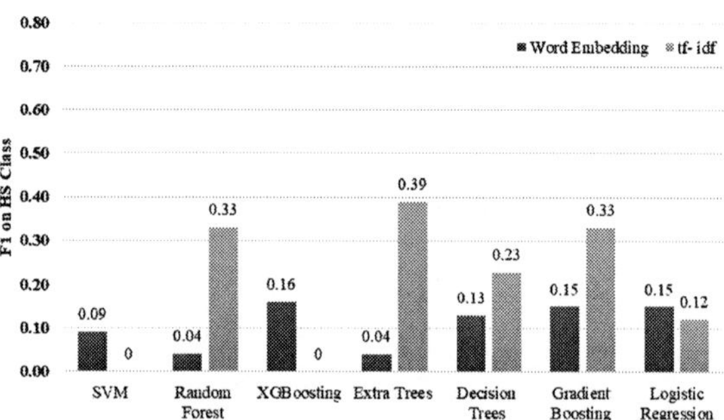

Figure 3: F1 on HS class of classical learning models.

4.3 RQ2: Classical vs. Neural Models

We now turn our attention to RQ2, which is concerned with comparing classical and neural models. We considered the best-performing classical model, i.e., Extra Trees with tf-idf features, as the *baseline*, which we compare against eight neural models:

- The first three are RNN models, namely LSTM, BLSTM, and GRU.
- The fourth is CNN.
- The next three are combined CNN and RNN models, one for each RNN type.
- The last one is a combined CNN and LSTM version that is trained on an oversampled training data to address the unbalanced data problem, where some HS (i.e., the minority class) examples are replicated.

Due to time constraints, we only trained the neural models using word embeddings. According to the results of the first experiment in Section 4.2, using tf-idf features is worth trying too. We defer this to future exploration.

Tweet	True label	Predicted (Extra Trees, Embeddings)	Predicted (Extra Trees, tf- idf)	Predicted (CNN+LST M)
إحنا أتباع إيران يا آل سلول يا نسل اليهود We are followers of Iran, O family of Salul, descendants of the Jews.	HS	**HS**	**HS**	**HS**
بس يا فاشل يا خاين يا عميل Shut up, O loser and traitor!	NOT_HS	**NOT_HS**	**NOT_HS**	**NOT_HS**
يا هنيدي يا عمرو ياديب الاهلي ف الصداااااارة خبوا الحصالة ادددددا◼◼ #للخلف_درر_يا_زمالك O Hinaidi, O Amr Adeeb, Al-Ahly is taking the lead. #GoBack_Zamalek team.	HS	<u>NOT_HS</u>	HS	<u>NOT_HS</u>
يا كافر يا زنديق يا مرتد يا انت عاوز يبقى عندنا ديمقراطية زى الكفرة اللى ما يعرفوش ربنا O bastard and Godless! You want us to have a democracy like the infidels, who do not believe in God.	NOT_HS	**NOT_HS**	**NOT_HS**	<u>HS</u>
هههههههههههههههههه يا طحلبي يا صغير جدة يا جاهل شوف بطولات الاتحاد قبل 1417 Hahahahahaha! You, little kid of Jeddah, you ignorant. Check the Al-Ittihad [tournaments/ championships] before 1417.	HS	<u>NOT_HS</u>	<u>NOT_HS</u>	**HS**

Table 2: Examples (from the dev-set) of correct (bolded) and incorrect (underlined) classification using Extra Trees models with word embeddings and tf- idf and the combined CNN+LSTM neural model.

Figure 4 depicts the performance of all tried neural models along with the baseline measured in macro-averaged F1. Similar to the first experiment, we have several interesting observations. First, the figure shows that combining CNN and RNN models improved performance over individual models. Second, the classical model unexpectedly exhibits a comparable performance to several neural models. Third, combining CNN and LSTM exhibited the best performance, outperforming all other neural models in addition to the baseline classical model. Finally, oversampling did not help, at least when applied to the best performing model.

Figure 5 indicates the same exact performance patterns measured in F1 on the HS class. However, the performance gap between the best neural model and the baseline is even widened.

Table 2 shows examples (from the dev-set) of correct and incorrect classification using both of tf-idf and word embeddings with Extra Trees classifier and combined CNN and LSTM neural model. The table shows that the models made different mistakes.

4.4 Submitted Runs

Based on the results above, we chose the combined CNN and LSTM model in addition to its oversampling version to submit results on the test set to the shared task. Table 3 shows the results of the two models as reported by the task organizers, compared to the results on the dev set. As expected, the performance on the test set is slightly lower than on the dev set, however the unsampled version still outperforms the oversampled one.

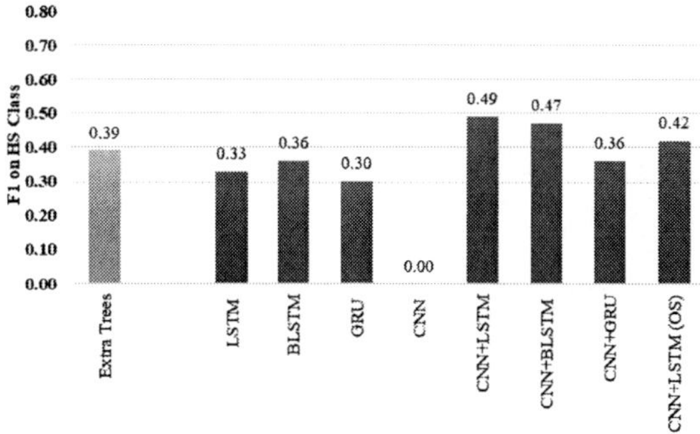

Figure 5: F1 on HS class of neural learning models compared to the best-performing classical model.

Model	Macro F1 (dev-set)	Macro F1 (test-set)
CNN+LSTM	**0.73**	**0.69**
CNN-LSTM (OS)	0.70	0.65

Table 3: Macro F1 scores of submitted models.

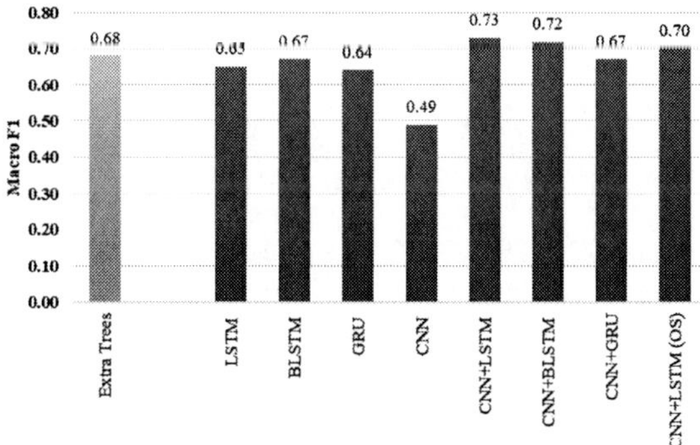

Figure 4: Macro F1 of neural learning models compared to the best-performing classical model.

5. Conclusion and Future Work

In this paper, we presented a quick and simple approach to tackle the problem of detecting hate speech in Arabic tweets. Our approach adopts simple problem-independent features to represent terms in tweets and leverages the quick development service supported by existing powerful machine learning libraries. We compared 15 classical and neural learning models along with two different term representations (tf-idf and word embeddings). Our experiments over 8k labelled dataset of Arabic tweets showed that tf-idf representation is more effective than word embeddings when used in classical models, and that the best neural learning model (a joint CNN and LSTM architecture) outperforms the classical ones. To our knowledge, this is the first time a combined CNN and LSTM is used to detect hate speech over Arabic tweets. The classification performance achieved by this combined model exhibited a significant improvement over the majority-class baseline, proving the effectiveness of our "quick and simple" approach.

For future work, we plan to conduct several experiments. Firstly, as it shows better performance with classical learning models, we will consider using tf-idf representation with neural models as well. Secondly, we plan to experiment with transfer learning techniques to leverage the models that are trained for related tasks such as offensive language detection. Thirdly, we will further investigate the sampling techniques to overcome the unbalanced data problem. Finally, since the pre-trained model BERT yields the state of the art performance in several natural language processing tasks (Devlin et al., 2018), it is worth trying for hate speech detection too.

6. References

Alakrot, A., Murray, L. and Nikolov, N.S., 2018. Towards accurate detection of offensive language in online communication in arabic. *Procedia computer science*, 142, pp.315-320.

Albadi, N., Kurdi, M. and Mishra, S., 2018, August. Are they our brothers? Analysis and detection of religious hate speech in the Arabic Twittersphere. In 2018 *IEEE/ACM ASONAM* (pp. 69-76).

Chowdhury, A.G., Didolkar, A., Sawhney, R. and Shah, R., 2019. ARHNet-Leveraging Community Interaction for Detection of Religious Hate Speech in Arabic. In *Proceedings of ACL: Student Research Workshop* (pp. 273-280).

Devlin, J., Chang, M.W., Lee, K. and Toutanova, K., 2018. BERT: Pre-training of deep bidirectional transformers for language understanding. *arXiv preprint arXiv:1810.04805*.

Malmasi, S. & Zampieri, M., 2018. Challenges in discriminating profanity from hate speech. *Journal of Experimental & Theoretical Artificial Intelligence*, 30(2), pp. 187-202.

Mikolov, T., Sutskever, I., Chen, K., Corrado, G.S. and Dean, J., 2013. Distributed representations of words and phrases and their compositionality. *In Advances in neural information processing systems* (pp. 3111-3119).

Mohaouchane, H., Mourhir, A. and Nikolov, N.S., 2019, October. Detecting Offensive Language on Arabic Social Media Using Deep Learning. In *IEEE SNAMS* (pp. 466-471).

Mondal, M., Silva, L. A. & Benevenuto, F., 2017. *A Measurement Study of Hate Speech in Social Media.*. New York, USA, ACM, p. 85–94.

Mubarak, H. & Darwish, K., 2019. Arabic Offensive Language Classification on Twitter. *In International Conference on Social Informatics* (pp. 269-276). Springer.

Mubarak, H., Darwish, K. and Magdy, W., 2017, August. Abusive language detection on Arabic social media. *In Proceedings of the First Workshop on Abusive Language Online* (pp. 52-56).

Mubarak, H., Darwish, K., Magdy, W., Elsayed, T. and Al-Khalifa, H., 2020. Overview of OSACT4 Arabic Offensive Language Detection Shared Task. *In Proceedings of the 4th Workshop on Open-Source Arabic Corpora and Processing Tools (OSACT)*, vol. 4.

Ousidhoum, N., Lin, Z., Zhang, H., Song, Y. and Yeung, D.Y., 2019. Multilingual and Multi-Aspect Hate Speech Analysis. *arXiv preprint arXiv:1908.11049*.

Smedt, T., De Pauw, G. and Van Ostaeyen, P., 2018. Automatic detection of online jihadist hate speech. *arXiv preprint arXiv:1803.04596*.

Soliman, A.B., Eissa, K. and El-Beltagy, S.R., 2017. Aravec: A set of arabic word embedding models for use in arabic nlp. *Procedia Computer Science*, 117, pp.256-265.

Wang, X., Jiang, W. and Luo, Z., 2016. Combination of convolutional and recurrent neural network for sentiment analysis of short texts. In *Proceedings of COLING 2016: Technical papers* (pp. 2428-2437).

Watanabe, H., Bouazizi, M. & Ohtsuki, T., 2018. Hate speech on Twitter: A pragmatic approach to collect hateful and offensive expressions and perform hate speech detection. *IEEE Access*, 6, pp. 13825-13835.

Zhang, Z. & Luo, L., 2018. Hate speech detection: A solved problem? the challenging case of long tail on Twitter. CoRR abs/1803.03662 (2018).

Zhang, Z., Robinson, D. & Tepper, a. J., 2018. Hate Speech Detection Using a Convolution-LSTM Based Deep Neural Network. *In Proceedings of ACM WWW conference (WWW'2018)*. New York, NY, USA.

Zhou, C., Sun, C., Liu, Z. and Lau, F., 2015. A C-LSTM neural network for text classification. arXiv preprint arXiv:1511.08630.

Association for Computational Linguistics
209 N. Eighth Street
Stroudsburg, Pennsylvania 18360

ISBN 978-1-7138-1272-2